William Brownfield and Son(s): 1837-1900

A most prolific Staffordshire pottery

An illustrated guide to
Brownfield wares 1837-1900

TIM H. PEAKE, M.A., M.LITT.

Book Number in Limited Edition of 1000

No 428.

1 November 1995.

Author's Signature *Tim Heake*

PUBLISHED BY T. H. PEAKE. SEPTEMBER 1995
COPYRIGHT 1995 T. H. PEAKE. WORLD COPYRIGHT RESERVED

Professional photography by Ray Massey, Camden Park Studios,
The Church Hall, Camden Park Road, London NW1 9AY.

Printed by The Acanthus Press Limited, Wellington, Somerset

ISBN 0 9525952 1 4

WILLIAM BROWNFIELD

THE SECOND MAYOR OF HANLEY

Born 1812, Died 1873

CONTENTS

CHAPTER | | | PAGE

1   The early years with John Wood   1837-1850   1- 16

2   The challenge of independence   1850-1862   17- 38

3   The heyday of William Brownfield   1862-1873   39- 51

4   A new age — the sons' management   1873-1883   52- 69

5   Decline, co-operative and failure   1833-1900   70- 80

6   Teapot and tea service designs   1850-1900   81- 86

7   Plate designs   1837-1900   87-126

8   Majolica and porcelain   1871-1900   127-163

9   Appendices 1-10   1837-1900   164-189

APPENDICES

1   Registration of Brownfield Designs and Shapes   1848-1900   164-167

2   Known Porcelain Pattern and Shape Numbers   1871-1900   168-169

3   All Known Brownfield Plate Designs   1837-1900   170-172

4   All Known Brownfield Jugs   1837-1900   173-174

5   Markings on Brownfield Jugs and Plates   1837-1900   175

6a   Introduction of Factory Pattern Numbers   1837-1900   177

6b   Painted Pattern Numbers on Jugs, Plates etc.   1837-1900   177-180

6c   Brownfield 'Numbered' products   1851-1870   181

7   All Known Brownfield Teapots and Teacups   1850-1900   182-183

8   International Exhibitions   1837-1890   183

9   General Factory Registration of Products   1834-1860   184-185

10   Price Guide to Jugs and Plates   186-189

ACKNOWLEDGEMENTS

I have received invaluable assistance in the research and writing of this book. In the initial stages, I relied considerably on the scholarly historical survey of William Brownfield's firm and career written by Rodney and Eileen Hampson in Volume 4 of the *Northern Ceramic Society Journal* (1980-81). The historical detail and framework provided by this work saved me months of ferreting through countless sources. Inevitably, much of that detail is incorporated in this book. I am extremely grateful to them for this and much subsequent help and advice. My first literary introduction to nineteenth century jugs came from Dr R K Henrywood's book *Relief-Moulded Jugs 1820-1900*. This enabled me to proceed with confidence to research in the Design Register at the Public Record Office.

Last, and by no means least, I have gained continued help, assistance and advice from a group of ardent fellow jug collectors. Their jug collections provided me with much of the raw material used in illustration in this book. Their enthusiasm and fascination have been infectious and it has been vital throughout the preparation and writing of this book.

Above all, I would like to thank my wife for her long suffering tolerance of my passion for collecting Brownfield jugs, plates, etc. Without that, no book would have been possible. To her and the following collector friends, I would like to dedicate this book.

R&EH   KVB   PLlD   RL   MM   BM   GM   MR   WR

I would like to thank J.T.D. for invaluable help with proofreading.

The 'Hotei' teapot illustrated on the front cover is reproduced courtesy Phillips Auctioneers, Alphington, Exeter. The porcelain cherub spill holders are courtesy Beagle Antiques, Essex. The Oriental jug made by Wood & Brownfield in about 1842-44 is courtesy East Reach Antiques, Taunton, Somerset.

NOTES TO THE READER

There are three kinds of illustrations in the book. The first is Marks, the second is Figures (reproduced in black and white) and the third is Colour Plates. The abbreviations used to denote these are: (1) Marks, (2) Fig, (3) Col Pl. The Marks and black and white illustrations appear in the text.

Chapters 1-5 concentrate on designs for jugs and jardinieres, Chapter 6 deals with teapots and teasets, Chapter 7 covers dinner and dessert service plates. Chapter 8 covers the production of jugs, plates, teacups, lamps and figures in majolica and porcelain.

INTRODUCTION

Most recent authors of books on pottery and porcelain have concentrated much of their attention on the 'body' of the products manufactured by a particular factory or factories — be they earthenware, stoneware, parian, porcelain etc. This author has turned his attention much more to the written sources relating to the firms of Robinson, Wood and Brownfield, Wood & Brownfield and William Brownfield, a sphere in which, as an historian, he feels much more qualified to make a detailed appraisal.

Research has been concentrated on the historical background to the respective firms and to their products. It seeks to explain both to collectors and specialised dealers what jugs, teapots, plates, dinner services etc. were manufactured, when they were first introduced and (where possible) why they were given particular design names. In particular, a detailed breakdown of annual manufacturing output in the period 1837-63 has been established for the first time. This has facilitated accurate dating of many individual items to within about three months.

A close inspection has been made of the Design Register introduced in September 1842 and a detailed analysis has been attempted of the slow and spasmodic use made of it by many leading Staffordshire manufacturers in the 1840s. The attribution of some jugs to Wood & Brownfield in the early 1840s and especially 1842 will be considered contentious because of the lack of definitive proof. This should, at least, encourage further research on an important period when the new Design Register was slowly being employed by the Staffordshire pottery factories and when the manufacturers were clearly engaged in a battle with the London retailers over the marking of their wares.

Evidence has been provided of William Brownfield's early attempt in the late 1850s to obtain the legal enforcement of penalties on a fellow manufacturer for pirating his registered products. In addition to the firm's registered products, many unregistered items have been attributed to the various Brownfield firms for the first time, including a sizable collection of 'numbered' but otherwise unmarked items. Over fifty different markings of the different firms' wares have been established.

Attention has also been given to the displays submitted by the pottery producers to the various great Exhibitions, both at home and abroad, and to the very real probability that even if a factory's own personnel were not present, it may have exhibited through an agent. This suggests that William Brownfield may have exhibited considerably earlier than the date of 1863 hitherto accepted. Evidence has been discovered of established, if not exclusive, Brownfield retailers, not only in the United Kingdom but also in several overseas countries.

Concentration on written historical sources makes it possible to appreciate just how important a factory William Brownfield was in the nineteenth century and why it met its demise in 1900. This was at the end of two extremely difficult decades during which the economic climate caused the downfall of many important Staffordshire pottery firms including Davenport and many others. For over ninety years William Brownfield's pottery has been in oblivion and few people in Staffordshire today will have even heard the name. This historical account seeks to place the firm's true importance in its proper perspective.

September 1995   Tim Peake

CHAPTER 1

THE EARLY YEARS WITH JOHN WOOD: 1837-1850

In late 1836, William Brownfield was invited to join a partnership with Noah Robinson and John Wood, thus launching his career as a pottery firm director lasting from early 1837 until his death in 1873. However, strike action in 1836 probably delayed production until the new year. John Wood, his partner, was born in about 1796, and was about forty years old, not much older than Noah Robinson, the second partner. William Brownfield, twenty-five, was the junior partner, probably responsible for sales.

Industrial disputes over the terms and timing of the annual hiring in 1836 closed the factories. The bosses insisted that the workers should only be paid 'piece-rate' for wares that emerged satisfactorily from the ovens; the workers argued that they should be paid for all good work prior to its entry to the ovens — believing (rightly) that the malfunctioning or imperfect performance of the ovens could lose them pay. This issue led to a major lock-out of the workers that took place between November 1836 and 28th January 1837. The premises occupied by the new partnership from January 1837 had been vacant for two years ever since the bankruptcy of R & J Clews, its previous management. The new business appears to have commenced early in 1837, but it was probably four to five months before they began their operations. The factory contained six gloss and three biscuit ovens and a proportionate number of kilns, but it is unlikely that the new firm chose to operate all the ovens immediately. The workforce was built up to about one hundred and fifty by 1842 — producing earthenware and stoneware goods only.

The new venture, located between the Waterloo Road and Blackwell's Row, Cobridge, did not have an auspicious beginning. On 5th September 1837, within four months of the firm's inception, Noah Robinson died. His place in the business appears to have been taken by his father John, a man with many years experience in the potting industry. As the administrator of his son's will, he looked after the widow's interest in the firm until his death on 12th September 1840. However, the markings on products manufactured after Noah's death in September 1837 ("W&B" only) show that John Wood and William Brownfield now acted in joint charge, although the dissolution of partnership agreement shows that the legal withdrawal of the Robinson family was not completed until 12th March 1841.

It has not, hitherto, been possible to date the pattern numbers of the wares made by the firm between 1837-41, nor indeed the years thereafter. Marks on the base of products manufactured between 1837-41, pattern numbers on the bottom of jugs, and information provided by William Shaw the foreman from 1842 to 1863, show that in each of the first four years 1837-41, only about forty new patterns were introduced. We know from William Shaw that only 200 patterns had been introduced by the beginning of 1842. Detailed estimates are now provided of the patterns introduced each year from 1842-1850, from 1850-64 and from 1864-94 (Appendix 6A); these suggest that 1400 patterns had been introduced by November 1844 , 3150 by November 1847 and 5100 by November 1850.

This dating of patterns 1840-51 is based partly on a steady progression in output and partly on the painted pattern numbers on the bottom of a number of specific jugs. This numbering suggests that about 5100 patterns had been used by the autumn of 1850. The assumption of a steady progression in output can, of course, be questioned, but a carefully reasoned estimate of pattern dating is much better than none at all. Dating of patterns in the years 1837-63 is accurate to within three to four months.

The transfer printed floral jug with enamel decoration, marked clearly "RW&B" and with the pattern number '30', is one of the earliest jugs manufactured by the firm (**Col Pl. 1**). This was made in the very first year of its existence — in about September 1837. Although this jug is a rare find, there is nothing very spectacular about it. The shape, especially that of the handle, is very typical of the 1830s — much more elaborate than the simplified shapes of the later 1840s and 1850s. The picture of leaves, flowers and Greek-type wine ewer is done by a transfer print and the enamelling is done by one of the young girls in the paint shop. The picture shown on the front side of this 1837 jug is repeated on the reverse. The handle is an extremely good example of those that followed on the vast majority of Brownfield jugs — invariably having a degree of relief-moulding, sometimes substantial as here. Another example (Pat No 70) was produced in about August 1838 on the same shaped body, but with a quite different transfer print (**Col Pl. 2**). This same handle was used on the registered Robinson, Wood & Brownfield jug of 1st September 1839.

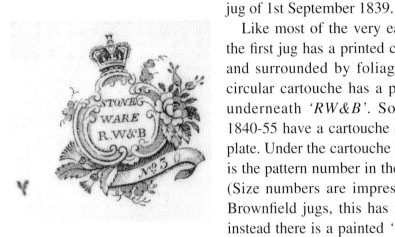

Marks 1. RW&B. Pat No '30' Jug. Printed Floral Cartouche with Crown. 'Stone-ware'/'RW&B'/'No 30'. Enameller's Mark 'Y'. cSep 1837.

Like most of the very early RW&B products discovered to date, the first jug has a printed cartouche on the base, headed by a crown and surrounded by foliage and flowers (**Marks 1**). The roughly circular cartouche has a printed 'STONEWARE' and immediately underneath 'RW&B'. Some of the later products in the years 1840-55 have a cartouche containing the pattern name of the jug or plate. Under the cartouche is a printed scroll containing 'No 30'; this is the pattern number in the system inaugurated by the firm in 1837. (Size numbers are impressed and not printed.) Unlike most later Brownfield jugs, this has no impressed potter's mark on the base; instead there is a painted 'Y' — a letter which appears in impressed form on a large number of subsequent jugs. This was probably the enameller's mark necessary to assess payment based on piece-rates. The second jug has only a pattern number.

The RW&B 'Versailles' water ewer has recently been identified; this twelve inch ewer and basin set is produced with an elaborate blue transfer printed pattern. It has no printed pattern number, but is clearly marked 'ROBINSON, WOOD & BROWNFIELD' which would date its introduction as 1837. No picture of this is as yet available. The 'Canton' transfer printed ewer (**Col Pl. 3**) was also introduced in 1837. Both an ordinary brown transfer-printed and an enamelled version have been found. Its marks include a cartouche containing 'CANTON' and 'RW&B', and an impressed '5'. One example, identical to the ewer illustrated here, has been found with most unusual printed marks. These include the lion and unicorn, a coat of arms with coronet at the top, the letter 'S' printed to the left of the coronet, the letter 'H' to the right. Underneath the coat of arms is a printed cartouche containing 'DIEU ET MON DROIT' and below that 'PATENT LONDON'. There is also an impressed '5' and a blue printed 'clock key' mark, both of which have been found on other Wood & Brownfield products. The Wood & Brownfield marked 'Amoy' plate of February 1838 (Pat No '54') indicates that the marks RW&B were only used until Noah Robinson's death. Dorothea Robinson remained a partner until March 1841, but virtually all goods made from the beginning of 1838 were only marked 'W&B', with the exception of the rare registered 1839 jug. Experienced collectors will, therefore, find such 'RW&B' marked products rare collectors items. The last one will have a factory pattern number somewhere between thirty-one and fifty-four.

In about May 1839 Wood & Brownfield produced a chinoiserie jug (Pat No '103') (**Col Pl. 4**) using the same transfer print as the one employed on the later 'Nankin' jug of August 1843. Close inspection of the printed marks on the 'Nankin' jug indicated that an earlier example would be found, with one even manufactured prior to Noah Robinson's death in September 1837. The precise location in the cartouche of the letters 'W&B' on the 1843 jug, the letters appearing in the right hand side instead of in the centre of the cartouche suggest that the 'R' for Robinson has been deleted (**Marks 2**). This jug has no other attributive marks. It is likely that other transfer prints will be found on this same shape.

The Robinson, Wood & Brownfield 'Vertical Columns' jug (**Col Pl. 5**) is totally unknown to many collectors of twenty years' experience. Authentication is easy as the jug is clearly impressed on the base *'PUBLISHED BY ROBINSON, WOOD & BROWNFIELD, COBRIDGE, STAFFORDSHIRE POTTERIES, SEPTEMBER 1st 1839'* (**Marks 3**). It is not a distinctive, elaborately moulded jug like the 'Willie' and 'Judgment of Solomon' jugs of 1841, and it has some design characteristics in common with Elijah Jones' 'Vertical Leaves' jug which was produced in 1838 under the old registration law of 1811. This gave fourteen years' copyright protection to jugs with human or animal figures. The jug spout is the most elaborately shaped of all the early Wood & Brownfield jugs and, like the relief-moulded handle, is very reminiscent of the 1830s. This six inch jug is not produced in the normal buff coloured stoneware so common in the 1830s and the bright greyish green glaze is unusual on a Wood & Brownfield jug. No decorated examples have yet been discovered.

Left: Marks 2. (R)W&B. 'Nankin' jug. Printed 'Nankin'/'No 773'/ 'W&B'. Position of 'W&B' in Cartouche indicates that this was a 'RW&B' pattern from 1837. This example cAugust 1842.

Right: Marks 3. WW&B. 'Vertical Columns' Jug — Impressed 'Published by 'Robinson Wood & Brownfield'/ 'Cobridge'/'Staffordshire Potteries'/ 'September 1st 1839'.

The markings on the jug base offer further food for thought because they contrast with the procedures adopted with plates manufactured in the years 1838-41. The absence of any 'Robinson' mark on the 'Amoy' plate (February 1838) suggests that it would not appear on a jug produced over a year and a half later. It may be that the requirements of the 1811 statute demanded that all legal partners in the company should be recorded on the base. If that is so, then the Robinson referred to here is Noah Robinson's widow who remained a partner until March 1841. Noah had been dead for two years when this 'Vertical Columns' jug was registered.

This registration by RW&B is only the fourth known to the author, effected by a Staffordshire pottery to ensure legal protection of a jug or plate in the 1830s. This gave fourteen years 'copyright' protection to a jug with human or animal figures. It had been preceded by Machin & Potts in 1834, Elijah Jones in 1835 and 1838, and W Ridgway in 1835 and 1836. It is an enigma that Wood & Brownfield then followed it with just two more registered jug designs in 1841, but no more thereafter. A partial explanation almost certainly lies in the 'battle' waged in the 1840s between the manufacturers and the powerful London retailers. This was over the marking of goods in a way that might enable prospective purchasers to by-pass the London middle-men and go straight to the factory with their orders.

The Wood & Brownfield relief-moulded 'Willie' jug (**Col Pl. 6**) was registered on 1st January 1841

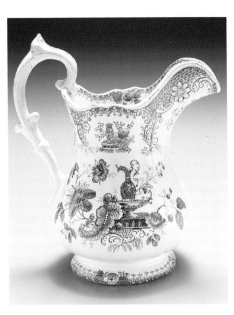

1. RW&B Transfer printed Flower Jug. Printed Cartouche and Crown. 'RW&B'. Pat No '30' cSeptember 1837. Jug 6¼" — 16cm.

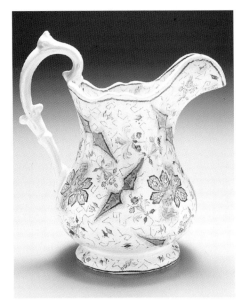

2. RW&B Transfer printed jug. Pat No '70'. Circa Aug 1838. Otherwise unmarked. 7" — 17.5cm.

3. RW&B 'Canton' Ewer. Printed Cartouche — 'RW&B'/'Canton'/ c1837-38. 12" — 30.5cm.

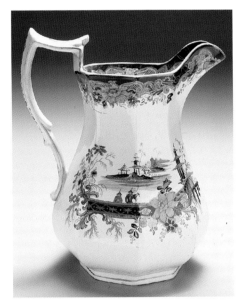

4. W&B. 'Amoy' Chinoiserie Jug. Pat No '103'. Unmarked example. cMay 1839. 8¼" — 21cm.

5. RW&B 'Vertical Columns' Jug. Moulded Cartouche — Published by Robinson, Wood & Brownfield, Staffordshire Potteries, Cobridge. 1st September 1839. 7" — 17.5cm.

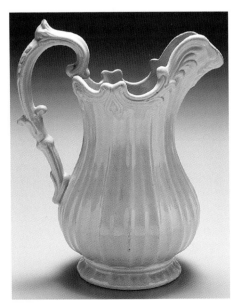

6. W&B. 'Willie' Jug. Impressed Cartouche — Publihsed by Wood & Brownfield, Staffordshire Potteries, Cobridge. 1st January 1841. RL Collection. 7" — 17.5cm.

7. Pankhurst. 'Willie' Jug. c1853. Unmarked example. Courtesy Mr Nigel Daniels, Taunton Antique Centre.

10. W&B. 'Judgement of Solomon' Jug. Impressed cartouche — Published by Wood & Brownfield, Staffordshire Potteries, Cobridge. 1st September 1841. WR Collection. 8¾" — 22cm.

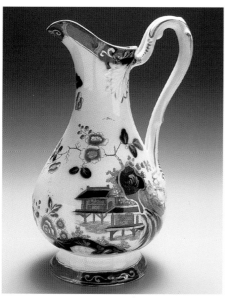

11. W&B. Chinoiserie Print Jug. Jug Pat No '3008' — cSeptember 1847,. 10" — 25.5cm. Courtesy Hutchinson Antiques, Plymouth.

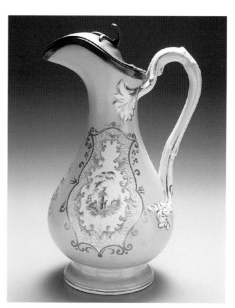

12. Jas Dixon & Son, Sheffield. Chinoiserie Print Jug. Published by Jas Dixon & Son, Sheffield, 1st March 1842. 9½" — 24cm.

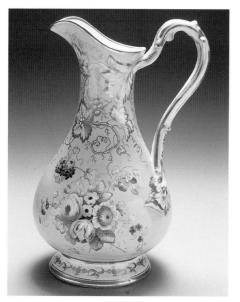

13. Attributable to W&B? Hand Painted Floral Jug. August 1842. Unmarked Example. Shape registered by Jas Dixon — March 1842,. 9½" — 24cm.

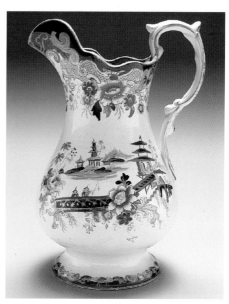

15. W&B. 'Amoy' jug — Pat No '333'. cJune 1842. 8" — 20.5cm.

5

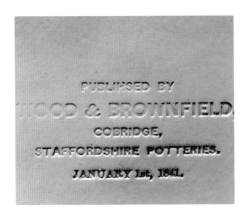

Marks 4. W&B. 'Willie' jug — Impressed Inscription — 'Publihsed by Wood & Brownfield'/'Cobridge'/Staffordshire Potteries'/'January 1st 1841'.

Fig 8. Unattributed 'Willie' Jug. c1850-53 Unmarked. WR Collection. 8" — 20.5cm.

Fig 9. W Ridgway. 'Willie' Jug. Reg 21 Oct 1851. Engraving — the Design Register. Courtesy the PRO.

under the old Registration Act of 1811 **(Marks 4).** Printed on the base of the jug are the words '*PUBLIHSED* (a quaint misspelling!) *BY WOOD AND BROWNFIELD, STAFFORD-SHIRE POTTERIES, COBRIDGE, JAN 1 1841*'. This jug has no impressed or printed markings that recognise Dorothea Robinson's continued presence in the partnership. The 'Willie' jug is of a quite remarkable quality — much superior to that of J W Pankhurst c1853 and an unattributed example c1850-53. The principal scene depicted on all three is a group of three men in a tavern, based on a watercolour by John Masey Wright (1777-1866) and recording an incident from Robert Burn's poem "Willie Brew'd a Peck of Malt".

This 'Willie' jug can be compared with the Pankhurst version and another unattributed example **(Col Pl. 7)** and **(Fig 8)**. It is noticeable that while the shape and handle of the Pankhurst jug follows that of Ridgway's registered 'Willie' jug **(Fig 9),** the relief-moulding has some variations.

'The Judgment of Solomon' **(Col Pl. 10),** the next registered relief-moulded jug appeared nine months later — the registration being taken out on 30th September 1841. The story behind this jug was explained by Dr R K Henrywood in an article in 1989, *Relief-Moulded Jugs — Some recent discoveries.* Solomon, King of Israel 1015-977 BC was renowned for his wisdom and was called upon to adjudicate the conflicting claims of two mothers to a new-born child. Solomon's judgment of human nature led him to award the child to the mother, who at the final hour, had preferred to abandon her claim rather than risk the child's life. Those with a good knowledge of the Bible will know that the story is recorded in the Old Testament, 1 Kings 3: 16-28. This jug is of the same very high quality as the 'Willie' jug and is known to have been made in blue, buff and a green-grey stoneware.

It was not accepted only a few years ago that (Robinson), Wood and Brownfield were capable of making jugs of such high quality. With a workforce of at least 150 to be kept busy, it is most unlikely that these were the only jugs. Clearly there were others — although precisely how many others will remain a matter of contention. The 1842 Government Report on the employment of children can be used to estimate the approximate workforce of Wood and Brownfield in 1842 and the figures work out at fifty-eight men, thirty-six women, thirty boys and twenty-four girls — a total of 150 workers. Plain business logic shows that a firm of this size must have needed a large number of products throughout the 1840s to keep the workforce occupied and among these there must have been a range of jugs. William Shaw, the foreman, indicated that 200 patterns and shapes were introduced between 1837-41 and some of these would have been jugs, possibly further relief-moulded jugs of a similar quality to 'Willie' and 'Judgement of Solomon'. *If* only five percent of these 200 patterns were designs for jugs, that would represent ten jug shapes; *if* the percentage was ten or twenty percent that would mean twenty or forty jug shapes.

The number of patterns introduced during the years 1841-50 probably rose considerably: the analysis in Appendix 6A suggests that about 5000 patterns had been used by October 1850. The same reasonable hypothesis used above would suggest that five percent of the 4800 items (5000 less 200 manufactured during the years 1837-41) were jugs; this would mean no less than 240 jugs (not necessarily relief-moulded ones). Even if the same jug was produced in several different enamelled colours, it clearly leaves a large number of unidentified Wood & Brownfield jugs. Between 1841-50 the Wood & Brownfield workforce expanded from one hundred and fifty to about four hundred and fifty, an increase of two hundred percent. Such a growth could only be supported if there was a corresponding increase in the number of new products launched. Perhaps five to ten percent of the new range of goods introduced by Wood and Brownfield between 1842-50 were jug shapes.

JAMES DIXON & SON'S REGISTERED JUGS:
1st MARCH AND 2nd SEPTEMBER 1842

In about May 1842 Wood and Brownfield produced a clearly marked *'REAL IRONSTONE'* plate with the pattern number *'303'*. Its transfer printed chinoiserie scene shows two houses on stilts surrounded by flowers and foliage enamelled in orange, green and deep blue. There is a pagoda in the left background and in front of it a small lake. The scene is in many respects typical of those produced by many manufacturers in the 1840s but an exact copy (down to the finest detail) on a jug of the same period would suggest that the jug was probably made by the same factory.

The Sheffield Britannia metal lid makers James Dixon & Son registered a jug design on 22nd September 1842 — the first under the very recently introduced law. It is clear that while James Dixon & Son registered this jug, they manufactured nothing more than the lid itself. Another pottery manufacturer Jos Wolstenholme, also a Sheffield Britannia metal lid manufacturer, registered another jug on 3rd November 1842. For some six months after the introduction of the new Design Register, no Staffordshire pottery factory was prepared to take the initiative and register a product in their own name until Samuel Alcock did so on 21st February 1843. Other firms took even longer before they followed Samuel Alcock's example: Josiah Wedgwood first used the 1842 act on 1st March 1843, Jones and Walley on 13th May 1843 and Minton on 10th November 1843, fourteen months after the new system had been in operation. Quite remarkably, leading firms like Ridgway & Abington and Davenport, made no use of the 1842 law until as late as 3rd November 1846 and 20th January 1849 respectively.

The clearly marked Wood & Brownfield plate of May 1842 has an identical transfer printed scene to that on a jug based on the James Dixon & Son registered shape of March and September 1842. This chinoiserie jug **(Col Pl. 11)** has a pattern number *'3008';* in the Wood & Brownfield sequence this would date it as cSeptember 1847. (See Appendix 6A.) Although based on the Dixon registered shape of 1842, this jug has no printed registration mark on the base. The absence of this mark could mean that it might be another factory's copy, but the additional data recorded on the jug base suggests not. Three different examples have been seen, all with the pattern number '3008', and each with a printed '3', also found on other Wood & Brownfield plates in the late 1840s and early 1850s (including Palmyra). Each jug carries a potter's mark (or marks) common to other Brownfield products **(Marks 5)**.

At least three more patterns were produced on this jug shape, each having a different transfer print

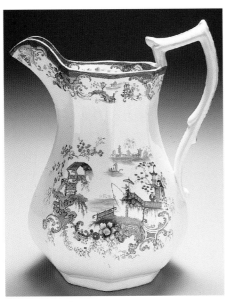

16. W&B. 'Nankin' Jug. Printed
Cartouche and Crown — 'Nankin'/
'W&B'/No '773'. cAugust 1843.
8½" — 21.5cm.

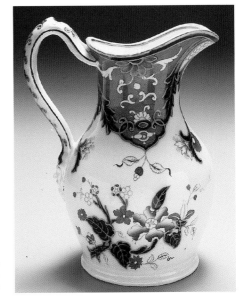

19. W&B. Portland Shaped Floral Jug.
Pat No '3134'. cNovember 1847.
8¼" — 21cm.

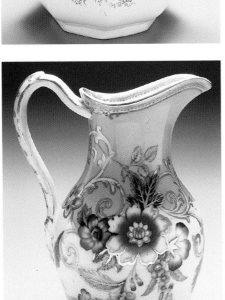

20. W&B. Portland Shaped Floral
Jug. Pat No '3368'. cApril 1848.
7" — 17.5cm.

21. W&B. Portland Shaped Floral
Jug. Pat No '3371'. cMay 1848.
6¼" — 16cm.

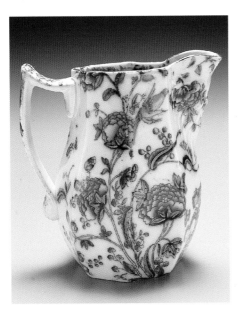

22. W&B. 'Snipe' Masked jug.
circa Oct 1848. Printed
'Snipe'/'W&B'/ Pat No '3665'.
5¾" — 14.5cm.

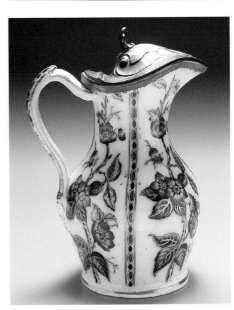

23. W&B. 'Turin' Jug. Printed
Cartouche and Crown.
'Turin'/'4088'/ 'W&B'. cJune
1849. 7¼" — 18.5cm.

25. W&B? Chinoiserie Jug. Unmarked. c1840-50. Forerunner to 'Lotus' Jug? 8¼" — 21cm.

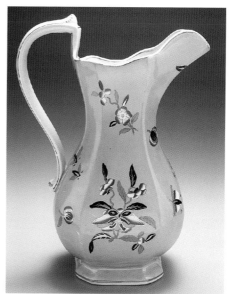

26. W&B. Oriental jug. Printed Marks — 'Oriental, W&B, Cobridge'. c1842-48. 8½" — 21.5cm.

28. WB. Portland shaped Floral jug. cNov 1850. Impressed 'o': Pat No '5049/::/H'. Printed blue factory mark '.)'. Height 7¼" — 18.5cm.

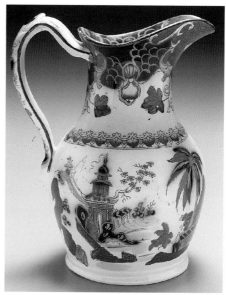

29. WB. Portland Shaped 'Palm Tree' Jug. Pat No '5348'. cFebruary 1851. 7¼" — 18.5cm.

30. WB. 'Patent No 1' Jug. c1850-1. Printed 'Patent No 1'. Height 6¾" — 17cm.

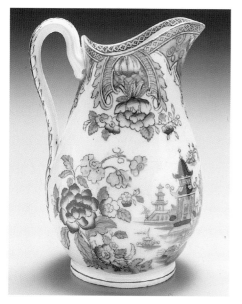
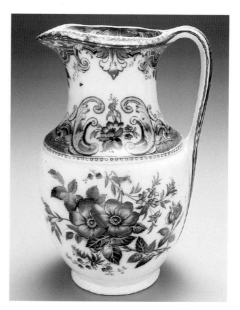

31. WB. 'Eureka' Jug. Printed Garter Mark — 'Eureka'/'5272'/WB. cOct 1851. 11½" — 29cm. Courtesy Jan Roach, Bristol.

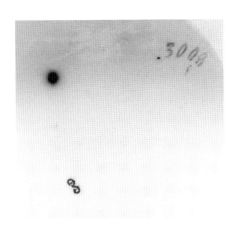

Marks 5. W&B. Chinoiserie Jug c1847. Printed '3'. Pat No '3008'. Blue Printed Factory Mark 'o'.

filled in with enamels. The first of these shows an oriental man carrying a sun umbrella over his shoulder while a child stands at his side **(Col Pl. 12)**; it has on its base *'PUBLISHED BY JAS DIXON & SON, SHEFFIELD, MARCH 1st 1842'*. This same transfer print has very recently been found on a marked Wood & Brownfield dessert service with a pattern number *428*, dating it as cDecember 1842. Moreover, this set **(Fig 12)** is filled in with the same yellow enamel as the Dixons jug. A second jug, having a floral transfer print, has *'REGISTERED BY JAMES DIXON & SON, 22nd SEPTEMBER 1842'*. Somewhat surprisingly, James Dixon & Son took the trouble to register the same jug shape under both the old law of 1811 and the new one of 1842. We have, therefore, to assess the likelihood of all the patterns on this jug shape being produced in the same factory. Identification of the different examples will be helped by the minimal relief-moulded leaves at both the top and bottom of the jug handle — a common Brownfield practice in later years — evident on the Brownfield 'No 1', 'No 18', 'No 21', 'No 28' and 'No 45' jugs manufactured in the 1850s. (These are reviewed in Chapter 2.)

Fig 12. W&B. Chinoiserie Dessert Plate. Impressed Cartouche — 'W&B/Pearl White/Cobridge'. Pat No. '428'. cDec 1842.

Yet another unmarked example has no pattern number at all **(Col Pl. 13)**; its hand painted flowers, not based on an underlying transfer print, suggest that it may have been a one-off. Both the design and the type of enamelling found on this jug are typical of Wood & Brownfield production in the 1840s, but it was not a style exclusive to this firm. The excellent moulding of the jug (especially the upper terminal on the handle) suggests that it was one of the very first to emerge from this mould; this would imply a date of late 1841 or early 1842 rather than later in the decade. The absence of any registration data on the base also suggests that it probably preceded the jug shape registered by James Dixon & Son on 1st March and 22nd September 1842. The manufacture of four or five patterns on the same jug body would be consistent with the same practice adopted by both Wood and Brownfield and William Brownfield with the 'Portland' Jug shape, first introduced in 1845-46 and subsequently used for no less than six other patterns introduced between 1847-52. However, this was a common practice operated by other factories in this period.

There is a further example of a jug produced on this exact shape on page 147 of Geoffrey Godden's *Illustrated Encyclopedia of British Pottery and Porcelain* **(Fig 14)**. The relief-moulding at both the top and bottom of the handle appears to be identical and matches that on the three jugs already shown. This is another transfer printed jug with enamel decoration, showing flower heads and foliage with a butterfly just under the jug spout. This latter floral design has some characteristics in common with the '3008' chinoiserie jug. This jug has *'JAMES DIXON & SON'* printed on the base and a date *'22nd SEPTEMBER 1842'*. However, other 1840's jugs show that at least one or two distinctive shapes were copied by other firms. Examples of this include the 'Ino' jug of about 1850-51, manufactured by

Samuel Alcock, Charles Meigh, Edward Walley, Bradbury Anderson & Bettany, and possibly Cork & Edge, but the 'Ino' jug shape was not registered either under the old legislation of 1811 or the new of 1842 and so factories were free to copy this exactly if they so wished.

Evidence from the 1840s shows that the transfer prints used on this kind of jug were sold not just to a single factory but to a number of them. The same chinoiserie pattern found on the W&B '3008' plate has also been found on a Careys' plate in the 1840s and on a Doulton plate in the 1890s. It has also been found on an unattributed plate with the pattern number '2768'; the presence of a blue printed 'o' on the back of this last plate suggests that this was a Wood & Brownfield product. If so, it would date from about April 1847, just five months before the chinoiserie '3008' jug. However, while this precise transfer print may not have been exclusive to the Wood & Brownfield factory, the right to use it on this jug *SHAPE* was restricted to the factory that manufactured the James Dixon & Son jug. Under the old law of 1811, no other firm could copy it before 1855 and under the 1842 act not before September 1845. This might suggest that it was the same firm producing all the patterns on the 1st March and 22nd September 1842 jug shape.

Fig 14. James Dixon & Son. Transfer Printed Floral Jug. Printed 'Registered by James Dixon & Son. 22nd September 1842'. Courtesy Geoffrey Godden.

All the markings on the '3008' chinoiserie jug of 1847 strongly suggest that *this* jug was manufactured in the Wood & Brownfield factory. The dessert service (Pat No 428) suggests that the James Dixon & Son jugs of March 1st 1842 and 22nd September were also made by Wood & Brownfield, but it is harder to be completely sure about the exquisite hand painted floral jug of early 1842. Minute inspection will be necessary of other patterns discovered on the same shape to see if there are pattern numbers and factory printed or painted marks. Investigation also needs to be carried out to try and ascertain the manufacturer of the jug registered by Jos Wolstenholme on 3rd November 1842.

OTHER WOOD & BROWNFIELD JUGS

Wood and Brownfield introduced the transfer printed 'Amoy' plate (Pat No '54') in about February 1838. Just over four years later, perhaps inspired by the recent events of the Opium War fought between Britain and China 1839-42, the firm decided to use the same transfer print on a jug. The only markings on this 'Amoy' chinoiserie jug **(Col Pl. 15)** are a painted pattern number *'333'* and a printed blue '+', the latter being one of the blue printed marks ('+', '*', 'o', 'v', '§' etc) used on many Brownfield transfer-printed wares in the late 1840s and early 1850s. A full 'Amoy' dinner service, clearly marked Wood & Brownfield and with the adjacent pattern number 335 supports the attribution of this jug to the same factory. The style of the jug is very reminiscent of the 1840s with an elaborately shaped rim and handle, and the historical background of the Opium War strongly suggests that this was a jug design introduced in 1840-42.

Wood & Brownfield may well have re-issued the 1838 'Amoy' pattern to commemorate the treaty of Nankin (August 1842), in the same way that it later commemorated many of the incidents of the Crimean war 1853-56. The Wood & Brownfield pattern number '333' would date this jug at about June 1842, but it could well be that '333' was in fact introduced two months later in August 1842, just after the Nankin treaty had been finally signed. The marked Wood & Brownfield 'Amoy' plate clearly uses the same transfer print as the transfer-printed jug. The design of the scrolls and the enamelling of the dog roses under the lip of the jug follow very closely those in the border of the plate. The 'Amoy' jug uses not just one but both the transfer prints employed on the 'Amoy' plate. This evidence indicates that this is a hitherto unidentified Wood & Brownfield jug emanating from about June-August 1842.

The 'Nankin' jug **(Col Pl. 16)** has a pattern number *'773'*, suggesting an introduction date of about August 1843, just after Parliament had debated the Nankin Treaty that concluded the Opium War. The jug has the same transfer printed scene with enamelled decoration on each side of the jug; this shows a Chinese man sitting on a veranda outside his house, fishing in the lake. Various trees, foliage and other affluent residences are shown in the background and these are also painted around the inside rim of the jug. A border of scrolls and flowers appear at the bottom of the scene and the same scrolls continue along and down the jug handle. There is no relief moulding on the jug itself, only two ornaments on the inside and outside of the handle. Insignificant though these may seem, it is possible that they may help to identify other examples produced on the same jug shape.

The jug has a printed cartouche on its base, containing the pattern name *'NANKIN'*, *'No 773'* and underneath this the printed letters *'W&B'*, but this does not in itself prove that it was a Wood and Brownfield product. Very little has been pieced together about the marking system employed by Wood and Brownfield on unregistered and non relief-moulded jugs in the 1840s. Similar printed cartouches have been found on several other wares, but these mostly originate in the years 1851-55 and thus are William Brownfield products. However, it is likely that William Brownfield chose to continue the marking system operated in the years 1841-50. This opinion is confirmed by the type of marks found on the Wood & Brownfield 'Cable' plate of 1848 which are virtually copied on the William Brownfield edition of 1850-51.

This does not, however, guarantee accurate attribution of the 'Nankin' jug. It could conceivably have been produced by Wood and Bowers, but they were operating for less than twelve months in 1839. However, a pattern number '773' suggests that it is highly unlikely that a tiny, short-lived pottery could have produced so many patterns in less than a year. Wood and Brownfield's estimated output in the 1840s (a firm known to have at least 150+ employees) shows that even they were not introducing this number of different patterns in one year. (See Appendix 6A.) On this basis therefore, it is safe and reliable to attribute the 'Nankin' jug to the Wood and Brownfield firm and this particular jug would have been produced in about August 1843.

'Japanese' was also produced on the same jug shape, with a pattern number '885', dating it about December 1843 and it is marked in the same way. 'Viola' is another pattern produced on the same jug shape. Its pattern number *'1009'* suggests that it was introduced in about February 1844. This jug was produced with an identical relief-moulded handle and it shows transfer printed flowers and foliage with enamelled decoration in blue and a reddish orange. There is also slight gilding on the leaves and under the rim of the jug. It has a printed cartouche and a pattern number on the base, similar to that found on the 'Nankin' jug. 'Oriental' is the last pattern so far found on this jug shape: its pattern number *'2109'* suggests an introduction date of about March 1846. It has a printed cartouche with the pattern name and *'W&B'*. More examples of the 'Nankin' jug shape may still be discovered and will be identified from the relief-moulded handle and the shape of the jug spout.

The Wood & Brownfield 'Portland' jug **(Fig 17),** was probably introduced some time between late 1845 and the beginning of 1847. In 1845 a maniac had destroyed the famous Portland Vase kept in the British Museum. Many manufacturers were quick to commemorate the original vase by producing 'Portland' jugs. Wedgwood, Alcock, Adams, Pearson, Copeland, Bradbury, Anderson & Bettany and

T & R Boote were among those to do so. Wood and Brownfield also produced a "Portland" jug although there are no obvious marks to link the jug to their factory. The first evidence proving attribution comes from the 'Turin' jug of 1849 and from William Brownfield's 'Bouquet' jug of February 1851. Both these jugs have clear printed marks attributing them to the Brownfield factory and both are manufactured in an identical shape to the 'Portland' jug. The second piece of evidence linking the 'Portland' jug with the Wood and Brownfield factory is the rare and distinctive potter's mark *(Ẅ)*, found on some 'Portland' jugs and on other Brownfield products in the early 1850s and on *no other* firm's goods.

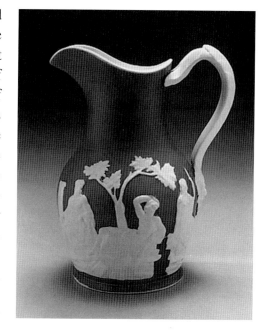

Fig 17. W&B. 'Portland' Jug. c1846-47. Unmarked Example. 6" — 15cm.

Three characteristics distinguish the Wood and Brownfield 'Portland' jug from others. The basic scene depicted on each jug is the same, but the neck of the Brownfield jug is broader than that on the Alcock, Adams, Pearson and other versions. The biggest difference, however, lies in the handle which has a clearly discernible thumb rest at the top while the head is moulded at the handle terminal rather than on both the handle and the terminal. This will be seen by comparing the picture of the Wood and Brownfield version with Alcock's **(Fig 18).**

Further examples have been attributed to Wedgwood and, on the basis of their 1855 Paris Universal Exhibition catalogue, to Cork and Edge. The last of these is possibly not Cork and Edge's own jug; Cork and Edge are more likely to have been acting for a number of firms which individually did not have the courage to have their own display stands in Paris. The uncertainty, financial risk and the current tight tariff restrictions imposed by the French government make this understandable. The Catalogue printed for the Great Exhibition of the Industry of all Nations (1851) held at Crystal Palace, shows that further editions of the Portland jug were being made at that time by both Copeland and T & R Boote, giving at least seven different examples of this famous jug. Another version has also been found produced by T Sneyd of Hanley, a firm that existed only from 1846-47.

Wood and Brownfield next introduced a different transfer printed pattern on the 'Portland' jug shape, **(Col Pl. 19)** the pattern number *'3134'* suggesting an introduction date of about November 1847. (See Appendix 6A.) The enamel decoration under the spout of this eight inch jug is identical to that on a later 'Portland' shape jug of April 1848, while the pattern of leaves and flowers is very similar to several on Brownfield plates of the early 1850s. This is, without question, the identical shape to the three Wood & Brownfield 'Portland' jugs of 1847-48, the 'Turin' jug of 1849, the sixth 'Portland' shaped jug of 1851 and the 'Bouquet' jug of 1852. Unlike the great majority of jugs produced in the period 1850-60, the

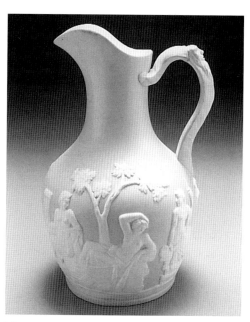

Fig 18. S. Alcock. 'Portland' Jug. c1846-47. Printed Coat of Arms, Lion & Unicorn, *'Patent'*, *'113'*. 7" — 17.5 cm.

1847-1848 examples have only a painted pattern number. Wood and Brownfield produced two further editions on the 'Portland' jug shape in about April 1848. These have pattern numbers '3368' and '3371', the first having an impressed 'Ẅ', the second a 'D' **(Col Pl. 20) (Col Pl. 21)**. The soft pink enamelling on the first is unusual for Wood & Brownfield. Patterns '3369-70' may well be two more editions of this same Portland shaped jug, with a different enamelled colour combination.

By about September 1848 Wood & Brownfield were producing a transfer-printed 'Snipe' jug **(Col Pl. 22)**. The example shown has a masked spout and a predominantly floral transfer print which continues about an inch into the jug itself. The relief moulding of the masked spout indicates that the jug body had been used for an earlier jug, probably another with a transfer-print, but one which did not encroach on the masked spout. Its marks include a printed cartouche containing the pattern name, 'W&B' and a pattern number '3665'. A second example of the 'Snipe' pattern has been found on a jug of entirely different shape, a small water jug with accompanying basin. This has the same pattern name and even the same pattern number. It is unlikely that these were the only jugs produced on these two shapes. Frustratingly, most other Wood & Brownfield jugs appear to be unmarked.

IDENTIFICATION OF WOOD AND BROWNFIELD JUGS IN THE 1840s

The absence of any registration diamond on Wood & Brownfield jugs and other wares during the years 1842-50 is a major handicap as is the absence of any clearly defined firm's mark — ie the Staffordshire knot, the circular trade mark or the twin globes of later years. However, a third type of mark did begin to appear on some firms' jugs in some exceptional instances in the 1820s and 1830s. In Wood and Brownfield's case, it only appeared in the later 1840s, possibly 1846-50 although no precise date can be imposed. This mark was invariably a single impressed letter or sign. Much conjecture has taken place over the years as to its meaning. Three possibilities have been pinpointed: first that it indicated some form of dating system, second, that it represented a model letter and third that it was a potter's mark impressed to make payment by piece rates possible and to assist in quality control.

A study of over 2000 individual Brownfield jugs suggests that the third explanation is correct although some enigmas remain to be solved. The first of these is that prior to the years 1846-50, the potter's mark is an exceptional occurrence rather than the norm. Individual letters or marks do appear on some Ridgway jugs in both the 1820s, 1830s and 1840s. The examples found of Wood & Brownfield's two relief-moulded jugs of 1841 do not bear potter's marks which is rather strange because the workers were still being paid piece-rate for output and the prolonged strike showed that workers and management were still in conflict over whether they were paid 'good from hand or good from oven'. Without any impressed potter's marks on the jug base, it is difficult to know how piece rates were calculated or quality control maintained.

The Wood & Brownfield 'Portland' jug impressed with the very distinctive potter's mark 'Ẅ' suggests that the factory introduced this practice in the 1840s, although we do not know the precise year in which this jug was made. It could have been made in 1846-47, but equally it might have been produced by William Brownfield in the early 1850s. Some potter's marks were common to workers in more than one factory, but the author believes that this mark is exclusive to Wood & Brownfield and William Brownfield jugs, having also been identified on William

Marks 6. W&B. 'Turin' jug — Printed Garter Mark — 'W & B'/Factory Sunburst Mark '*'. Pat No '4088'. Enameller's Mark '∴'. cJune 1849.

Brownfield's 'Fuchsia' jug of 1851, the 'Ivy' jug of 1856, the 'Jewel' jug of 1858 and the 'Shamrock' jug of 1859. A fair number of potters' marks were common to the factory workers of Ridgway, William Brownfield and Dudson, but this '*Ẅ*' mark is only found on Brownfield wares. The discovery of a marked Wood and Brownfield 'Turin' jug **(Col Pl. 23)**, produced on this same 'Portland' jug shape, and with a pattern number *'4088'* (June 1849), suggests that it was Wood and Brownfield that

Fig 24. WB. 1870s 'Lotus' shaped Jugs — 1880 Brownfield Catalogue. Courtesy Spode Ltd and Keele Univ Library.

made the initial 'Portland' jug with the potter's mark '*Ẅ*', rather than William Brownfield after 1851 **(Marks 6)**. The 1902 Pottery Gazette list of Brownfield pattern names tells us that Wood & Brownfield's 'Turin' pattern was also produced as 'Rome'. The fourth, fifth and sixth patterns produced on the 'Portland' jug shape (Pat Nos '5049', '5348' and '6099') are reviewed in Chapter 2.

Another unknown Wood & Brownfield jug has been detected from p68-69 of the 1880 Brownfield factory catalogue where there is a description of a 'Lotus' jug. This is a plain jug with a minimum of relief moulding around the base of the jug and again under the jug spout **(Fig 24)**. The Wood & Brownfield precursor to this 'Lotus' jug is manufactured on exactly the same jug shape although the handle is slightly different. The relief moulding is sufficiently unusual to suggest that, unless this is another firm's imitation, this transfer printed chinoiserie jug filled in with enamels was probably produced in the Wood and Brownfield factory **(Col Pl. 25)**. There are no printed marks on the jug base as there are on 'Nankin' and there is not even a pattern number. The only marks are two painted enamellers' letters, painted in yellow — the final colour used to paint the jug rim and the side of the handle. These are *'o'* and *'x'*, the first of which appears on a great number of enamelled Brownfield products in the early 1850s. Attribution would, of course, be much more straightforward if there were more specific markings, but many of the early plates have been found both with and without clear attributive marks. However, another 'Ironstone Vine' jug has recently been found with this same relief moulding, with clear attributive marks indicating manufacture by Livesey, Powell & Co. This indicates that this unusual relief-moulded jug was not exclusive to Wood & Brownfield.

A second 'Oriental' jug **(Col Pl. 26)** has recently been discovered, another of the transfer-printed jugs filled in with enamel decoration, produced in the 1840s. The pattern is a naturalistic one, depicting roses and butterflies on a green enamelled body: the latter is similar to the 1840 Jas Dixon transfer-printed floral jug, also produced on a green enamelled body. The jug has

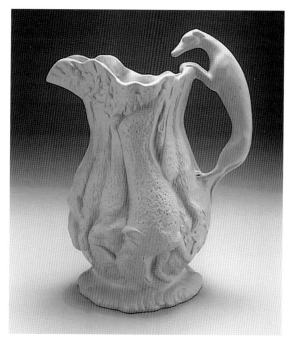

Fig 27. Attributed to W&B. 'Hanging Game' Jug. c1845-50. Unmarked Example. Impressed Potter's Mark '&'. WR Collection. 9½" — 24cm.

clear printed marks, *'ORIENTAL, W&B, COBRIDGE'*, but it has no pattern number which facilitates an accurate date. The pattern is similar but not identical to that on the 'Oriental' jugs and plates already identified by the author as being in production between 1842-46. This unusual shaped jug body has also been found with the same Wood & Brownfield transfer-printed chinoiserie scene found on the 1847 jug (Pat No. 3008). Unmarked, it is likely to be a Wood & Brownfield product.

The possible attribution of one 'Hanging Game' jug **(Fig 27)** is now reviewed. This jug has not been found with a printed or impressed name or coat of arms that can link it to a particular factory. But examples have been found with impressed potter's marks, while others have had an applied numbered rosette. These *may* provide us with slim clues to a specific attribution. This particular jug has the impressed potter's mark *'&'* and an impressed number *'6'* (the latter refers to the jug size). In over 2000 jugs that the author has examined, this impressed potter's mark has only been found on known Brownfield jugs. In all, it appears on over fifty different jugs introduced in the Brownfield factory between 1858-71. The absence of any precise date marking on this jug means that it could have been made c1845, c1850 or c1855. This most unusual potter's mark suggests that one version of the 'Hanging Game' jug was made in the Wood and Brownfield or William Brownfield factory.

The discovery of another 'Hanging Game' jug with the potter's mark *'FG'* supports this view. Other similar double letters have appeared on a large number of other Brownfield jugs. Jugs marked with twin letters ('FG', '&P', 'WG' etc) may have involved the collaborative work of two potters, possibly in the context of one experienced worker supervising another in his early months of employment by the firm. Very rarely did the other manufacturers employ twin potters' marks. This may be an additional reason for attributing one version of the 'Hanging Game' jug to the Brownfield factory. This argument can, however, only be applied to this jug. Dr R K Henrywood has identified another 'Hanging Game' jug with an applied rosette, containing the number '64', and this is not a system known to have been operated either by Wood and Brownfield or by William Brownfield thereafter. Clearly *two* case studies are not sufficient to warrant any generalisations about the 'Hanging Game' jug, but the hitherto insuperable difficulties in attributing this and other famous jugs made in the 1830-50 period suggest that this line of research may ultimately produce some unexpected conclusions. It must now be appreciated that the firm of Wood and Brownfield was well capable of producing quality jugs, and it must be considered as a possible manufacturer of some of the many unattributed ones, along with Ridgway and Abington, Charles Meigh, T & J Mayer, Davenport, Jones & Walley, and Samuel Alcock. Until very recently, this is not a thought that would have been seriously entertained, if considered at all.

CHAPTER 2
THE CHALLENGE OF INDEPENDENCE: OCTOBER 1850-JUNE 1863

The partnership with John Wood was terminated in October 1850. The workforce of 475 had increased by 200% in the previous nine years and in sheer numbers, William Brownfield employed a greater number of workers than Ridgway & Abington and only a few less than T & J Mayer and John Ridgway.

William Brownfield is known to have registered twenty three jug designs in the thirteen years 1850-63, in addition to many others relating to different wares. (See Appendix 1.) To that twenty-three, we must add the 'Patent No 1' jug of c1851-2, 'Bouquet', 'Cuba', the 'Portland' shaped jugs of 1850-1851, the 'Eureka' jug of 1851, the 'No 7' jug of 1851, the 'Rope' jug of June 1852, the 'Moldavia' Ewer of 1853, the 'Cape Ivy' painted ewer, the 'No 18' jug, the 'No 21' enamelled floral jug of March 1855, the 'No 28' water ewer first registered in April 1855, the 'Greek' jug of 1859, the 'No 38' Chinoiserie jug, the 'No 45' water ewer, 'Swiss', 'Universe', 'Barley Ear' and 'Burton', none of which was registered. Two further designs related to jardinières and in some cases a jardinière design also produced a jug. This was true of 'Tradescantia' (1857), 'Jewel' (1859) and 'Fern' (1859). However, two early jardinière designs 'Grapevine' (8th May 1854) and 'Passion Flower' (4th December 1861) did not produce a jug.

The next Portland shaped transfer-printed jug **(Col Pl. 28)** (Pat No '5049') is the first illustrated jug known to have been manufactured by William Brownfield after John Wood's retirement. This employed the fourth of six different transfer prints used on the same jug shape and was probably produced in about November 1850. The transfer printed 'Portland' shaped jug with enamelled decoration **(Col Pl. 29)** (Pat No '5348'), originated in about February 1851. (See Appendix 6A.) The scene in the lower half of the jug body shows a pagoda with a nearby palm-tree while a man fishes from an adjoining bridge. The same transfer print is found on Brownfield's 'No 17' jug of cSeptember 1854.

The 'Patent No 1' jug **(Col Pl. 30)** was probably introduced in 1851 or early 1852. This transfer printed jug with enamel decoration is one of several manufactured by William Brownfield between 1850 and 1863. There are no overt marks on the jug base that facilitate unquestioned attribution, but the same transfer print is found on the 'No 38' jug of December 1856 and on another later jug made in 1863. The 'No 38' jug does have both a pattern number *'9638'* and the blue printed sunburst '*' found on a host of proven Brownfield products made in the 1850s. Only the very first jug in this numbered series has *'Patent No'* on it, the remainder have just a blue or mauve printed 'No' **(Marks 7).** This is, as yet, impossible to explain. In isolation, the evidence for this jug's attribution may not seem wholly convincing, but it is much stronger in the broader context of the whole numbered series. No less than thirty-nine out of the forty-nine numbered items found have attributive marks denoting the Brownfield factory: some of these have printed blue marks found only on other known

Marks 7. WB. Patent No 1' jug (c1851-2). Printed 'Patent No 1'.

Marks 8. WB. 'Bouquet' jug. Printed Floral Cartouche — 'WB'/'Bouquet'. Pat No '6099'. cMar 1852.

Brownfield factory wares in the 1850s. (See Appendix 6C.) Both the 'No 18' and 'No 21' transfer printed jugs of 1854-55 were manufactured on the same jug shape as the registered Brownfield 'Mother and Child' jug of 14th March 1862. The type of print used to denote the No in this series is exactly the same in all instances except one — 'No 68'.

The first registered jug appeared on 10th October 1851 (Reg No 80910). The engraving in the design register shows that the shape was for a plain water ewer, but several transfer printed patterns were probably produced on this shape. The first of two known patterns produced on this shape is the 'Eureka' water jug **(Col Pl. 31)**. The pattern (and colours) of the flowers are very typical of Brownfield products in the early 1850s. This eleven and a half inch jug has a pattern number '5272' which would date its introduction at about February 1851 — six months before its registration. (See Appendix 6B.) Its printed garter mark contains the pattern name and underneath it the letters 'WB': it also has the printed sunburst mark '*', a virtually illegible registration diamond and the clearly impressed number '19'. This cannot be a size number, but it could possibly indicate another of the Brownfield numbered wares. (See Appendix 6C.) The pattern number '5272' refers to its initial introduction date in the Brownfield factory and this example was possibly produced later in 1852-53. Unfortunately, Brownfields did not at this early stage impress a month and year number on the base of their jugs; this was a practice only introduced after 1863. However, the paucity of evidence on which these estimated dates for pattern numbers had to be based, means that they may be inaccurate by three to four months.

The 'No 7' water jug with a pattern number '6150' **(Col Pl. 32)** is the second jug produced on the registered shape of 10th October, dating its original production about March 1852. This example may or may not have been the first jug produced in the actual month of its registration; if it was, the estimated date of its pattern number would be just over four months wide of the mark. It has the appropriate registration diamond, a pattern number, the blue printed sunburst mark '*' found on many Brownfield products in the 1850s and an impressed star and cross. Another toilet set with the pattern name 'Clarendon' was produced on this same registered shape in about August 1854. This has a registration diamond for 10th October 1851 and a printed cartouche containing the pattern name: under this is a printed No (left blank), the printed letters 'WB' and a painted pattern number '7787'. The latter would indicate an introduction date of about August 1854. (See Appendix 6A.)

'Fuchsia' **(Col Pl. 33)** is the first registered relief-moulded jug of 1851 (Reg No 80989) — introduced on the 16th October. This eight inch deep blue enamelled jug has white flowers while other examples have been found in plain white stoneware. Lidded jugs were produced from a different mould from the un-lidded ones. This is clear from a comparison of the enamelled blue jug with the plain white stoneware example **(Col Pl. 34)**. The shape of the jug lip has been changed to facilitate the use of a Britannia metal lid, but the remainder of the relief-moulding is the same; in some subsequent jugs, both the handle design and the jug lip had to be altered. The jug markings at this stage are a simple registration diamond, a size number and a potter's mark. The first of the two illustrated Fuchsia jugs has the rare impressed potter's mark '*W*' — found only on the earliest Brownfield jugs.

Only two new registered jug designs were introduced in 1851, the first full year of William Brownfield's firm, a remarkably low number for a firm with 475 employees. 1851 was also the year of the famous exhibition at Crystal Palace, at which many of the Staffordshire potteries demonstrated their

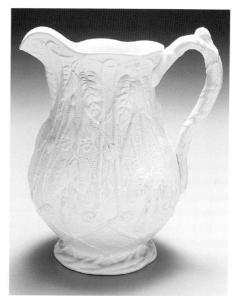

32. WB. 'No 7' Water Jug. Printed 'No 7'/'6150/6'. cMarch 1852. Height approx 10" — 25.5cm. Courtesy Simmon's Antiques, Lewes.

33. WB. 'Fuchsia' Jug. Moulded Reg D — 16th October 1851. Height 7¹/₂" — 19cm.

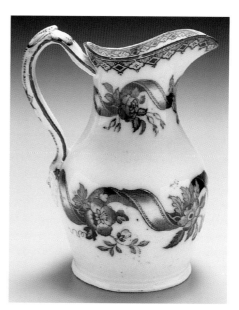

34. WB. 'Fuchsia' Jug. Moulded Reg D — 16th October 1851. Height 7¹/₂" — 19cm.

35. WB. 'Bouquet' Jug. Printed Cartouche — 'Bouquet'/WB/6099'. cMarch 1852. Height 6¹/₄" — 16cm.

40. WB. 'Cuba' Jug. Printed Garter Mark — Cuba'/'WB'/'6932'. cOctober 1853. Height 5³/₄" — 14.5cm.

41. WB. 'Kent' Jug. Moulded Reg D. 1st April 1853. Pat No '8616'. 6¹/₂" — 16.5cm.

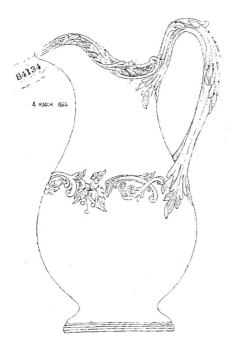

Fig 36. WB. Water jug. Registered — 4th March 1852. Engraving from the Design Register. Courtesy the PRO.

products. The official Exhibition catalogue shows that about sixty firms exhibited, including famous ones like Minton, Copeland, Samuel Alcock, Charles Meigh, F & R Pratt, T & J Mayer, Wm Ridgway, John Ridgway and Wedgwood to name but a few. There is no evidence that William Brownfield had his own stand at the Crystal Palace Exhibition in 1851.

'Bouquet' (Pat No '6099') **(Col Pl. 35)** is another 'unregistered' jug manufactured before the end of 1851 — the seventh and last manufactured on the Portland jug shape of 1846-47. The 'Bouquet' jug has less decoration than any of its predecessors, having only two rows of intermittent flowers linked together by an undulating scroll of foliage. The link with the registered 'Bouquet' plate of 10th February 1851 is the undulating scroll which is found inside the perimeter of the plate. (See Chapter 7.) The jug has an unusual printed cartouche on its base giving the pattern name, printed initials *'WB'*, and a pattern number **(Marks 8)**. The number dates the introduction of this particular jug as cMarch 1852. A water jug was introduced on 4th March 1852 **(Fig 36)** (Reg No 84134). This has minimal relief-moulding around the base of the handle and in the centre of the jug body. Like many of the earliest jugs, this appears to be a rare collector's item and the author has only seen one example (accompanied by a basin). This was a six inch enamelled jug, but the minimal pattern can only be illustrated from the Design Register engraving at the Public Record Office. Its only markings are, like its immediate predecessors, a registration diamond, a size number and an impressed potter's mark.

The 'Mazeppa' jug **(Fig 37)** followed six months later. Ivan Stepanovich-Mazeppa (who lived in the seventeen and early eighteenth centuries) ultimately became 'het-man' of the Cossacks, but he had

Fig 37. WB. 'Mazeppa' Jug. Moulded Reg D — 25th October 1852. Engraving — the Design Register. Courtesy the PRO.

been born into a poor family, where he remained until he became a page at the court of Poland. (See P D Gordon Pugh's *Staffordshire Portrait Figures*.) At some stage, he was discovered by a nobleman to be involved in an 'intrigue' with that nobleman's wife. He was bound naked upon his horse as a punishment and set loose and he somehow found his way back to the Ukraine (some versions of the story say to his own town). In 1687, at the age of forty-three he joined the Cossacks and was subsequently elected 'het-man'. He won the confidence of the famous Peter the Great and was made Prince of the Ukraine. For a while fame and fortune seemed to be assured, but Mazeppa incurred the wrath of Peter The Great by intriguing with Charles XII of Sweden. He fought on Charles's side against the Russians, experiencing a heavy defeat at the Battle of Pultowa (1709) and he died in the same year, humiliated and impoverished. No example of Brownfield's 'Mazeppa' jug has come to light but the engraving taken from the Design Register shows quite clearly what it was like.

Dramas about Mazeppa continued in popularity for the next fifty years. Interestingly, in the Romantic revival of the mid nineteenth century, it was not only jugs that were made to commemorate Mazeppa. In January 1990 the Antiques Road Show illustrated a silver snuff box, hall-marked in 1836, with an engraving of the naked Mazeppa on horseback. There were also at least four Staffordshire figures produced, one depicting Mazeppa on a Zebra, but most of these are thought to have emanated from c1864, the year when the beautiful Adah Isaacs Menken played the title role of Mazeppa at Astley's theatre.

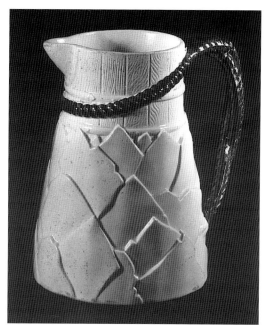

Fig 38. Attributed to WB. 'Interlocking Rope' Jug. Impressed Mark 'GP ' Pat No '6280'. cJune 1852. 8" — 20.5cm. Courtesy Kathy Hughes, Tudor House Galleries, Charlotte, NC, USA.

The 'Interlocking Rope' jug of 1852 **(Fig 38)** might be attributed to the Brownfield factory. This jug has been found not only with unusual twin potters' marks identified on other Brownfield jugs but also with painted pattern numbers *'6280'* and *'6287'* which fit into the pattern numbering system employed by Brownfields in the early 1850s. (See Appendix 6A.) This number would date the jug as cJune 1852. Seven different examples of this have been found with typical Brownfield potters' marks: four examples have the impressed letters 'GP', one the mark '*' and two the unusual mark '§'. The letters 'GP' have also been found on an 'Union' jug first registered in 1861, the '*' has been seen on eleven other Brownfield jugs including 'Kent' (1854) and 'Eglantine' (1860) and the '§' has been identified on a 'Shamrock' and an 'Union' jug also. This evidence is not water-tight, but the precise and unusual potters' marks found impressed on these jugs suggest that this 'Interlocking Rope' jug was made in the Brownfield factory. Unless the potters' marks are most unusual, it is dangerous to attribute a jug to a particular factory on this basis alone.

No jugs were registered in 1853, indeed the firm made no use of the Design Register during this year. It is almost certain that new unregistered jugs were produced — a view supported by the firm's need to keep the large workforce fully employed. 'Moldavia' **(Fig 39)** is the first one identified — a water ewer with a pattern number '6827', dating it as cMay 1853. (See Appendix 6A.) Moldavia and Wallachia were two provinces in the eastern Balkans, the first of which had borders with Russia. Both were involved in the Crimean War of 1853-54 — in which Turkey, Britain and France fought against the Russians. This is one of a considerable number of products manufactured by William Brownfield, many of which are named after locations in and around the Black Sea and Crimean peninsular area. (An 'Azoff' plate presumably refers to the Sea of Azov.)

'Cuba' **(Col Pl. 40)** is another unregistered jug with a pattern number *'6932'*. This is a transfer printed jug with enamel

Fig 39. WB. 'Moldavia' Ewer. Printed Garter Mark — 'Moldavia'/'WB'. Pat No '6827'. cMay 1853. Approx 10" — 25.5cm.

42. WB. 'Kent' Jug. Moulded Reg D
— 1st April 1853. 8½" — 21.5cm.

44. WB. 'No 17' Chinoiserie Jug.
Impressed '17'. Painted '7871'.
cSeptember 1854. 6½" — 16.5cm.

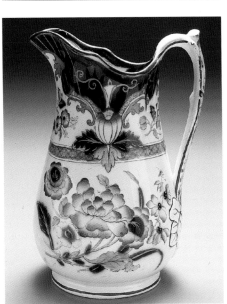

45. WB. 'No 18' Jug. Printed 'No
18'. Pat No '7867'. Printed Factory
Marks */o. cSeptember 1854.
8¾" — 22cm.

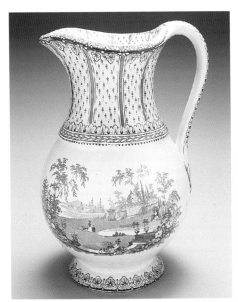

46. WB. 'Kew' Ewer. Printed
Garter Mark. 'Kew'/'WB'.
c1845-54. Private Collection.
12" — 30.5cm.

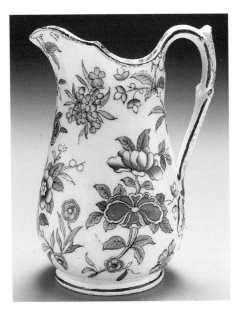

49. WB. 'No 21' Jug. Printed
'No 21'/Pat No '8379'. cMarch 1855.
7½" — 19cm.

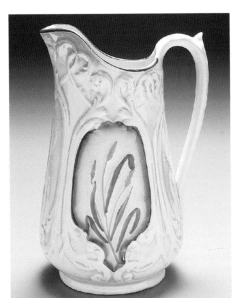

50. WB. 'Barley Ear' Jug.
Moulded Staffordshire
Knot/'WB'./'8428'. cApril 1855.
8¼" — 21cm.

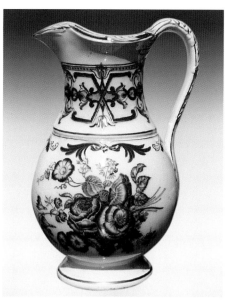

51. WB. 'No 28' Jug. Moulded Reg D — 26th April 1855. 'No 28'/'9474'. cApril 1855. 10" — 25.5cm. Courtesy Moulton's Antiques, W Bridgford, Nottingham.

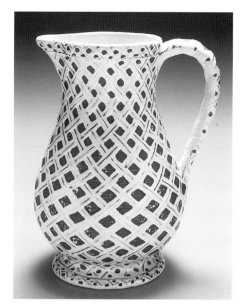

52. WB. 'Wicker' Jug. Moulded Reg D — 28th November 1855. 7¹/₂" — 19cm.

53. WB. 'Cape Ivy' Ewer. Printed 'Cape Ivy'/'WB'. c1850-55. 11¹/₂" — 29cm.

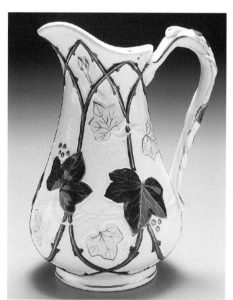

54. WB. 'Ivy' Jug. Moulded Reg D — 30th April 1856. Pat No '9401/2' 7³/₄" — 19.5cm.

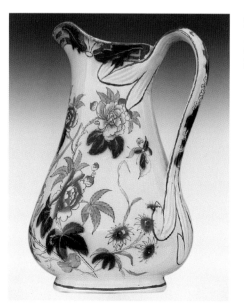

55. WB. Transfer Printed Floral Jug with Enamel Decoration. Reg D — 30th April 1856. 6" — 15cm. Courtesy Victoriana Antiques, Exeter.

56. WB. Transfer Printed Floral Jug with Enamel Decoration. Reg D — 30th April 1856. Pat No '9429'. Approx 7" — 17.5cm. Private Collection.

23

decoration dating from cOctober 1853. The floral pattern is the same on each side of the jug and is very similar to many on the Brownfield plates produced in the early 1850s. (See Chapter 7.) The shape is rather more bulbous than any other transfer-printed floral jug of the 1850s and the enamelling on this particular six inch jug appears to have been done by an apprentice rather than a more experienced member of the paint shop. The jug markings include a printed cartouche, the jug name and 'W.B': additionally there is a painted ':.' and a blue printed 'o'.

'Kent' (Col Pl. 41) is the first of two new designs introduced on 1st April 1854 (Reg No 95510). The design draws heavily on a naturalistic motif so commonly used by many of the pottery manufacturers in the 1850s. Minton had introduced his 'Hops' jug in May 1847: this is a very similar style — it has a deep blue enamelled background and white stoneware leaves. The body shape and handle of the Brownfield versions are markedly different. Separate moulds were used for lidded and un-lidded 'Kent' jugs

Marks 9. WB. 'Kent' jug — Moulded Reg D for1/4/54. Impressed Size '30'. Painted Pat No '8418/7'. N.B. The Moulded Registration Diamond is the only mark on new registered jugs introduced between 1851-1859.

(Col Pl. 42): not only is the lip of the jug different, but so too is the relief-moulding of the hops. The cluster of hops in the top centre of the jug body is quite different from that on the lidded example: further down and a little left of centre, a group of three hops on the lidded jug becomes a group of four on the unlidded one. This use of separate moulds was to continue with the 'No 17' and 'No 18' transfer printed jugs of cSeptember 1854 (both produced on the same jug shape), the 'No 21' jug of cMarch 1855 and the 'Arrowhead' jugs of December 1857. The introduction of the 'Jewel' jug in October 1858 saw a change in the styling of the handle so that only one mould was needed thereafter. The Brownfield 1880 factory catalogue tells us that the firm called the jug 'Kent'; with an abundance of hops, it is named after a county renowned for its plentiful crop. The only markings continue to be a registration diamond, accompanied usually by a size number and a potter's mark (Marks 9).

Fig 43. WB. 'Grapevine' Jardinière. Registered 8th May 1854. Engraving from the Design Register. Courtesy the PRO.

'Grapevine' (Fig 43) was the first of thirteen jardinières registered by William Brownfield between 1854-78 (Reg No 95751). It is included here because five of the thirteen designs led to both a jug and a jardinière — 'Tradescantia' 1857, 'Jewel' 1858, 'Fern' 1859, 'Argos' 1864 and 'Sisyphus' 1876: it does not appear to have done so in the case of 'Grapevine' 1854, 'Passion Flower' 1861, 'Gothic' 1863, 'Glenny' 1867,' Barlaston' 1869, and three other unnamed designs, two of 1870 and one of December 1878. It has, hitherto, been assumed that these last eight designs were those of jugs, but this does not appear to be the case. Most of Brownfield's jardinières appear to have no attributive markings at all and the author has seen an unmarked Brownfield 'Gothic' jardinière described as Minton. No example of the

Brownfield jardinière of 8th May 1854 has yet been found, and only time will tell if there is a jug of the same design. The picture of the 1854 jardinière is taken from the Design Register.

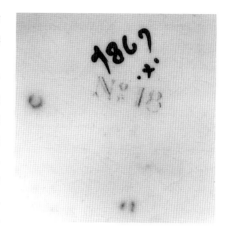

Marks 10. WB. Transfer printed Floral jug. Printed 'No 18'/'o'. Pat No '7867'. Enameller's Mark '.x.'. c Sep 1854.

Four more unregistered jugs have been found — initially introduced in 1854. These attributions are suggested by the pattern numbers found on the base of the jugs, the potter's impressed letters and what appears to be special factory numbers found on the bottom of some jugs. The 'No 17' and 'No 18' are two unregistered Brownfield jugs introduced in about September 1854 **(Col Pl. 44)** **(Col Pl. 45)**, the first having an impressed 'No 17', the second a printed 'No 18' **(see Marks 10)**. Their Brownfield attribution is confirmed by the later production of the registered 'Mother and Child' jug in the same shape as the 'No 17', 'No 18' and the 'No 21' transfer printed floral jugs with enamelled decoration; this was registered on 14th March 1862. Detection was facilitated by a growing awareness that William Brownfield used the same jug shape for two, three or more designs. The minimal relief moulding on all three jugs is identical; the 'No 17' has no pattern number, but is likely to have been produced shortly before the 'No 18' which has a pattern number '7871'. This pattern number suggests an introduction date of about September 1854. The scene portrayed on the 'No 17' jug is also identical to that on the 'Portland' shape transfer printed jug with the pattern number '5348' **(Col Pl. 29)**.

The third known unregistered jug introduced in the early years 1851-54 is the 'Clarendon' water ewer referred to earlier. No picture of this is available, but its transfer-printed floral pattern with enamel decoration follows very closely those on the jugs numbered '18' and '21'. The fourth and last of the known unregistered jugs made in 1854 is the 'Kew' ewer **(Col Pl. 46)**. This design is very reminiscent of the 1840s and it has much in common with the Palmyra plate, hitherto thought to have been first introduced by Wood and Brownfield in 1845. (See Chapter 7.) The 'Kew' ewer was produced on the same shape as the 'No 28' Water Ewer and this ewer shape was registered later by William Brownfield on 26th April 1855. There is a profusion of printed detail on the ewer base — a printed garter mark containing the title name 'KEW' and under that a printed *No* (left vacant) and the letters 'WB'. The garter mark is topped by a crown and there is an impressed potter's mark 'G'. It is a moot point whether this was first produced in 1855 or earlier in the years 1845-54. Its design characteristics suggest that it was introduced by the Wood & Brownfield factory in the 1840s.

The year 1855 saw the registration of three new jugs — the first 'Linenfold' **(Fig 47)** appearing on 26th April, accompanied on the same day by the second — a plain jug or probably a ewer. The second registered design was the shape of a jug, introduced almost certainly with a view to manufacturing different patterned versions in later years — an opinion confirmed by subsequent

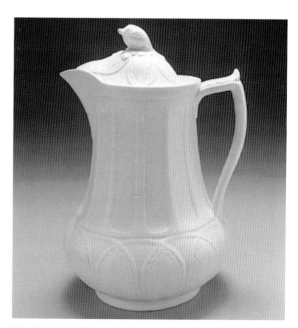

Fig 47. WB. 'Linenfold' Jug. Moulded Reg D. 26th April 1855. WR Collection. 7½" — 19cm.

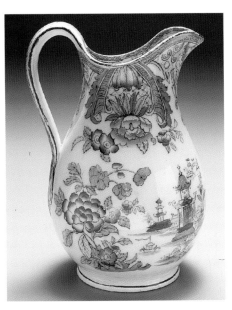

57. WB. 'No 38' Jug. Painted 'No 38'/'9638'/Factory Marks '*o'. cDec1854. 8½" — 21.5cm. Courtesy Schofield Antiques, Exeter.

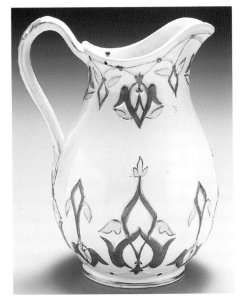

58. WB. Stylised 'Tradescantia' Jug. Moulded Reg D — 5th June 1857. Pat No '10,227'. 6¾" — 17cm.

59A. WB. Unlidded 'Arrowhead' Jug. Moulded Reg D — 9th December 1857. RL Collection. 7" — 17.5cm.

59B. WB. 'Arrowhead' Jug. Moulded Reg D — 9th December 1857. WR Collection. 8" — 20.5cm.

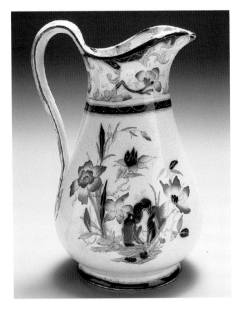

60. WB. 'No 45' Jug. Unmarked. Printed 'No 45'/'10,408'. cSeptember 1857. 8½" — 21.5cm.

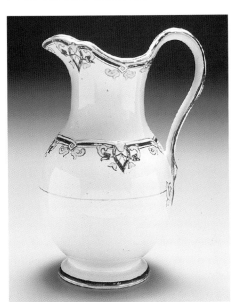

61. WB. Water Jug. Illegible Moulded Reg D — 24th August 1858. Size number '1'. 7¾" — 19.5cm.

discoveries. The name accorded to the first jug of April 1855 is not the one given to it by William Brownfield; the jug has only a registration diamond, a size number and a potter's mark and it is not one of the many designs illustrated in the firm's 1880 salesman's catalogue, now to be found in the Spode Manuscripts in Keele University. Its original and proper design name is not therefore known and the title 'Linenfold' was accorded to it by one of a group of Brownfield jug collectors, whose collaborative efforts went into the initial preparation for this book. This seven and a half inch 'Linenfold' jug is the only one the author has so far discovered — produced in plain white stoneware. The jug is extremely unusual for a Brownfield in having a stoneware lid.

A plain water ewer design was registered on 26th April 1855 **(Fig 48)**. Such a registration would normally imply that this was a *new* design, but in this instance this was clearly not the case. The review of the 'Kew' ewer earlier in the chapter indicates that this shape had been in production for a number of months or years prior to April 1855 without being registered. Exactly how long cannot be specified. One wonders why William

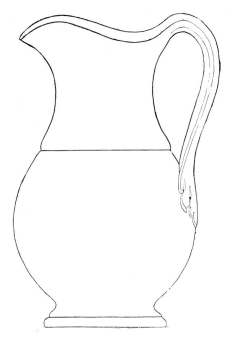

Fig 48. WB. Plain Ewer. Moulded Reg D. 26th April 1855. Engraving from the Design Register. Courtesy the PRO.

Brownfield, in this and other instances, did not register the ewer (or jug) shape when it *first* came into production. Two other patterns have been found on this ewer shape; the first, 'Anapa' of cFebruary 1855 has a pattern number '8221' and the Brownfield factory blue printed marks '*o', an impressed '48' and a printed '10'; the second is the 'No 28' Water Ewer of cJune 1855 with the pattern number '8474'. (See Appendix 6A.)

The 'No 21' jug **(Col Pl. 49)** is the next known unregistered jug manufactured in about April 1855. This is another in the Brownfield numbered sequence of transfer printed jugs with enamelled decoration. It is just one in a group of similarly numbered jugs, plates and other products that is so distinctively marked — the *only* ones during the years 1850-1900. There are no positive markings on the jug base that make definite attribution possible. There are, however, two clues that enabled the author to confirm that this is a Brownfield product. The first is minimal relief moulding (the outline shape of a tree leaf), both under the top of the jug handle and at its base. Close inspection shows this to be identical to the moulding on a later Brownfield jug — the 'Mother and Child' jug registered on the 14th March 1862. The whole jug shape and the handle are *exactly* the same as this earlier jug, ie it has come from the same mould. The second clue is a painted pattern number '*8379*' which fits into the Brownfield sequence in the 1850s and tallies with the approximate date of manufacture of the jug. Appendix 6A shows that the pattern number dates this jug as approximately March 1855 — seven years before the same shape was re-used for the 'Mother and Child' jug. It is possible that even more patterned examples of this 'No 21' jug may yet be found.

A 'Barley Ear' jug **(Col Pl. 50)** was possibly introduced in 1855. The earliest examples of this jug with enamelled decoration do not have a pattern number nor do they have any specific marks linking them with the Brownfield factory, but another identical jug has been found with the pattern number '8428'. This dates the introduction of this latter jug as cApril 1855. (See Appendix 6A.) It seems likely that the unmarked examples emanated from c1853-55. It is known that by 1855, Brownfields were marketing a plain white stoneware version of this jug with a moulded Staffordshire knot on the base

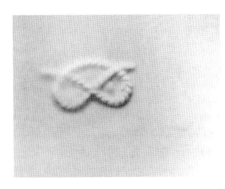

Marks 11. WB. 'Barley Ear' jug. Moulded Staffs Knot/'WB'. Size '24'. Impressed '5/90'. Potter's mark 'S'. The illustrated jug is unmarked. NB. The Staffordshire knot was used by William Brownfield for new jugs introduced between 1855-1863.

(containing the letters 'WB') and the same jug was still in production in 1890. The 1890 example has a Staffordshire knot, an impressed potter's mark 'S' and an impressed date for May 1890 *(5/90)* (**Marks 11**). Because the jug was never registered, Brownfields continued to produce it with its original markings instead of the twin globes that would normally be found on other Brownfield jugs from this very late period. For the student of exceptional marks, therefore, this jug is most unusual. Like some of the firm's other products it was in production for well over thirty years.

The 'No 28' transfer printed water jug (**Col Pl. 51**) with accompanying toilet set, all with enamelled decoration, was produced on the ewer shape registered by William Brownfield on 26th April 1855. The water jug is ten inches tall, and has a moulded registration diamond. Additionally, the base of the ewer has a painted pattern number '9474', two impressed potters' marks 'JH' and a printed number 'No 28'. The pattern number shows that this example of the jug was manufactured from about September 1856, but the registration diamond clearly indicates that it was first registered on 28th April 1855 and the Kew ewer (made on the same shape) indicates that this jug shape was in production earlier than that — probably some time between 1845-54.

There followed later in November 1855 the production of the 'Wicker' jug (**Col Pl. 52**) (Reg No 102785). One of these jugs is very unusual in that it has no registration diamond like all the others and its only markings are an impressed cartouche containing the title 'WICKER' and an impressed '18' — its size number. This would suggest that this was a prototype of the jug registered on 28th November 1855. Many previous authors have given this jug the title 'Basketweave' — this was done by Hugh Wakefield in his *Victorian Pottery* (1962), but the title is misleading because another Brownfield pattern 'Basket' was in fact introduced in January 1880. There is no doubt that this was the pattern name given to the jug by William Brownfield as it appeared under this name in the 1880 salesman's catalogue. The only markings on the jug base are those standard to the years 1850-58, a registration diamond, the size number and a potter's mark. Another 'Wicker' jug has been found without any clear attributive marks except the potter's mark 'W' — a mark identified on other early Brownfield jugs. This more elegantly shaped 'Wicker' may have been another prototype, discarded in favour of the shape registered in November 1855.

1855 was an important year for many of the Staffordshire potteries because of the Paris Universal Exhibition. William Brownfield did not participate *directly* in this. At this time the French exercised a prohibition on the importation of 'all English stoneware or untransparent ware except stoneware for professional purposes'. The immediate prospect of generating worthwhile sales from exhibiting at Paris was therefore minimal and only twenty-three Staffordshire firms were present at Paris; of these, Minton and Copeland took up no less than 55% of the available 2600 square feet of display space. The 1855 Paris Universal Exhibition has been, perhaps, renowned in pottery circles for the Cork and Edge display of no less than nineteen different jugs, a display that has given rise to a great deal of controversy among ceramic historians. There is no evidence that Cork and Edge displayed any Brownfield jugs on their 'collective' stand.

The 'Cape Ivy' Ewer (**Col Pl. 53**) is another unregistered Brownfield jug which originated in this period. Precise dating of this jug is difficult because there is, unusually, no painted pattern number on the base of the jug. However, given the style of this eleven and a half inch, transfer printed ewer with enamel decoration, it seems likely that it emanated from the years 1850-56 and preceded the relief-moulded 'Ivy' jug. Its markings include a printed *'CAPE IVY'* and *'WB'*. The relief-moulded 'Ivy' jug (**Col Pl. 54**) was introduced on 30th April 1856 (Reg No 104603), the same day as the registration of an accompanying plain jug. Of all the naturalistic designs in the period 1820-60, 'Ivy' must have been one of the most popular. The first and arguably the most famous was that of J D Bagster in 1828. There followed in July 1846 the Ridgway and Abington version, with Samuel Alcock producing his own edition in January 1854, and Pankhurst and Dimmock theirs in December of the same year. Minton went one better — producing two jugs on the same theme — the first on 22nd November 1845 and the second in June 1852. This most attractive Brownfield 'Ivy' jug is produced in damson, gold and white; the only markings on the jug base are the registration diamond, (in one instance a pattern number *'9070'*), the size number and the potter's mark *'W'*: 'Ivy' was the only registered relief-moulded jug introduced in 1856.

Marks 12. WB. 'No 38' jug. c1856. Printed Factory marks '*'/'o'/Printed 'No 38'/'5'. Pat No '9638'. Impressed 'J'. c Dec1856.

The engravings in the Public Record Office show that a plain jug shape was registered at the same time. The registration of a plain jug suggests that the design was almost certainly used to produce additional transfer printed examples of it, an opinion confirmed by the discovery of two such jugs with enamel decoration (**Col Pl. 55**), although it is unlikely that these are the only ones. The only markings on the jugs are a moulded registration diamond and an impressed potter's mark, unaccompanied by any jug pattern name. A set of three jugs has been found with the same transfer-printed pattern, but enamelled in a different colour combination: the one illustrated (**Col Pl. 56**) has the pattern number *'9429'*, suggesting an introduction date of about September 1856.

Towards the very end of 1856, probably in about December, William Brownfield introduced the 'No 38' transfer printed jug (**Col Pl. 57**), filled out with enamel decoration. This chinoiserie scene is identical to that on the 'Patent No 1' jug of 1851-2. It is produced on the same jug shape, but a slight alteration has been made to the jug handle. It has no obvious markings that facilitate attribution to the Brownfield factory, but it has the factory blue printed sunburst mark '*' and a 's' found on many other known Brownfield plates and jugs in the 1850s (**Marks 12**). It also has the impressed potters' marks *'JT'* and a pattern number *'9638'*, showing that this jug was introduced in about December 1856. (See Appendix 6A.) Other transfer printed examples of this jug will probably be identified by the relief moulding found at the base of the jug handle.

The only other development in late 1855 and early 1856, and a very interesting one, was the formation in November 1855 of a Brownfield employees 'Free Trade' association. This intriguing development shows twelve workers, probably with little education and no great political or economic awareness, taking the initiative in the formation of a free trading branch. Normally the impetus would come from the management, but this movement was only taken over and organised by the bosses a few weeks later. It seems likely that the initiative for the Anglo-French Free Trade Association stemmed as much from the dynamic leadership of one of the Brownfield workforce, the radical Enoch Stevenson. There is no incontrovertible evidence at this juncture, 1856, that William Brownfield's firm had entered the export market. The group's action is, therefore, intriguing and it supports the *possibility* that the firm had already taken its first small steps to expand their sales overseas, if only in the context of a collective venture or on a stand organised by a Paris agent at the 1855 Paris Universal Exhibition.

It has, hitherto, been argued that Brownfields only entered the export market in 1867 — at the Paris Universal Exhibition, over twelve years after the workers formed this group. The discovery of the 'Universe' jug marked with a Staffordshire knot, suggests that this may well have been produced for display at the 1855 Paris Universal Exhibition (this particular 'Universe' jug was not produced *before* 1855 — the earliest known date for the Staffordshire knot). Production was probably delayed until after 1859 because in 1855-58 there was still a prohibition on the export of most categories of English earthenware to France. William Brownfield may well have decided to delay the sale of 'Universe' in France until tariffs were markedly reduced — ie about 1859-60. It could be that Brownfield used a Parisian agent or an English retailer to exhibit his goods. This possibility is endorsed by evidence from 1862 when Furnivals displayed in London on the stand of Pellatts — the well known London dealer. Several Staffordshire pottery firms also used French agents to display at the 1867 Paris exhibition.

Three new registered Brownfield products emerged in 1857, two of which were relief-moulded jugs while the third was a jardinière. The first two of these were the stylised 'Tradescantia' jug **(Col Pl. 58)** and its fellow jardinière, both being registered on 5th June (Reg No 110097-98). This is not the name accorded to the jug by William Brownfield, but the only markings are the registration diamond, the size number and the potter's mark. The jug did not appear in the 1880 catalogue, and so its original pattern name is not known. The jug illustrated is just under seven inches tall and is the only fully enamelled version of this jug yet found. There is a painted pattern number *'10,227'* on its base. This scarce jug is known predominantly in plain white stoneware although three examples have the motif picked out in blue, green or crimson enamel; this adds to its attraction but does not wholly succeed in comparison to those jugs where the jug background is enamelled in colour. Indeed, like many Brownfield jugs, it is transformed with an enamelled or glazed background to bring out the floral motif much more sharply.

Nowhere is this more true than in the case of the next jug — 'Arrowhead' **(Col Pl. 59A)** registered on 9th December 1857 (Reg No 112354). This is the title that Dr R K Henrywood gave to this jug in his chapter 'Little-Known makers and Puzzle Pieces' in his book *Relief-Moulded Jugs 1820-1900* (p216). The example shown there is in white stoneware with the motifs picked out in blue enamel — quite attractive but unexciting in comparison to a fully enamelled jug produced in blue, white and gold. The jugs illustrated have a quite different dimension; the first is seven inches tall, and is transformed from the ordinary to the exceptional by superb, deep blue enamelling, augmented by gilding of the white arrowheads and flowers. The second **(Col Pl. 59B)** shows the lidded edition with altered handle, enamelled in green, yellow and gold on a white body. No further alteration to the relief-moulding has been made in this instance. The markings on the jugs are a moulded registration diamond, an impressed size number and a potter's mark.

Another unregistered, transfer printed floral jug was introduced by Brownfields in 1857. The only marks on the jug illustrated **(Col Pl. 60)** are a painted pattern number *'10,408'* and a blue printed clock-key mark found on other Brownfield products of this period. It resembles closely the registered Brownfield jug of 30th April 1855, but in this instance there is a slight variation in the relief moulding. The jug shape in each case is identical, but this example only has the relief-moulding at the base of the handle and it has to be said that, while very similar, this is not identical to that on the registered jug of April 1855. However, the enamelling of the orange flower heads is exactly as on the earlier jug, and the likelihood of it being another firm's imitation is diminished by the discovery of another identical jug, ten inches tall, also with the pattern number '10,408'. Crucially, it also has a printed *'No 45'* — in the same blue print as on many of the numbered Brownfield products and it also has the 'clock-key' printed

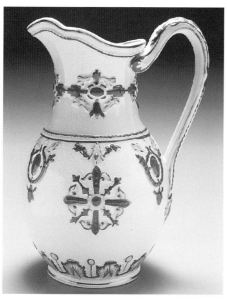

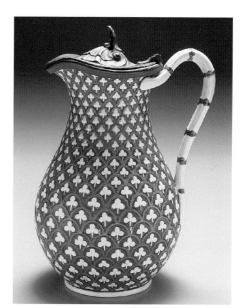

62. WB. 'Jewel' Jug. Moulded
Reg D — 5th October 1858.
Pat No '11,358.' 6½" — 16.5cm.

63. WB. 'Shamrock' jug. Moulded
Reg D — 20th May 1859.
Pat No '11,949'. 7¼" — 18.5cm.

64. WB. 'Fern Jug. Moulded
Staffordshire knot and 'WB'
Reg D for 5th November 1859.
Private Collection. 8" — 20.5cm.

65. WB. Unusual 'Fern' Jug.
Moulded Reg D for 5th November
1859. WR Collection. 7¼" — 18cm.

66. WB. 'Greek' Jug. Pat No '12,883'.
Factory Mark '*'/Impressed 'Greek.'.
6¾" — 17cm.

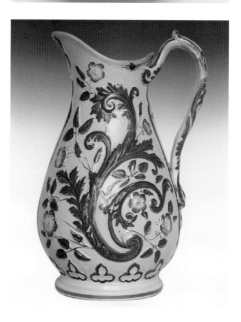

67. WB. 'Eglantine' Jug. Moulded
Staffordshire knot and 'WB' Reg D
for 6th June 1860. 8" — 20.5cm.

mark. This suggests that it was introduced in about September 1857. (See Appendix 6A and 6C.) A 'Farmers' Arms' jug was also produced on the same relief-moulded body, suggesting that this was probably made in the Brownfield factory.

Only two jugs were registered in 1858 — the first, registered on 24th August, was produced as a small water jug and basin **(Col Pl. 61)** (Reg No 114763). Only one example of this has come to light and this is enamelled in blue and yellow with additional gilding on a brightly glazed white body. Its markings include an illegible moulded registration diamond and a size number. The minimal relief moulding has much in common with that found on the stylised 'Tradescantia' jug which preceded it in June 1857. The second registered jug was 'Jewel' **(Col Pl. 62)** — the registration being effected on 5th October (Reg No 115902). No separate registration was taken out for a jardinière of the same design, but the salesman's book of 1880 shows that the pattern was also used for that purpose. The name of the jug does not appear moulded on the base and this is only known because it is given in the Brownfield 1880 catalogue. The jug illustrated shows an unusual colour combination of orange, yellow and gold on a white background body. Different pattern numbers show that a new colour range was being introduced for 'Jewel' in 1864 and the jug was still in production in 1880, twenty-two years after its initial registration. 'Jewel' was the last in the sequence of jugs to be marked only with the registration diamond, the size number and a potter's mark. Several examples have an additional painted pattern number on the jug base — these range from '11,341' to '11,358'. At least ten different colour combinations have already been found.

'Shamrock' **(Col Pl. 63)** was the first of two new registered jugs in 1859, introduced on 20th May (Reg No 119968). In its plain white stoneware form, the jug is not exciting, but the seven and a quarter inch jug illustrated here comes in an attractive mauve enamelled background body. For the first time we now have on the jug base a moulded Staffordshire knot containing the initials *'WB'*, the registration diamond, the size number and a potter's mark. Contrary to earlier opinion, this precise form of marking on new registered jugs was only used between 1859-63. One green and white enamelled example of 'Shamrock' has what would appear to be an erroneous painted pattern number — *'11,343'* dating it as October 1858, whereas the design was not registered until May 1859. Given that '11,341' and '11,342' were both 'Jewel' jugs, it seems probable that this number should also have been a 'Jewel' design.

'Fern' **(Col Pl. 64),** the second relief-moulded jug registered on 5th November 1859 (Reg No 123816), was probably the most successful of all Brownfield's jug designs. Like its immediate predecessor, its proper markings should include the Staffordshire knot, the registration diamond for 5th November 1859, the size number and a potter's mark. The jug illustrated is eight inches tall and is enamelled in an attractive and very unusual mauve, gold and white. 'Fern' provides us with the first of eight examples of erroneous moulded markings on the jug base. Having been registered on 5th November 1859, the correct markings should show the appropriate information for that date. However, there are a number of 'Fern' jugs with the later moulded circular trade mark and a registration diamond for 14th October 1863 **(Marks 13)**. This is the appropriate registration date for the 'Albion' jug. Similar errors were to be made later in the case of the 'International' jug which can be found with no less than three 'wrong' registration dates, with the 'Ivy' jug, the 'Argos' jug (three different dates), the 'Cupid' jug, the 'Severn' teapot and with the 'Hudson' jug of 22nd December 1877.

Marks 13. WB. 'Fern jug — Erroneous Moulded Reg D for 14 Oct 1863 (Albion Jug). Moulded twin Globes trade mark — 'WB'/'Cobridge'. Impressed potter's mark 'S'.

The 'Fern' jug proved to be so popular that imitations quickly appeared on the market — within the three years allotted for the protection of the registered design. In his book *Relief-Moulded Jugs 1820-1900,* Dr R K Henrywood commented: 'It is difficult to understand how Dudson could successfully register this close copy (of Brownfield's Fern) when the original Brownfield version was still protected'. The full explanation of this, and another allied controversy, has now been unearthed in the *Staffordshire Advertiser's* coverage of a court case held before the Hanley magistrates in May 1861. Surprisingly, the summons issued by William Brownfield for 'fraudulent conversion' of the Fern jug was taken out, not against James Dudson, but against the firm of Samuel Bevington — a manufacturer and wholesaler in Hanley. William Brownfield, called to give evidence, told the court that during a visit to London (precise date unspecified) he had discovered that one of his customers in the retail trade had been selling 'Fern' jugs at a price less than he had been charging the retailer. Mr.Brownfield then told the magistrates that he had first brought home the fraudulent conversion to Mr.Dudson, but he had made some amends and accordingly he had not brought Mr Dudson to court. William Brownfield asserted that Mr.Bevington's 'Fern' jug differed slightly only in the form of the handle and on the body of the jug the representation of the wheat or barley ears had been omitted.

Called to account for this, Samuel Bevington protested that the jug produced in court in evidence (bought directly from his factory by one of Brownfield's employees) was made before W Brownfield ever made a jug. He added in increasingly intemperate manner that there were fifty men (in Staffordshire) making the same jug. Samuel Bevington clearly felt very aggrieved that he was being prosecuted and he had initially ignored the Magistrates' summons for several weeks. He tried to convince the court that his tiny firm was being bullied by Brownfield's much bigger one, telling the magistrates that while his firm had only one jug maker, Brownfield employed sixty. The magistrates ignored Bevington's emotional outburst and told him that all forged jugs were to be handed over to William Brownfield or be destroyed. The moulds were to be broken up and Bevington was to pay all the expenses incurred in the court case. The magistrates concluded with a stern admonition — saying that if he had persisted they would have convicted him. Disappointingly, the report of the case throws no light on the 'atonement' made by James Dudson. The picture of a different 'Fern' jug **(Col Pl. 65)** could possibly be one of Samuel Bevington's imitations (or of one of the many others to which he referred), although this example only shows an alteration to the handle and no corresponding differences to the ears of the barley. It may have been a precursor to the 1859 'Fern' made in the Brownfield factory.

Soon after the legal protection expired in November 1862, variations and near copies of the 'Fern' jug were produced by Worthington and Green on 20th March 1863, by James Macintyre of Burslem on 11th April 1863, by F R Pratt on 18th December and by Wood and Sale on 2nd July 1864. This last registration is particularly interesting as it was done on behalf of James Dudson, to whom the registration was transferred on 13th February 1865. (It is interesting to note, as a final observation on illegal copying, that a John Bevington (probably a relative) later employed the mark '✗' on his wares in what would appear to have been a deliberate attempt to imitate Meissen and thus deceive the buying public. This may well have been sharp practice in one generation continued in the next!)

In addition to 'Shamrock' and 'Fern', Brownfields were producing at least two other unregistered jugs in 1859 — 'Greek' **(Col Pl. 66)** and 'Antique'. 'Greek' is a transfer-printed jug filled in with enamel decoration, its floral pattern being typical of the 1850s and similar to the 'Cuba' jug of 1855. There are no easily identified impressed or printed marks that facilitate attribution, but there is the Brownfield factory printed sunburst mark '*', accompanied by the pattern name *'GREEK'*, and a pattern number *'12,883'*. The latter indicates an introduction date for this example of about November

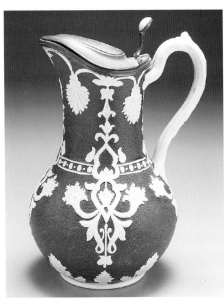

68. WB. 'Floral' jug. Moulded Staffordshire knot and 'WB' Reg D for 29th October 1860. BM Collection. 9" — 23cm.

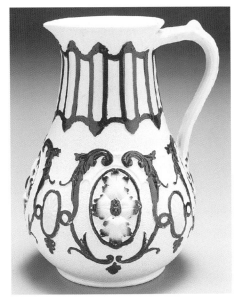

69. WB. 'Donatello' Jug. Moulded Reg D — 6th July 1861. Moulded Staffordshire knot. Moulded Cartouche 'Donatello'/'WB'/36/'13,507'. 7½" — 19cm. MM and MR Collection.

70. WB. 'Union' Jug. Moulded Reg D — 4th December 1861. Moulded Staffordshire knot. Cartouche — 'Union'/'WB'/'30'. 8" — 20.5cm. Courtesy Von Bulow Antiques, Dorking, Surrey.

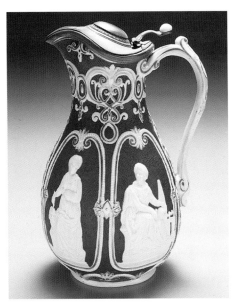

72. WB. 'International' Jug. Moulded Reg D — 25th January 1862. Moulded cartouche/Staffordshire knot 'International'/'WB'/'18'. 8½" — 21.5cm.

73. WB. 'Mother and Child' Jug. Printed Reg D — 14th March 1862. 8½" — 21.5cm.

74. WB. 'Universe' Jug. Moulded Staffordshire knot and 'WB' Cartouche — 'Universe'/'WB'/'18.' Pat No '16,164/3'. 7¾" — 19.5cm.

1859. This is the only evidence linking the jug to the Brownfield factory and 'Greek' does not appear in the 1880 factory catalogue, by which time this type of floral jug was no longer in vogue. 'Antique' is another transfer-printed jug with a handle very closely resembling that of 'Greek'. Its marks are also minimal, just a pattern number '12,397' and the factory sunburst mark '*'. The author has no doubts about the significance of the sunburst mark, as well over a hundred different pieces have been found with the printed sunburst, many of them with other unquestionable Brownfield marks. The great majority of these products emanate from the years 1847-65, but one 'Yeddo' jug from the late 1870s has also been found with the same sunburst mark.

Marks 14. WB. 'Donatello' jug. Moulded Cartouche — 'Donatello'. Moulded Reg D for 6/7/61. Moulded Staffordshire Knot — 'WB'/'36'. Impressed 'B'.

'Eglantine' (**Col Pl. 67**) is the first of two registered jugs introduced on 6th June 1860 (Reg No 129861) but, like many of Brownfield's jugs, there is no obvious reason to explain the pattern name. The seven inch jug illustrated here is enamelled most attractively in green and gold on a highly glazed white body: it was still in production twenty years later. The discovery of an unmarked 'Eglantine' jug suggests that this may have been a forerunner of the registered Brownfield product or another of Samuel Bevington's fraudulent copies. The legal proceedings against him were not held until May 1861, and so this second possibility is quite feasible. 'Floral' (**Col Pl. 68**) is the second jug registered on 29th October 1860, the name accorded to it because its original pattern name is not known. The example shown is seven inches tall and is enamelled in purple. It is one of the rarer early jugs and it is the last in a sequence of four jugs to have been marked with the Staffordshire knot.

Three new designs were registered in 1861 — two for relief-moulded jugs and one for a jardinière. 'Donatello' (**Col Pl. 69**) was registered on 6th July (Reg No 141732): this was the first jug to carry a new type of marking on the base — a moulded cartouche containing the pattern name of the jug, a Staffordshire knot, a moulded registration diamond, a size number and a potter's mark. The jug illustrated is seven inches tall and is enamelled in a very attractive ruby, gold and white. There is also a close-up picture of the new marking system introduced with this jug (**Marks 14**).

Donatello (full name Donato di Niccolo) was the name of a medieval Italian sculptor born in Florence in 1386. He came to be acknowledged as the founder of modern sculpture, being the first to produce statues independent of a background and thus capable of being viewed from all angles. The date of registration does not appear to coincide with any obvious centenary and there is no clear reason why Brownfield chose to produce this particular design in 1861. The markings on the enamelled 'Donatello' jugs raise one technical problem — its pattern numbers don't fit into the progression employed in the years 1859-1862. One discrepancy could be ascribed to a potter's error, but with several, it remains something of an enigma. One possible explanation is that the two 'Floral' jugs (whose pattern numbers should precede those of Donatello) are later editions, rather than the first ones of October 1860.

The 'Union' jug (**Col Pl. 70**) was registered on the 4th December 1861 (Reg No 147309). The jug illustrated is enamelled in green, yellow and gold on a brightly glazed white stoneware body which shows the English rose, the Scottish thistle and the Welsh leek. The markings follow the pattern set by 'Donatello'. There seems no obvious reason why Brownfield should have chosen the theme of Union in December 1861. The original Act of Union had been passed in 1707 and 1861 does not appear to coincide with any obvious centenary. It has been assumed until now that 'Passion Flower' (**Fig 71**) was

Fig 71. WB. 'Passion Flower' Jardinière. Reg 4th December 1861. Engraving from the Art Journal Illustrated Catalogue for the 1862 International Exhibition.

the design name of a new jug. However, this was registered for a jardinière and no jug of this name has yet come to light. Unfortunately, William Brownfield does not appear to have been consistent in his registration of designs where both a jardinière and a jug were concerned. Previous examples have already shown that although 'Jewel' and 'Fern' were only registered as jugs, the pattern was also used to produce jardinières. Later in January 1876, he adopted the opposite policy: the design 'Sisyphus' was only registered as a jardinière (29th Jan: Reg No 298029) and yet a jug emerged from the same pattern. The author has yet to discover a 'Passion Flower' jug and it remains an open question whether one was produced. The engraving shown here to illustrate the pattern is taken from the *Art Journal Illustrated Catalogue for the 1862 Exhibition*. 'Passion Flower' is on the left of this picture.

'International' **(Col Pl. 72)**, probably the second most popular of all Brownfield jugs (after Fern), was registered on 25th January 1862. (Reg No 148870). This was almost certainly produced specially for the London International Exhibition of 1862 and it appeared in the range of goods illustrated in the Exhibition catalogue. The jug was made in at least ten different colour combinations. The design shows four panels revealing classical figures representing 'Science', 'Art', 'Music' and 'Commerce'. The example shown has white stoneware figures on a blue enamelled body with the panels picked out in gilding. Examples have been found produced in parian, made after 1871. The correct markings are a cartouche containing the jug name, a Staffordshire knot, the registration diamond for 25th January 1862 and an impressed potter's mark. Jugs manufactured after 1873 may well have the twin globes instead of the Staffordshire knot, but they should still have the correct date of registration. Three erroneous diamonds have been identified on this jug — including one for 14th October 1863, the correct date for the registration of 'Albion', one for the 12th October 1864, the appropriate date for the registration of 'Tyrol' and another for 30th October 1865, the registration of 'Tiverton'. (The first of these is illustrated in **Marks 15.**)

Marks 15. WB. 'International' jug — Reg 25th Jan 1862. Erroneous Reg D for 14/10/63 (Albion jug). Moulded Cartouche/ Staffordshire Knot — 'WB'/'International'. Impressed 'Y'.

According to the Design Register, 'International' was the only new jug registered in 1862 but another has recently come to light. This is the 'Mother and Child' jug **(Col Pl. 73)**, a design based on a pattern for a plate registered on 14th March 1862. (Reg No 149957.) The jug is different from all preceding Brownfields in that it has a printed registration diamond instead of an moulded one **(Marks 16)**. There are no overt marks linking the jug with William Brownfield and full identification can only be made by consulting the Design Register. The artist responsible for the 'Mother and Child' jug was the well known H K Browne (PHIZ) — formerly the illustrator of many Dickens characters including Micawber, Mrs Gamp, Pecksniff and Samuel Weller. A contemporary review of the design described it as 'Bacchanal though without grossness — the engraving is excellent and the ground colour a delicate peach and there is an appropriate border by the same artist'. A Bacchanal was a worshipper of Bacchus, the God of Wine. Members would participate in feasts in honour of Bacchus which would often finish in drunken revels. In the foreground of the picture, we can see a thyrsus — the wand of Bacchus — a staff wreathed in ivy, while close by is a pomegranate, which because of its numerous seeds may be symbolic of fertility.

Marks 16. WB. 'Mother and Child' jug — Reg 14 March 1862. Printed Reg D for 14/3/62.

This pattern is just one of a hundred and fifty that William Brownfield displayed at the 1862 London Exhibition. This is the first time that we are sure that the firm exhibited publicly under its own name. William Brownfield had taken 90 square feet of space, a fairly humble involvement compared to that of some of their competitors. Copeland had taken 600 square feet, Minton 600, Brown Westhead-Moore 180, Ashworth Bros 80 and J Locket 90 square feet. The Exhibition appears to have been a great success — the public was admitted for the last time on the Saturday prior to November 8th and by the time the doors had closed, 3,626,934 people had visited it, 906,530 of them through the Fine Arts department in which Brownfield and other ceramic manufacturers had exhibited.

All the jugs registered by William Brownfield between 1851-63 have now been reviewed. However, there are at least three other unregistered ones, the first being 'Universe' **(Col Pl. 74),** which was possibly made specially for the Paris Universal Exhibition of 1855. A superb example of this was shown in Griselda Lewis's *A Collector's History of English Pottery* (1988) — a ten inch jug with white stoneware figures on a rich plum coloured enamelled body. It is one of the rarest early Brownfield jugs. The four main panels show figures symbolizing the four continents of 'America', 'Africa', 'Europe' and 'Asia' and this might suggest that it was designed for the export market. Two subsidiary panels depict the Eastern and Western hemispheres. Initial thoughts were that the jug was made for the 1867 Paris Universal Exhibition, but the markings on the jug base indicate an initial production date at least five years earlier — prior to 1863 when the Staffordshire knot was replaced by the circular trade mark. The most probable explanation of the 'Universe' jug is that it was exhibited at Paris in 1855, albeit by a wholesaler or Parisian agent, and that William Brownfield delayed its sale in France until tariffs had been reduced — ie about 1859-61. In this context the markings on the 'Universe' jug would be consistent with manufacture and sale abroad in about 1860. Only one enamelled jug with a pattern number has been found — '16,164' — indicating an introduction date for this jug of about March 1863.

The second unregistered jug is 'Swiss' **(Col Pl. 75) (Col Pl. 76).** Although its precise date of introduction cannot be specified, it has a moulded cartouche, the Staffordshire knot and a potter's mark. Four jugs with pattern numbers '16,238', '16,254', '16,256' and '16,2—' suggest an introduction date of 1863. The sequence of pattern numbers (see Appendix 6A) shows that this system was changed towards the end of 1863 — probably after the departure of William Shaw, the firm's foreman from 1841-63. This would, therefore, mean that all these 'Swiss' jugs emanated from about April 1863, just months before the system was changed. Two examples of 'Argos', the first registered jug in 1864, have painted numbers '23' or '55'. The first 'Swiss' jug shown has a blue enamelled body with white stoneware

Marks 17. WB. 'Swiss' jug (c1863). Moulded Crescent shaped Cartouche — 'Swiss'. Moulded Staffs Knot — 'WB' Size '18'. Impressed 'J.B.'.

horizontal lines, each of which is picked out in intermittent gilding. The second is, perhaps, a prototype with a different handle which was discontinued because of the probable damage done by the lid when fully opened. A brown majolica example produced after 1871 has also been seen. It is surprising that William Brownfield did not register the design. **(Marks 17).**

'Burton' **(Col Pl. 77),** is the last unregistered Brownfield jug of this period, seemingly introduced in 1863. One such enamelled jug has been found with the pattern number *'16,176'*, suggesting an introduction date of about March 1863. However, the great majority of the 'Burton' jugs discovered have an impressed month and year date for the late 1870s. Both the barrel shape and the pattern name suggest that it may well have been made for the famous Burton brewery.

CHAPTER 3
THE HEYDAY OF WILLIAM BROWNFIELD: JUNE 1863-JULY 1873

During 1863, the factory introduced a new trade mark on its goods — the circular mark that appeared for the first time on the 'Albion' jug of October 14th. At the end of 1863, the pattern numbering system operated since 1837 was replaced by a new one. The workforce remained on or about 475 throughout most of the decade and there was, from 1867 onwards, a significant increase in the number of items registered, but this did not include any increase in the number of jugs.

There were only seventeen, possibly eighteen jugs, registered between 1863-73. However, five different patterns were produced on the unregistered 'Lotus' jug shape introduced probably in the late 1860s. This suggests, perhaps, that greater emphasis was now being given to dinner services, tea sets, flower stands, candelabra, vases, feeding bottles, umbrella stands and a multitude of other objects. It also reflects the large number of jugs introduced in the 1850s which were still being made. Rarely in the previous decade had jugs represented less than 40-50% of all new registered products: in the 1860s, that percentage begins to drop below 35% especially after 1867 and this trend accelerated in the 1870s and early 1880s. The management was broadened by the inclusion in 1871 of William Etches, William Brownfield's eldest son. The other major strides taken by the firm in the years 1863-73 include the beginning of china, parian and majolica production in 1871 and the ambitious appointment in 1872 of Louis Jahn as art director, brought over from Mintons.

The 'Gothic' jardinière **(Fig 78),** the first item to be registered in 1863, was introduced on June 8th (Reg No 163189). The only example seen by the author is unmarked and therefore its attribution can only be made by reference to the design register. The illustration of its design is taken from that source. To date no jug of this design has been discovered. The first registered jug of 1863 is the commemorative 'Albion' **(Col Pl. 79)** introduced on October 14th (Reg No 167289). This was the last of five jugs produced to celebrate either the engagement or marriage of Edward, Prince of Wales, to Alexandra, daughter of Christian IX of Denmark. It had been preceded by J & M P Bell's version of March 1862, Thomas Cooper's superb 'Edward and Alexandra' jug of December 9th 1862, Beech & Hancock's 'Alexandra' jug of March 21st 1863 and by Bodley & Harold's Denmark jug of March 23rd. The 'Albion' jug shows the four heraldic shields of 'England', 'Scotland', 'Ireland' and 'Wales' and these are accompanied by the royal coat of arms and the Prince of Wales' feather and motto. Between the panels showing the shields are the national emblems of the rose, thistle, shamrock and leek. 'Albion' is the first new jug to have the moulded circular trade mark

Fig 78. WB. 'Gothic' Jardinière. Registered 8th June 1863. Engraving from the Design Register. Courtesy the PRO.

Marks 18. WB. 'Albion' jug — Moulded Circular Trade mark — 'Albion'/'WB'/ 'Cobridge'. Size '24'. Moulded Reg D for 14/10/63. NB. The Moulded Circular Trade Mark was used on new jugs introduced between 1863-1874.

(Marks 18). So few enamelled versions of this jug have been found that a painted pattern number has yet to be discovered. 'Albion' was followed later in the month by the registration of another plain jug (Reg No 170418), introduced on December 23rd 1863. Its markings should include the recently introduced circular trade mark: it is highly likely that the jug shape was used for a variety of transfer printed patterns.

'Argos' **(Col Pl. 80)** was the first of two jugs registered in 1864 — introduced on April 29th (Reg No 174168). In plain white, blue or grey stoneware, the jug is unexciting to say the least, but in an enamelled version, it is quite attractive. The design is a very simple one — there is a band containing the Greek key motif around the neck and there are stylised anthemions in the lower half of the jug. This is the first jug to reveal the new pattern numbering system — two examples having the numbers '23' and '55' painted on the base. The jug can be found with different moulded trade marks **(Marks 19):** the one first employed in April 1863 is more common, the one illustrated is a post 1871 alteration; it also has the impressed date '2/72'. 'Argos' has also been found with an erroneous moulded registration date.

'Tyrol' **(Col Pl. 81)** was the second jug, appearing six months later on October 12th (Reg No 179656). Undistinguished in plain stoneware, whether blue, grey, green or white, justice is only done to the pattern of Arabesque type scrolls when it appears in enamelled form. Among the most attractive of all, perhaps, are three examples found with gilded scrolls on either a lavender, green, or crimson body. Its markings are the circular trade mark containing the registration diamond for 29th April 1864, accompanied by an impressed potter's mark and occasionally by a pattern number.

'Florence' **(Col Pl. 82)**, the first of two registered jugs in 1865, was introduced on April 1st (Reg No 185520). Once again the design is a simple one, based on vertical fluting of the jug body, with a goat's head moulded on the top of the handle. The latter is a feature found identically on the unregistered 'Truro' jug produced later, probably in the mid to late 1870s. The occasional jug can be found with gilded rings around the jug neck, a further one at the base of the jug and with more gilding on the handle. The example illustrated has the vertical fluted stripes enamelled in blue on a white stoneware body.

The next registered jug, 'Tiverton' **(Col Pl. 83),** followed after a six month interval — being introduced on October 30th 1865 (Reg No 191407). This has a slightly more elaborate design than its three predecessors — having an abundance of stylised flowers, vines and leaves. Somewhat unusually, most surviving jugs are to be found in enamelled form. Some of these have a white body with the stylised flowers picked out in damson and gold, while others have an enamelled body in blue, pink or mauve with the flowers picked out in white, sometimes with additional gilding. There is one most unusual example of the 'Tiverton' jug — one of only two such jugs the author has seen. One side of this jug is enamelled in pink while the reverse side is enamelled in mauve; this would appear to be a travelling salesman's specimen jug.

Marks 19. WB. 'Argos' jug. Correct Moulded Circular Trade mark and Reg Diamond — 29/4/64. 'WB'/'Cobridge'/ 'Argos'. Impressed '11/78'.

The pattern name, like many of Brownfield's jugs, is most unusual and rather intriguing. It is just conceivable that the jug name might be explained by William Brownfield's ardent commitment to the Liberal cause. As long ago as 1841, William Brownfield and his close friend and fellow Liberal John Ridgway, had actively campaigned on behalf of their candidate John Ricardo in the General Election in Stoke-on-Trent. The possible political link with Tiverton is that it had been the Parliamentary constituency of Henry John Temple, better known later as Lord Palmerston. Temple was MP for Tiverton from June 1835 to February 1865 and he played a considerable role in the transition of the Whig to the Liberal Party. To some, this might seem a

Fig 85. WB. 'Glenny' Jardinière. Reg D for 15th March 1867. Engraving from the Art Journal.

rather far fetched link, but it is interesting to note that Lord Palmerston died on October 18th 1865, just two weeks before William Brownfield registered this jug. The precise date of its registration suggests that this jug was William Brownfield's tribute to a great politician for whom he had long held a great admiration.

'Alloa' (Col Pl. 84) was the only new registered jug in 1866 — introduced on April 7th (Reg No 196672). The pattern name is more enigmatic than that of its predecessor, and one for which an explanation is even harder to find. One possibility is that it may have been a trade jug ordered by the Scottish Alloa Brewery Co. Charles McMaster's 'Alloa Ale', kindly sent to the author by the current company secretary, points out that from 1860-66 the Brewery was run by Robert Roy. But in 1866, the year in which the 'Alloa' jug was made, the firm was taken over by Archibald T Arrol of Glasgow. If the take-over negotiations had begun earlier in 1865, it is quite conceivable that the new owner commissioned the 'Alloa' jug as part of a publicity venture to launch his newly acquired brewery. However, no documentation has yet been found to substantiate this. The jug design is based on the shape of a barrel, with hop vines and barley depicted around the neck. The most attractive jugs have an enamelled body in green, blue or brown, with gilding picking out the vines and the barley and the horizontal bands. Its markings include the circular trade mark employed since 1864.

1867 was to be a very busy year — preparing for the Paris Universal Exhibition. Many dinner service designs were brought out specially and there were several new stoneware jugs — notably the 'Cashmere' jug seemingly made for the Paris exhibition. William Brownfield was one of only four 'principal' exhibitors (the others were Doulton & Watts, J & C Price of Bristol and Mr Jones of Stoke-on-Trent). Brown-Westhead, Moore & Co decided not to exhibit in their own right but to do so through a Parisian agent. Three of the twenty-four silver medals awarded went to the firms of Wedgwood, Doulton and Brownfield. Unfortunately, no details were given as to which item(s) won the medal.

The 'Glenny' jardinière (Fig 85) (Reg No 206762) and the 'Cashmere' jug (Reg No 206760) were the first of three new registered designs for 1867, being introduced on March 15th. The illustration of the first is taken from the Art Journal. To date no jug of this design has been found. The only 'Glenny' jardinière seen by the author is filled in with green enamel around the daisy and has an impressed registration diamond for 15/3/67. It has no impressed 'Brownfield'. The 'Cashmere' jug (Col Pl. 86) is one of the few designs introduced by William Brownfield where there is an obvious connection

Fig 87. WB. 'Napoleon' Jug. Registered 21st June 1867. Engraving from the Art Journal.

between the jug name and the pattern — the latter having clear Indian connotations. It used to be argued that the twin globes factory mark was inaugurated in 1867, but the markings on all known Cashmere jugs remain the circular trade mark; twin globes were not introduced until the Bangor jug of 1874. By some quirk of accident, the 'Cashmere' registration is not to be found in the Design Register for 1867.

It is a little surprising to discover that the 'Napoleon' jug **(Fig 87),** the third to be made specially for the 1867 Paris Universal Exhibition, was not actually registered until June 21st — some two and a half months after the exhibition had opened. It could be that William Brownfield waited to assess the reaction in Paris and then judged that it was worth registering. The 'Napoleon' jug must be the most scarce of all Brownfield jugs. Most jug collectors have never seen one in this country, although this is probably explained by it being made specially for the French market.

Dr R K Henrywood says that to his knowledge only one unmarked example has been found and a protracted search throughout France may be necessary to locate an example with a registration diamond. The jug was clearly designed to commemorate Emperor Napoleon III who had seized power by a coup d'état back in 1851.

The illustration of the jug is taken from the *Art Journal.* The portrait on the other side of the jug is now known to be that of Eugenie, Napoleon's wife whom he had married in 1853. There is no registration diamond on the earliest jugs which must have been produced by the Brownfield factory prior to the Paris Universal Exhibition. Many Staffordshire figures were produced of both Napoleon III and Eugenie, but nearly all these emanated from 1854-56 when England and France were allies in the Crimean War. By the 1860s, Anglo-French relations had become much more strained because of Napoleon's expansionism in Europe and in particular his annexation of Savoy and Nice in 1860. This deterioration in relationships suggests that William Brownfield made the 'Napoleon' jug specifically for the French and not for the domestic market.

Two of the three registered designs of 1868 are known to have led to the production of jugs: both 'Cone' and 'Hampton' were registered on June 12th. However, no 'Cone' jug has ever been found. Both the shape and pattern of 'Cone' are illustrated on page 125 of the 1880 Brownfield factory catalogue where it appears as a sugar box and bowl, and as a coffee and tea pot. The same is true for the 'Argyll' pattern and probably for 'Aston', 'Basket' and 'Butterfly' — also depicted in the same catalogue but only as teapots. The author has yet to see any of these five patterns in jug form, but it is possible that they have simply failed to come to light. However, the 'Westminster', 'Severn', 'Shamrock' and' Nile' patterns are also shown in teapot form and we know that they were produced as jugs.

'Hampton' **(Col Pl. 88),** registered on June 12th (Reg No 219317), is the second of the 1868 new designs. The essence of this pattern is a multitude of vine leaves covering most of the jug body while the branches are cleverly interwoven with both the top and bottom of the handle. It is a fairly scarce jug and one of the most attractive is in a brightly glazed white body with green leaves, the veins of which are picked out in gilding. The normal mark on this jug is the circular moulded trade mark —

75. WB. 'Swiss' Jug. Moulded Staffordshire knot and 'WB' Cartouche — 'Swiss'/'WB'/'18'. 7" — 18cm.

76. WB. Unusual 'Swiss' Jug. Moulded Staffordshire knot and 'WB' Cartouche — 'Swiss'/'WB'/'18'/. WR Collection. 7¼" — 18.5cm.

77. WB. 'Burton' Jug. Unmarked. Pattern Number — '16,176'. BM Collection. 6" — 15cm.

79. WB. 'Albion' Jug. Moulded Circular trade Mark. Reg D — 14th October 1863. 'Albion'/'WB'/'Cobridge'. MM/MR Collection. 5" — 12cm.

80. WB. 'Argos' Jug. Moulded Circular Trade Mark. Reg D — 29th April 1864. 'Argos'/'WB'/'Cobridge'/'18'. 7" — 18cm.

81. WB. 'Tyrol' Jug. Moulded Circular Trade Mark. Reg D — 12th October 1864. 'Tyrol'/'WB'/'Cobridge'. MM/MR Collection. 7½" — 19cm.

Marks 20. WB. 'Hampton' jug. Moulded Circular Trade Mark — 'WB'/ 'Cobridge'/'Hampton'. Size '30'. Moulded Reg D for 12/6/68.

Marks 21. (WB). W P & G P Phillips. 'Westminster' jug. Moulded Crescent shaped Cartouche — 'Westminster'. Moulded Reg D for 21/10/68. Impressed 'WB'/Size '24'/'F'.

in operation since 1864 **(Marks 20).** However, Kathy Hughes has identified a 'Hampton' jug marked only with a cartouche (a parallel example to the 'Wicker' jug reviewed in the previous chapter). This is the style adopted by W P & G Phillips on the 'Westminster' jug in October 1868, and it is possible that this example of 'Hampton' may have been made for the London retailer prior to Brownfield's registration of the jug. William Brownfield probably accorded it the name 'Hampton' because of the famous vines at Hampton Court Palace. The circular moulded trade mark (with plain WB) continued in use on jugs until 1872.

The last new registered jug design of 1868 is 'Westminster' **(Col Pl. 89),** introduced on October 21st (Reg No 223308), not by the Brownfield firm, but by W P & G Phillips of both Oxford and New Bond Street. This reputable concern is known to have represented Mintons and others at the 1862 London exhibition, but this is the first time that they are known to have acted for Brownfields. Later in September 1870 they were to register a jardinière, possibly made by Brownfields while in May 1871 they registered a Greek Key jug that may also have been produced in the Brownfield factory. Without confirmation from Phillips's own records we cannot be sure about the origins of the 1870 jardinière or the 1871 jug.

For the first time since 1864, there are different markings on most of the ''Westminster' jugs. There is a moulded cartouche containing the jug name, a registration diamond, sometimes a painted pattern number, and the letters *'WB'* **(Marks 21).** The main motif in this pattern is basketweave at both the top and bottom of the jug. Like so many Brownfields jugs, it needs to be enamelled to emphasise the motif. The example shown has a red enamelled body with the white basketweave picked out in gold. No less than five different pattern numbers have been found on the 'Westminster' jug. The first two of these are '140' and '151', numbers that suggest an initial production date of 1864, four years before W P & G Phillips registered the pattern. The third pattern number is '350', the fourth '445/3' and the last '550': only the last pattern number seems to relate to 1868. This strongly suggests that Brownfields had been making the 'Westminster' jug for Phillips for a considerable time before its registration.

Fig 90. WB. 'Barlaston' Jardinière. Registered 2nd April 1869. Engraving from the Design Register. Courtesy the PRO.

'Barlaston' **(Fig 90)** was registered on April 2nd

1869 and 'Severn' on June 19th. The pattern and shape of the first are illustrated on page 51 of the 1880 Brownfield catalogue along with Passion Flower', 'Argos', 'Gothic' and 'Glenny'. Of these five jardinière patterns, only 'Argos' has been found as a jug. 'Severn' **(Col Pl. 91),** introduced on 19th June 1869 (Reg No 230184), is the first of several jugs all named after rivers. The motif which helps a little to explain the pattern name of the 'Severn' jug is a band of fine-meshed netting just below the neck of the jug, a theme repeated towards the jug base; in between is a hexagonal mesh often picked out most attractively with gilding. Some 'Severn' jugs are produced in a blue enamelled body, offset by white bands at the top and bottom, while a few can be found in a white body enamelled in brown, some with the netting and jug handle picked out in gold. It was followed in subsequent years by 'Marne', 'Nile', 'Hudson', 'Clyde', 'Exe','Missouri' and 'Tiber'.

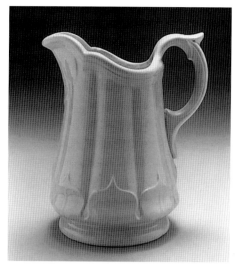

Fig 92. WB. 'Lotus' Jug — taken from the 1880 Factory Catalogue. Courtesy Spode Ltd and Keele University Library.

The next Brownfield jug of this period, produced perhaps towards the end of the 1860s or in the early 1870s, is 'Lotus' — the pattern and shape of the jug being identified from the Brownfield 1880 catalogue. The 'Lotus' jug **(Fig 92)** itself is shown on page 68 while four others, 'Bayonne', 'Strawberry', 'Alexandra' and 'Coblentz', appear on page 99. The first picture of 'Lotus' is somewhat indistinct, but it appears to be a relief moulded jug, while the four different transfer printed examples are produced on the same jug shape. It is something of a mystery that only a single plain and unmarked 'Lotus' jug has been found, but the names of three of the transfer printed jugs suggest that they may well have been made for export. The only 'Lotus' discovered is in a plain blue stoneware, has no impressed pattern name, no impressed date, nor is it marked Brownfield.

'Nile' **(Col Pl. 93)** and 'Marne' were the two registered jugs introduced in 1870. In addition, a jardinière **(Fig 94)** was registered by W P & G Phillips which may have been manufactured by Brownfields. Both the jugs have a more intricate and interesting pattern than those produced in 1869. The predominant motif of the 'Nile' jug, introduced on the 10th June, is the Greek key, augmented by a

central band of stylised floral scrolls. Just how this could lead to a pattern name 'Nile' is a mystery. Like many Brownfield relief-moulded jugs, it only comes to life in an enamelled form. The example shown in brown and gold is just one of the many colour varieties in which the 'Nile' jug was produced. The markings remain the moulded circular trade mark including a registration diamond and very occasionally a pattern number (No '763'). The jardinière registered by W P & G Phillips on the 27th September (Reg No 245229) is included because it may have been made by Brownfields as part of an agreement with the London retailers and, like 'Sisyphus', the pattern may also have been used for a jug. No jug has yet been found and we have to remember that this London firm did act for a whole

Fig 94. WP & GP. Jardinière. Registered 27th September 1870. Engraving from the Design Register. Courtesy the PRO.

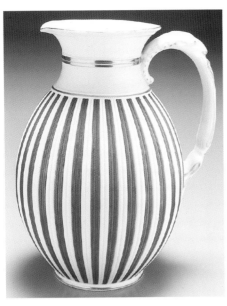

82. WB. 'Florence' Jug. Moulded Circular Trade Mark. Reg D for 1st April 1865. 'Florence'/'WB'/ 'Cobridge'/'244'. 7$\frac{1}{2}$" — 18.5cm. MM/MR Collection.

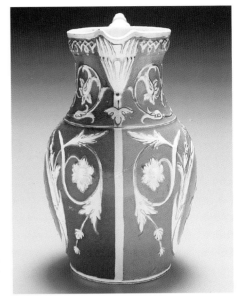

83. WB. 'Tiverton' Jug. Moulded Circular Trade Mark. Reg D for 30th October 1865. 'Tiverton'/ 'WB'/'Cobridge'. 6$\frac{3}{4}$" — 17cm.

84. WB. 'Alloa' Jug. Moulded Circular Trade Mark and Reg D for 1st April 1866. 'Alloa'/'WB'/'Cobridge'. 7$\frac{1}{2}$" — 19cm.

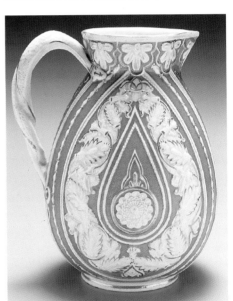

86. WB. 'Cashmere' Jug. Moulded Circular Trade Mark. Reg D for 15th March 1867. 'Cashmere'/'WB'/'Cobridge'. Pat No '275'. 6$\frac{3}{4}$" — 17cm.

88. WB. 'Hampton' Jug. Moulded Circular Trade Mark. Reg D for 12th June 1868. 'Hampton'/'WB'/'Cobridge'. Private Collection. 7$\frac{1}{2}$" — 19cm.

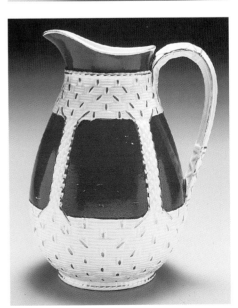

89. WB. 'Westminster' Jug. Moulded Crescent Cartouche. Reg D — 21st October 1868. 'Westminster'/'WB'/'24'. 7$\frac{1}{4}$" — 18.5cm. Registered by W P & G Phillips. Courtesy Brian Blisshill Antiques.

number of Staffordshire pottery firms during the years 1848-75.

'Marne' **(Col Pl. 95)** is the last registered jug of 1870 — introduced on 10th November (Reg No 247080). In a much simpler and more restricted form, this jug pattern has some similarities with the stylised flowers used around the neck of the 'Tiverton' jug made five years earlier. On 'Marne' they appear in the middle of the jug with only a basic border pattern above and below. The relative simplicity of the pattern only succeeds in an enamelled form: one example has a blue enamelled body with the stylised flowers and borders in a contrasting white, a second has a white body with damson and gold enamelling of the stylised flowers and borders. There is no ostensible reason why this pattern was entitled 'Marne'. The markings on the base continue to be the circular trade mark and registration diamond.

Fig 96. WB. Water Jug. Registered 2nd May 1871. Engraving from the Design Register. Courtesy the PRO.

1871 was the year of another International Exhibition in London, the third in a sequence since this venture was launched by Prince Albert in 1851. Two new vases, made for the Exhibition, had a finish very close to porcelain and the first of these was an arabesque pattern after Van Leyden. It was said that Brownfields would have had a much larger display but for a stock-taking necessitated by taking the eldest son into partnership. This does not sound a very convincing excuse for a much reduced display at the Exhibition. William Brownfield would surely have known of this necessity well in advance and made arrangements accordingly. Equally, the firm may have been hoping that its four new china producing ovens would have been brought on stream in time to exhibit their first china wares, but a delay seemingly inhibited this. The new ovens were certainly in the course of construction at this time, for in November the *Staffordshire Advertiser* announced that their installation had now been completed. In October-November the firm did display its first china wares at an exhibition in Stafford. It also exhibited the majolica 'Cockatoo' jug — our only dating for the introduction of this unregistered, splendid jug. (See Chapter 8.) There was important publicity to be gained from a domestic International Exhibition held only once a decade, and every effort would surely have been made to have the first china products ready by May when the London Exhibition opened. These endeavours did not succeed.

The next new jugs registered by Brownfields are a rather plain water jug (with basin) **(Fig 96)** and the much more attractive 'Worcester' **(Col Pl. 97),** both introduced on 2nd May (Reg Nos 252177-78). The first is a predominantly plain jug with minimal relief-moulding below the jug lip: a range of transfer prints was almost certainly used on it. The basic shape of the 'Worcester' jug is the same as the earlier 'Alloa' design of 1866, but most of the jug is covered in very fine relief basket weave while a hop vine grows downwards from just below the jug neck. It is hardly the most original or the most exciting of Brownfield's jug patterns and it very much needs enamelled colouring if it is to succeed. The hops in the 'Worcester' design suggest that, like 'Alloa', it may have been a trade jug made for a brewery in Worcester. Information received from the Worcester City Library shows that there was a

Fig 98. W.P. & G.P. 'Greek Key' Jug. Registered 6th May 1871. Engraving from the Design Register. Courtesy the PRO.

Worcester brewery operated at this time by Josiah Stallard & Sons, but there is no evidence that this firm ordered the jug. The markings remain the circular trade mark in use since 1864. The 'Worcester' jug illustrated has a white stoneware body with strips of dark blue enamelling around the jug neck and gilding of the edges of the hop vine leaves. The dating of the registration, co-inciding as it did with the opening of the London Exhibition, suggests that the new design may well have been introduced specially for this occasion. Painted marks on three different Worcester jugs ('1008', '1018' and '1019') suggest that 1020 new patterns had been introduced by June 1871.

Only four days later — on the 6th May 1871 — W P & G Phillips registered a 'Greek Key' jug (Fig 98) (Reg No 252258). However, there is so far no evidence linking this jug with the Brownfield factory and, unfortunately, no example has yet been found to ascertain the markings on the jug base. The shape of this jug is very close indeed to Brownfield's 'Sisyphus' jug introduced in January 1876 and it is just possible that Brownfields were testing the market with this prototype shape before launching it under their own name five years later. Such an explanation would also make sense of the 'Hampton' jug (another prototype?) identified by Kathy Hughes with a cartouche, instead of the customary Brownfield circular trade mark.

Despite the introduction of four china producing ovens, the workforce was still only 500 strong (10% more than in 1861) and just over ten years later, there were still only 530 workers. This suggests that from 1871 onwards Brownfields probably directed more and more attention to the production of china ware at the expense of earthenware and stoneware products. They would now be joining the league of 'giants', facing immense competition from firms with long established reputations for very high quality porcelain — Minton, Copeland and Wedgwood to name but three.

1872 was, perhaps, especially renowned for the installation of Louis Jahn as Art Director, an appointment doubtless motivated by the need to have the artistic creativity and originality essential if Brownfields were to make a successful challenge to the likes of Mintons, Copelands etc. Still only thirty-three, Louis Jahn had for the last decade been employed by Mintons and had modelled vases for them for the 1862 Exhibition. He was to remain with Brownfields until the early 1890s. During the next few years, Jahn evolved his dream of manufacturing a china vase, the like and the size of which had never been seen before. This led to the production of the eleven foot 'Earth Vase' in the years 1878-84 and to its ultimate display at Crystal Palace in 1884. It has been said that Jahn was responsible for Brownfield's greatest artistic achievements and doubtless in the sphere of china manufacture this was true, but his contribution to the design of stoneware, parian and majolica jugs in the years 1872-90 is very much less evident. Apart, perhaps, from 'Hudson' in 1877, the 'Cockatoo' jug and the majolica 'Swirling Fish' jug of 1879, there was little of outstanding artistic merit in this sphere.

'Cupid' (Col Pl. 99), introduced on 14th December (Reg No 268806), was the only registered stoneware jug produced in 1872, another indication, perhaps, that china production was receiving priority. This is very much a design based on the tankard shape originally developed and patented by T & R Boote in 1847. The central feature of the jug design is a Cupid figure sprigged onto the surface on each side of the jug, usually but not always in a contrasting colour to that of the jug. Kathy Hughes in her book showed a much more elaborately enamelled version — the jug enamelled in brown with the Cupid and stylised motifs done in white, producing a really splendid contrast. The example illustrated has a light brown body, the motifs and the Cupid in white and the oval centre piece enamelled in a pale light blue. The markings on this jug should be the circular trade mark containing the registration diamond — employed since 1864, but the jug illustrated by Kathy Hughes had a moulded cartouche, a registration diamond and a Staffordshire knot — markings employed in the 1850s and presumably wrongly effected by a worn-out potter late on a Saturday afternoon or by one with a major hang-over on Tuesday morning! Three different Cupid jugs have the pattern numbers '1348', '1374' and '1376'.

In addition, a very unusual and exquisite 'Cupid' jug (**Col Pl. 100**) has come to light, the oval centre piece having no Cupid figure at all, but some beautifully hand painted flowers. This six and three quarter inch jug may have been a 'one-off' made for a special commission, for the markings still show the 'Cupid' pattern name and the same registration date. 'Cupid' was the last jug to be registered during the lifetime of William Brownfield. There were no new registered jugs introduced in 1873 and no evidence has been found of William Brownfield and Son exhibiting in their own right at the Vienna Exhibition held in the summer. The firm may, however, have employed an agent to organise a stand: only three years later Herr G E Bossenroth, 39 C Bruder Strasse, was acting as Brownfield's representative in Vienna.

By July 1873 William Brownfield was 61 and in perfectly sound health for a man of his years. He worked Saturday morning on the 12th July in his customary manner, made his way home to Barlaston by train and retired to bed seemingly in good health. He died soon after midnight and an era going back to 1837 had come to an end. Such was the reputation that he had built up over 36 years that thousands joined the funeral procession to the cemetery in Hanley. His obituary in the *Staffordshire Advertiser* on 19th July tells us something about the man who had developed Brownfields so skilfully and with such dedicated commitment for just short of four decades. In the words of the paper 'Mr William Brownfield was a man of unimpeachable integrity . . . never satisfied with anything short of excellence'. At the time of his death he had been a Deputy-Lieutenant of the County, a Justice of the peace, A Director of the N Staffs Railway Co, Mayor of Hanley, an Alderman and Magistrate of Hanley, President of the Hanley School of Art, Vice-President of the Potteries' Mechanics Institute and leader of the local Liberal party ever since the death of his close friend John Ridgway in 1862. As a sign of tribute, all shops in Hanley were closed from 2-4 on Thursday afternoon, the day of the funeral. The newspaper did not mention that in terms of wealth (total assets including property) William Brownfield died a very rich man, bequeathing nearly a hundred thousand pounds. In today's values, that would make him a millionaire. It would be a major challenge to his sons to emulate his success.

CHAPTER 4

A NEW AGE — THE SONS' MANAGEMENT: JANUARY 1874-FEBRUARY 1883

William Etches was in charge of the firm from 1873 until 1883. The workforce over which he presided was still in the region of 500, rising to 530 early in the 1880s. He had the assistance of a general manager — a Mr E Harrison, and the Artistic Director for the next 17-20 years was Louis Jahn. Some design work was carried out for the firm by Carrier Belleuse during the period 1873-87. If the past success of Brownfields was to be maintained, much would depend on the managerial skills of William Etches and, after him, Edward Arthur.

Many of the special challenges that the company undertook were in the manufacture of porcelain rather than in earthenware; from late 1871 Brownfields had also begun production of parian and majolica wares. During the years 1874-83, the business seems to have concentrated considerably on increasing its exports and Brownfields attended International Exhibitions in Philadelphia in 1876, Sydney in 1879, Melbourne in 1882 and Calcutta in 1884. In addition to these, it had intended to exhibit at Paris in 1878 but withdrew ostensibly because of a disagreement over inadequate display space. We have no initial production date for all the unregistered jugs of this period and their attribution to these years stems from the impressed dates on surviving examples. It may be that some were in production before 1874.

It was not until June 1874 that the new management team under William Etches Brownfield launched the first registered jug/teapot shape since his father's death eleven months earlier. This was 'Aston', introduced on 6th June (Reg No 282799), the first of two new patterns registered in 1874. It has until now been thought that this was the name of a jug, but the only example identified is a teapot rather than a jug and it may be that in common with 'Butterfly', 'Basket', 'Cone', and 'Argyll', this pattern was only made for a tea set without a full sized jug. (See Chapter 6.) 'Bangor' **(Col Pl. 101)**, registered on 10th September (Reg No 285013), is in one respect the most remarkable of all

Marks 22. WB. 'Bangor' jug. Moulded Twin Globes Trade Mark — 'Brownfield & Son'. Moulded Reg D for 10/9/74. Moulded Crescent shaped Cartouche — 'Bangor'/ Size' 24' N.B. The Twin Globes Trade Mark was used on new jugs registered between 1874-1883.

Brownfield's designs, the shape being used for two different 'Mandarin' jugs, three different 'Hong Kong' jugs, one 'Audley' jug and two water ewers including one called 'Lincoln' — making ten jugs in all from the same registered shape. An eleventh, 'Sylvan' ('Bangor' shape) was registered separately on 10th June 1875. Only four examples of the jugs produced on the 'Bangor' shape have been found — one 'Bangor', two 'Mandarins' and 'Lincoln'. The ordinary stoneware 'Bangor' jugs seem to be a rather scarce collector's find and the Majolica example even rarer; the one illustrated has only been found in an enamelled form — unusual for a Brownfield, but understandable in view of its rather limited relief-moulded pattern. There is a very brief band of basket weave at the neck of the jug and a wider one at the bottom, both enamelled in a deep red, while the jug is in a bright white enamel colouring with minimal gilding of the very small motif and of the handle. For the first time, the moulded markings on the jug base are the twin globes trade mark, a cartouche containing *'BANGOR'* and the jug size, and a ribbon including

50

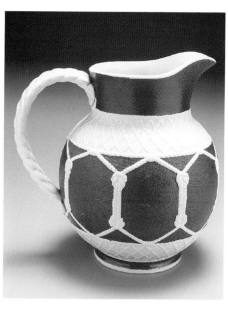

91. WB. 'Severn' Jug. Moulded Circular Trade Mark. Reg D for 19th June 1869. 'Severn'/'WB'/ 'Cobridge'/'638'. 7" — 17.5cm. MM and MR Collection.

93. WB. 'Nile' Jug. Moulded Circular Trade Mark. Reg D for 10th June 1870. 'Nile'/'WB'/'Cobridge'. Pat No '784'. 7" — 17.5cm.

95. WB. 'Marne' Jug. Circular Trade Mark. Reg D — Reg D — 10th November 1870. 'Marne'/'WB'/'Cobridge'/'842'. MM/MR Collection. 6" — 15cm.

97. WB. 'Worcester' Jug. Moulded Circular Trade Mark. Reg D — 2nd May 1871. 'Worcester'/'WB'/'Cobridge'. Pat No '1019'. 7" — 17.5cm.

99. WB. 'Cupid' Jug. Moulded Circular Trade Mark. Reg D — 14th December 1872. 'Cupid'/'WB'/'Cobridge'. MM and MR Collection. 9" — 23cm.

100. WB. Special 'Cupid' Jug. Moulded Circular Trade Mark. Reg D — 14th Dec 1872. 6³/₄" — 17cm. Courtesy Charterhouse Antiques, Teignmouth.

Fig 104. WB. 'Bangor' II Jug. Moulded Twin Globes Trade Mark. Reg D — 10th September 1874. Engraving from the 1880 Brownfield Catalogue. Courtesy Spode Ltd and Keele University.

'W BROWNFIELD & SON' (Marks 22).

The two 'Mandarin' jugs (Col Pl. 102) (Col Pl. 103), unlike 'Bangor', are produced basically in plain stoneware with a transfer printed pattern filled in with enamels. The illustrations of the other 'Bangor', 'Hong Kong' and 'Audley' jugs are taken from the Brownfield 1880 catalogue (Fig 104) (Fig 105) (Fig 106). The moulded markings on each of them should include the twin globes, the ribbon, the registration diamond, a cartouche and sometimes an impressed month and date.

Fig 105. WB. 'Hong Kong' Jug. Reg D — 10th September 1874. Engraving — courtesy Spode Ltd and Keele University.

'Sylvan' is the only new design for a jug in 1875, introduced on 10th June (Reg No 292005). This jug is an integral part of a dinner service shown on pages 85 and 122 of the 1880 Brownfield Factory catalogue. 'Sylvan' was produced in two different shapes; the first on the relief-moulded 'Bangor' shape, the second on a plain water jug. The theme of the dinner service is wild life in different parts of the world: species portrayed include deer, partridges, pheasants, ducks, the latter being sometimes hunted by retriever dogs. This is the subject material of the transfer print on the 'Sylvan' jug, but the print could possibly be any one of the thirteen scenes found on the plates in the dinner service. (See Chapter 7.) (This is similar to the variety of scenes shown on the 'Medieval' jugs introduced in February 1877.) No example of the 'Sylvan' jug has yet been found. 'Lincoln' (Fig 107) was produced on the same shape: its moulded markings include the twin globes, a registration diamond and a cartouche.

'Bass' (Col Pl. 108) is a third unregistered jug produced in 1875 (perhaps earlier), seemingly a trade jug made for the brewers of that name. It is one of at least two such trade jugs, introduced in the 1870s (the other being 'Alsopp', first known to have been made in late

Fig 106. WB. 'Audley' jug. (Bangor shape) Reg D — 10th September 1874. Courtesy Spode Ltd and Keele University.

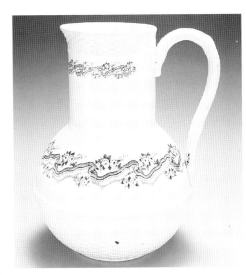

Fig 107. WB. 'Lincoln' Water Jug. Reg D — 10th September 1874. 12" — 30.5cm. Private Collection.

1877). In comparison with other Brownfield jugs, 'Bass' is, to say the least, unusual if not a little weird. The transfer-printed scenes on the jug show a mixture of animated flying bottles, teapots, kettles and barrels! Most examples are to be found in a rather heavy and unattractive brown and black, but the set of three illustrated has a white enamelled background — giving a much better colour contrast. The jollity of the pictures may have been considered appropriate to a public or saloon bar. The markings on this jug are quite different from those introduced in 1874: the only impressed marks should be Bass, the jug size, 'Brownfield' and a date (in this instance 3/84), perhaps because it is an unregistered jug. The potter has, however, managed to impress the wrong pattern name — calling it *'GIPSY'* instead of 'Bass'. Confirmation that 'Bass' was a trade jug comes from the Bass museum in Burton-on-Trent where examples of this jug are in the museum collection; somewhat strangely these jugs are not impressed 'Brownfield'. This suggests that they were prototypes made for customer inspection,

Marks 23. WB. 'Yeddo' jug. Moulded Twin Globes Trade Mark, cartouche — 'Yeddo', Impressed Reg D- 29th Jan 1876. Size '24', ' 11/76'.

subsequently retained by the brewery. Later examples produced in the early 1880s have an impressed date mark.

'Yeddo' **(Col Pl. 109)** is the first new jug in 1876, introduced on 29th January (Reg No 298028). At least four versions of this jug are known to have been produced, although only one shape was registered. Some are relief-moulded, others have transfer prints on a plain jug. The jug shape clearly shows the oriental influence prevalent in the later 1870s and 1880s. The central theme of the relief-moulded jug design is a pair of storks, sometimes gilded on a white or bluish-grey stoneware background. The moulded markings are the twin globes, a cartouche, a registration diamond, an impressed size number, a pattern number *'1695'* and an impressed month and year date **(Marks 23).** The plain 'Yeddo' jug is also found with a number of transfer prints. The first has a transfer printed picture of Pan and Dionysus **(Col Pl. 110),** while the second has a transfer printed picture from the series of 'Medieval' scenes **(Col Pl. 111).** The scene portrayed on the second of these is of three women in party costume with wings fitted to their backs, while there are two musicians on the reverse side, one carrying a trombone, the other blowing a bugle. This particular jug cannot have been introduced in 1876 because the 'Medieval' pattern was not introduced until February 1877 and, indeed, the date impressed on the base ('5/77') shows it to have been produced in May 1877. It is the only example found of this jug and time will tell whether it is unique. The fourth jug is a second version of 'Audley' **(Col Pl. 112),** a transfer-printed jug with enamel decoration, showing two storks in flight: this example is produced on the 'Yeddo', not the 'Bangor' shape. A very small number of these jugs have a printed cartouche with the pattern name 'Audley' and a pattern number '1757-T'. The markings on the base of all these jugs are the moulded twin globes trade mark, a registration diamond, and a cartouche containing 'Yeddo'.

Marks 24. 'Sisyphus' jug — Introduced January 1876. Moulded Twin Globes. Trade Mark — 'Brownfield & Son'. Crescent shaped Cartouche — 'Sisyphus'.

On the same day, Brownfields registered 'Sisyphus' **(Col Pl. 113),** a design for a jardinière. This was also used for a jug

101. WB. 'Bangor' Jug. Moulded Twin Globes Trade Mark. Reg D for 10th September 1874. 'Bangor'/'WB'/'Cobridge' 7" — 17.5cm.

102. WB. 'Mandarin' Jug. Moulded Twin Globes Trade Mark. Reg D — 10th September 1874. BM Collection. 7" — 17.5cm.

103. WB. 'Mandarin' II Jug. Moulded Twin Globes Trade Mark and Reg D — 10th September 1874. C.B. Collection. 7" — 17.5cm.

108. WB. 'Bass' Jug. Impressed 'Brownfield'/'3/84'.TEM Collection. 5½" — 14cm.

109. WB. 'Yeddo' Jug. Moulded Twin Globes, Cartouche and Reg D — 29th January 1876. 'Yeddo'/'24'/'Brownfield & Son'. 6¾" — 17cm.

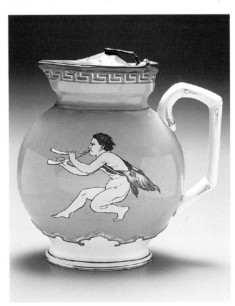

110. WB. Unusual 'Yeddo' Jug. Moulded Twin Globes, Moulded Cartouche, Reg D — 29th January 1876. Private Collection. 8" — 20.5cm.

111. WB. Unusual 'Yeddo' Jugs. Moulded Twin Globes, Moulded Cartouche, Reg D — 29th January 1876. 7³/₄" — 19.5cm.

112. WB. 'Audley'. (Yeddo shape) Moulded Twin Globes. Moulded Cartouche and Reg D — 29th January 1876. Pat No '1757/T'. 7³/₄" — 19.5cm.

113. WB. 'Sisyphus' Jug. Moulded Twin Globes, Cartouche. 'Sisyphus'/'Brownfield & Son'. 8" — 20.5cm.

115. WB. 'Medieval' Jug. Impressed 'Brownfield'. '7/77'. Impressed 'Medieval'. (Some jugs are impressed 'Carnival'.) 4" — 16cm.

116. WB. 'Olympus' Jug. Printed Reg D — 10/10/77. Impressed 'Brownfield'. Impressed '7/78'. Pat No '5414'. 12" — 30.5cm.

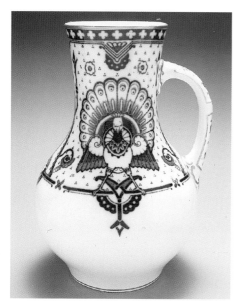

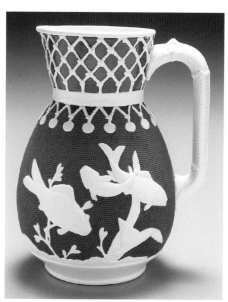

121. WB. 'Hudson' II Jug. Moulded Twin Globes, Cartouche. 'Hudson'/'Brownfield & Sons'. Reg D. for 22nd December 1877. WR Collection. 7" — 18cm.

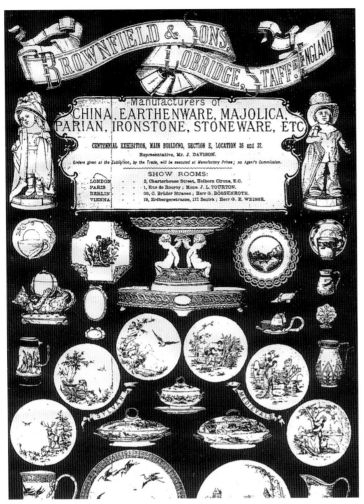

Fig 114. WB. Philadelphia Exhibition Advertisement from the Pottery and Glass Trade Review — May 1876.

although its markings do not include a registration diamond for this date. Sisyphus was the king of Corinth who had been condemned in Tartarus (the Greek hell) to roll a huge stone ceaselessly up a hill; it is impossible, however, to see any link between this and the design of the jug! The occasional example can be discovered with the ivy leaves, the uprights and the handle enamelled in blue, green, brown or pink. The markings are moulded twin globes, a cartouche with a size number, and an impressed date **(Marks 24)**. The illustrated jug enamelled in blue has a pattern number '*1572*' and an impressed date '*10/75*', indicating that its introduction preceded the registration by three months. Another example of the Sisyphus jug has been found with printed rather than moulded globes and registration diamond.

The Philadelphia Exhibition **(Fig 114)** opened on the 10th May 1876. Brownfields and Sons and Doulton were the only 'direct contributors', while Minton & Hollins, Doulton, and Daniel & Son, combined in the furnishing of offices at the exhibition. We know, however, that several other firms did have a display, perhaps on a collective stand organised by an American agent: these included Brown, Westhead-Moore & Co, Bates Walker & Co and Powell & Bishop. A special Brownfield vase had been designed for the exhibition by Carrier Belleuse — this, their most important piece, was five feet high. Further vases had been designed by Protat and Mollart and the painting of various pieces had been done by Sander, A Cartlidge, Hartshorn and Rouse. Several vases of a delicate silver grey were on show; this was the aventurine effect invented by Edward Arthur Brownfield. No mention is made of jugs specially commissioned for the exhibition and the bulk of Brownfields' efforts may have gone into developing their recent porcelain products.

The official Exhibition Catalogue, however, contains a full page Brownfield advertisement illustrating a wide range of stoneware and china products. The only five jugs shown are 'Argos' (1863), an unusual 'Bangor' (1874), a 'Medieval' jug (1877) and a second 'Medieval' water jug produced in a different shape. The fifth jug (seen on the extreme right just below a cup and saucer) is an unidentified, unregistered design. Both the 'Sylvan' and 'Medieval' dinner services feature prominently as do some of the recent porcelain items. Bates Walker had just begun at the Exhibition to make use of the original mould from which the Turners of Longton had produced jasper wares over eighty years ago.

'Medieval' **(Col Pl. 115)** is the first of three new designs for jugs registered in 1877, introduced on 7th February (Reg No 307570). This jug is produced in two different shapes — a toilet jug and an ordinary jug. It may have been offered with as many as eight to fourteen different patterns. The

Fig 117. WB. 'Suez' Jug. Courtesy Spode Ltd and Keele University Library.

Fig 118. WB. 'Crete' Jug. Courtesy Spode Ltd and Keele University Library.

registration copy at the Public Record Office shows over a dozen 'Medieval' scenes, any one of which *might* appear on this jug. The jug shown is of the ordinary 'Medieval' kind. 'Carnival' is another transfer-printed pattern produced on this same jug shape.

In September 1877 William Brownfield & Son displayed a remarkably artistic vase at their Charterhouse Street, London, showroom. This had a celadon body with white flowers in relief, supported by four cupids. The handles were twisted and sprung from four rams' heads. The vase was forty-six inches high, sixteen inches wide and the width of the handle was twenty-six inches. On 10th October the firm registered a series of toilet services including 'Suez', 'Olympus' (Harlech shape) and 'Crete'. They appear on p151, 169 and 176 of the 1880 Factory Catalogue, albeit without the details of their registration date. However, the transfer-printed 'Olympus' water jug **(Col Pl. 116)** has an impressed registration diamond for 10th October 1877. The transfer print is filled in with blue enamel with additional gilding of the top and base rims and of the handle. 'Suez' and 'Crete' are similar transfer-printed water jugs **(Fig 117) (Fig 118)**. In December Brownfields said that they were proposing to exhibit at Paris and as late as February 1878 the firm's name was still among those listed as intending exhibitors.

The next jug design appeared on 6th November (Registration Number 315954). The Brownfield design name for this jug is not known and it has been accorded the title 'Leek' **(Fig 119)**. So far no example of this has been found and the illustration is taken from the design register. The last registered jug of 1877 is 'Hudson' **(Fig 120)** introduced on 22nd December, of which five different examples have been found. This was done by using sprig-type moulds to construct a series of master models. The basic design shows a band of fine mesh netting around the neck of the jug, while underneath on a stipple dotted background, a variable number of fish swim among seaweed and seaplants. The illustrated jugs indicate that the collector has to study the permutations very closely. Even when the number of fish on different jugs is the same, they are not always found swimming in the same direction. The first of the five 'Hudson' jugs shows three fish swimming from right to left; this example is on a plain white stoneware body, but there are some that have minimal gilding of the weights on the netting. The reverse side of this jug usually shows a single fish. This basic 'Hudson' is fairly ordinary when compared to the subsequent enamelled examples. The markings

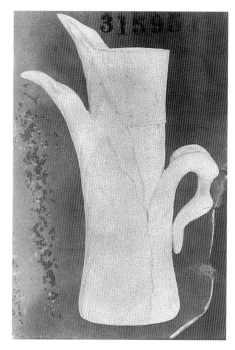

Fig 119. WB. 'Leek' jug. Registered 6th November 1877. Engraving from the Design Register — courtesy the PRO.

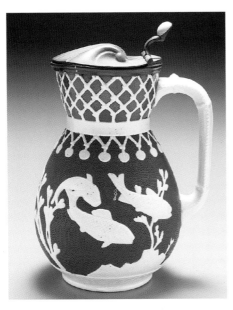

122. WB. 'Hudson' III Jug. Moulded Twin Globes, Reg D and Cartouche. 'Hudson'/'Brownfield & Sons'. Reg D. for 22nd December 1877. 6½" — 16.5cm.

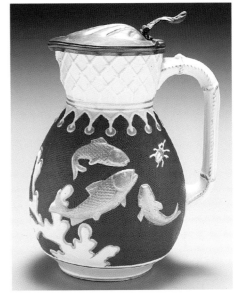

123. WB. 'Hudson' IV Jug. Moulded Twin Globes, Cartouche — 'Hudson'/'Brownfield & Sons'. Reg D. for 22nd December 1877. BM Collection. 6" — 15cm.

124. WB. 'Hudson' V Jug. Moulded Twin Globes, Cartouche — 'Hudson'/'Brownfield & Sons'/Reg D. for 22nd December 1877. RL Collection. 7¾" — 19.5cm.

125. WB. 'Alsopp' Jug. Impressed 'Alsopp'/'Brownfield'/'1/77'. Private Collection. 7½" — 19cm.

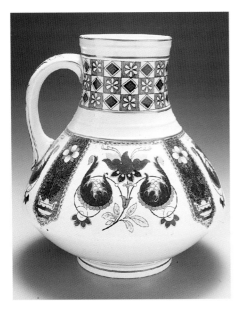

127. WB. 'Yesso' Jug. Moulded Reg D — 9/1/79. Printed Twin Globes, Printed Cartouche — 'Yesso'/'Ivory'/'11/80'. 10½" — 26.5cm.

128. WB. 'Sado' Jug. Moulded Regn D — 9/1/79. Printed Twin Globes, Impressed 'Ivory'/'Brownfield & Sons'/'2/81'. Pat No '5863'. Courtesy D Watson Antiques, Leominster.

58

on this and all 'Hudson' jugs include the twin globes, the moulded ribbon containing *BROWNFIELD & SON*, a cartouche with the jug name, an impressed month and year date and sometimes a pattern number (**Marks 25**).

The second 'Hudson' jug (**Col Pl. 121**) shows three fish, two swimming from left to right and the third swimming in the opposite direction. It is shown on a blue enamelled background, with both the fish and seaplants in white, while the netting around the jug neck is set against a brown enamelled background to give additional contrast. The third 'Hudson' jug (**Col Pl. 122**) also has three fishes, but this time they are all swimming from left to right, while the colour combination is the same. The fourth and fifth 'Hudson' jugs (**Col Pl. 123**) (**Col Pl. 124**) are the finest of all: the fourth has the fishes enamelled in gold with additional gilding of the seaplant and sea insect. However, the fifth is the most attractive because there are four rather than three gold fishes and there is a gold seaplant growing all the way up the jug body. The records in the Design Register show that George Jones of Stoke-on-Trent produced a very similar jug, registering it on 8th June 1880. This jug shows three fish, one crab and two seagulls.

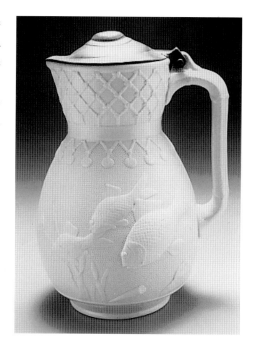

Fig 120. WB. 'Hudson' I Jug. Moulded Twin Globes, Reg D, Cartouche. 'Hudson/ 'Brownfield & Sons'/'10/79'. Reg D — 22nd December 1877. 7³/₄" — 19.5cm.

'Alsopp' (**Col Pl. 125**) is another unregistered jug from 1877, almost certainly made for the brewers who subsequently became a part of the Inde, Coope and Alsopp company. Surviving examples show that this was in production at least by January 1877 although further discoveries may show that it was being manufactured earlier than this. The two 'Alsopp' jugs discovered are produced in a highly glazed brown stoneware, each with a transfer printed picture of two elves, set on a light blue background. Both the naked elves have an animal skin over their shoulders; the first, in a semi crouched position, is pointing a finger at the other elf, while shielding his face behind a mask. On the opposite side of the jug, the second naked elf, also in a strange unbalanced crouch position, is playing a pair of cymbals. A second much larger version shows the naked elf playing a harp on one side of the jug and pouring some wine into a bowl on the other. The markings include a simple impressed jug name, a month and year date and 'BROWNFIELD'.

There were no new jug designs registered in 1878, perhaps because the firm was concentrating on the production of the giant earth vase. This was probably meant to be finished in time for the Paris Exhibition opening in May. However, preparation appears to have fallen behind schedule and by April Brownfields had cancelled their booking for Paris, alleging insufficient space had been allocated to them. (It was at this time that Brownfields commenced production of pate-sur-pate.) There was a preponderance of dealers at Paris, whereas the 1851 London Exhibition had insisted that displays were only to be shown by manufacturers. In October-November Brownfields got through their ovens a ten and half foot china group — displaying figures of the four seasons with a globe in the centre of the piece.

Marks 25. WB. 'Hudson' jug. Moulded Twin Globes Trade Mark — 'Brownfield & Son'. Crescent shaped Cartouche — 'Hudson'/Size '24'. Moulded Reg D for 22/12/77. Impressed '5/78'. Pat No '1899'.

Fig 126. WB. 'Stanley' Jug. Photograph from the 1880 Brownfield Catalogue. Courtesy Spode Ltd and Keele University.

This had reputedly cost £100 (over £2,000 in today's money) to model and mould.

The registered design for a jardiniere, introduced on 4th December 1878, may also have been used for a jug, but none has yet been identified. A theft in 1879 involved the 'London' cup and saucer design, the 'Madras' pattern and the 'Tunis' plate. In all eighty-two copper plates were alleged to have been stolen. A 'Tycoon' plate design was introduced at least by March 1878 and this was also used to produce a jug. 'Stanley' (**Fig 126**) is the only other jug known to have been issued in 1878, one of a series of unregistered engine-turned mosaic jugs illustrated in the 1880 Brownfield catalogue. It is, like most engine turned jugs with a mosaic pattern, a very unspectacular jug designed for a very cheap market. Its markings include the jug name, a size number, a month and year date and 'BROWNFIELD'.

The 'Yesso' jug shape (**Col Pl. 127**) was later used for different transfer-printed editions that include 'Sado', 'Ranga', 'Daisy', 'Denver', and 'Tudor': others have also been identified. 'Yesso', comes in the form of an ewer covered with a transfer printed picture. There is, unusually, a wealth of information on the base of this 'Yesso' ewer; a moulded registration diamond, two printed globes and a cartouche containing the design name 'YESSO'. There is also an impressed *'IVORY'*, an impressed *'BROWNFIELD'* and the impressed date *'11/80'*: 'Ivory' appears to indicate a special kind of earthenware body. The only difference on 'Sado' (**Col Pl. 128**) is a separate transfer printed picture. Both the 'Yesso' jug and the 'Sado' jug are ten inches tall, and 'Sado' has a moulded registration diamond, printed twin globes, an impressed *'BROWNFIELD & SONS'*, an impressed *'IVORY'* and an impressed date *'7/79'*.

'Ranga' shows a transfer print depicting the branches of a tree, with a further mosaic pattern around the neck. The markings on the jug base include a moulded registration diamond, a printed cartouche containing 'Ranga', an impressed 'Ivory', an impressed potter's letter 'T' and the date '12/77'. A fourth jug, 'Denver', is also produced on the 'Yesso' shape, but no illustration of this is available. 'Daisy' (**Col Pl. 129**) is a brightly coloured transfer print of clusters of daisies, its marks being similar to those on the other jugs. 'Tudor' is another transfer-printed pattern produced exclusively for Oetz Mann & Co. of Hampstead Road, London. Its marks include an impressed 'BROWNFIELD', 'IVORY' and '20', a registration diamond and a printed stamp detailing the retailer's address. The last example to be illustrated is an unnamed pattern (**Col Pl. 130**), the jug having no printed pattern name on the base, just an illegible registration diamond. The only other marks are an impressed *'6/83'* and a pattern number *'6201'*.

Two 'Dublin' jugs (**Col Pl. 131**) have been found dating from 1879 — the transfer printed scenes being two of several different ones used. Indeed there may be as many as ten or so different scenes on these jugs (as with the 'Medieval' pattern.) The first of the two 'Dublin' jugs has a transfer printed picture of two brightly coloured birds sitting on a branch, while on the other side of the jug three swallows are seen swooping down from the sky; this is the theme found on 'Spring' plates. The second 'Dublin' jug (**Col Pl. 132**) is the same shape, but shows two children playing at blowing bubbles, while on the other side two young boys are playing at the seaside — a scene from the 'Pastimes' series. (See also Chapters 7 and 8.) The impressed markings include *'BROWNFIELD'*, a size number and a month and year date — in these instances *'10/79'* and *'3/82'*. Both jugs have one further impressed mark —

'DUBLIN — a mark that the Hampsons have also identified on a 'Pastimes' tea kettle made in September 1881. The most likely explanation for this seems to be that while 'Merton' and 'Spring' were the design names used for the plates, the same patterns were used as 'Dublin' on transfer-printed jugs. The markings on the 'Pastimes' kettle could also be another 'Tuesday morning' mistake. In December 1886 a later example of the 'Dublin' jug was reissued with a newly patented device for a self-balancing removable jug lid. (This is illustrated in the next chapter.)

Fig 135. WB. 'Truro' Jug. Impressed 'Truro'/ 'Brownfield'/'B/85'. 7½" — 19cm.

'Missouri' **(Col Pl. 133),** introduced on 25th May, is the only new jug design registered in 1880 (Reg No 350098), another in the group of jugs that Brownfields named after famous rivers. This has a pattern showing a background of basket willow interwoven with upright bamboo canes. A number of willow leaves also emerge from the top of the handle. The jug name suggests that this may have been produced mainly for the American market. Its marks include the moulded twin globes, a registration diamond, a cartouche containing the name *'MISSOURI'* and sometimes an impressed month and year date.

We know that in addition to the jugs so far covered in this chapter, at least another sixteen unregistered jugs were in production by January 1880 at the latest; it is impossible, however, to pinpoint their precise introduction date. The first nine of these are all illustrated on page 61 of the 1880 Brownfield catalogue. Several of these are engine-turned jugs often with a mosaic type pattern — 'Exe', 'Adonis', 'Corinth', 'Solon', 'Stratford', 'Truro' and 'Tasso'. Although these are among the cheapest jugs manufactured by Brownfields, some of them have proved very difficult to find. No examples of 'Adonis', 'Dunedin' or 'Stratford' have yet been discovered. The only 'Tasso' jug discovered shows that it is a very ordinary engine turned mosaic jug produced for a very cheap market.

The most attractive of those that have been found is Corinth **(Col Pl. 134).** This has a narrow cylindrical body with the jug spout shaped as a goat's head. There is a double engine turned line of 'ovals' in the centre of the jug body, with a further single line both above and below. Very few examples have been found to date. The second of the illustrated engine turned mosaic jugs is 'Truro' **(Fig 135),** a very plain jug except for the blue pattern in the top half of the jug. Somewhat surprisingly, an elaborate handle with a goat's head has been added. It is a mystery why Brownfields accorded the jug this name. Its impressed markings include *'TRURO'*, *'BROWNFIELD'*, *'B'* and *'85'*; another has been found with 'D' and '85'. This seems to represent a change in practice from the marking system operated in the years 1874-80, during which time both the month and year of production were impressed. It was, perhaps, necessary to reinstate the potter's impressed mark for reasons of quality control and piece rate payment. 'Oxford' **(Col Pl. 136)** is another mosaic jug produced in a blue stoneware body, with an engine turned pattern similar to that of 'Truro'. Its marks include an impressed *'OXFORD'* and *'BROWNFIELD'*. Some may have an impressed month and year date.

'Clyde' **(Col Pl. 137)** is another jug usually produced in a rather drab white or grey stoneware, its only decoration consisting of a row of sprigged white flowers and berries just below the rim of the jug, while the bottom quarter of the jug has fluted vertical lines. However, the example shown here has the leaves enamelled in light greyish blue, the berries are gilded and there is a broad gold band round the

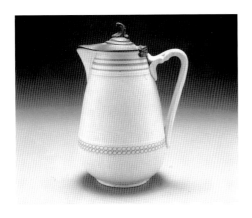

Fig 138. WB. 'Solon' Jug. Impressed 'Solon'/
'Brownfield'/'B/100'. 6" — 15cm.

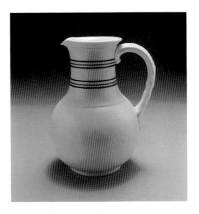

Fig 139. WB. 'Exe' jug. c1875-80.
Impressed 'Exe'. 7¾" — 19.5cm.
Courtesy Milverton Antiques,
Somerset.

Fig 140. WB. 'Adonis', 'Dunedin', and 'Stratford' Jugs. Photographs from the 1880
Brownfield Catalogue. Courtesy Spode Ltd and Keele University.

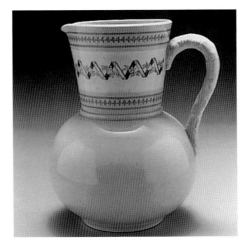

Fig 141. WB. 'Gipsy' Jug. Impressed 'Gipsy'/
'Brownfield'/'1/84'. 5" — 12.75cm.

129. WB. 'Daisy' Jug. Moulded Reg D — 9/1/79. Printed Twin Globes, 'Wm Brownfield & Sons', 'Daisy'. Impressed 'Ivory'. Pat No '5277'. 10½" — 26.5cm.

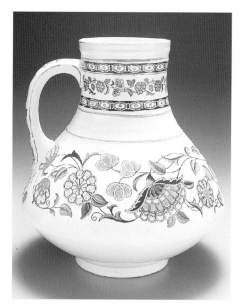

130. WB. Unnamed Yesso shape. Moulded Reg D — 9/1/79. Otherwise unmarked. 10½" — 26.5cm.

131. WB 'Dublin' I Jug. ('Spring' scene) Impressed 'Brownfield', '10/79'/'24'/'Dublin'. Pat No '2001'. 6¼" — 16cm.

132. WB. 'Dublin' II Jug. ('Pastimes' scene) Impressed 'Brownfield'/'Dublin'/'36'/'3/82'. Pat No '2416'. 5¼" — 14.5cm.

133. WB. 'Missouri' Jug. Moulded Twin Globes, Moulded Cartouche — 'Missouri'. Moulded Reg D — 25th May 1880. MM/MR Collection. 7" — 17.5cm.

134. WB. 'Corinth' Mosaic Jug. Impressed 'Corinth'/'Brownfield'. RH Collection. 7" — 17.5cm.

Fig 143A. WB. 'Dorking' Jug. Photograph from the 1880 Brownfield Catalogue. Courtesy Spode Ltd and Keele University.

Fig 143B. WB. 'Dorking' Jug. Photograph from the 1880 Brownfield Catalogue. Courtesy Spode Ltd and Keele University

Fig 144. WB. 'Taunton, Dartmouth, St. Germain' Jugs. Photographs from the 1880 Brownfield Catalogue. Courtesy Spode Ltd and Keele University.

body of the jug with additional gilding of the leaf edges and the jug handle. This shows that the design does come to life a little more when the jug had been produced in contrasting enamelled colours. 'Clyde' has much in common with the 'Ayr' jug reviewed later in the chapter; at best, both designs could be called functional. Unlike the 'Truro' jug, the markings are just 'CLYDE'.

The next mosaic patterned jug is 'Solon' **(Fig 138),** which has three engine turned blue bands just below the neck of the jug and two circular rows of blue ovals at the base of the handle. In contrast to the previous mosaic jugs, 'Solon' has vertical fluted lines from top to bottom and some jugs have quite attractive Britannia metal lids. This jug would have been named after Marc Louis Solon, the Sevres trained artist, who worked for Minton's and whose forté was the decoration known as pate-sur-pate — thin layers of china clay built up over a coloured ground to give a cameo type effect. The impressed markings include *'SOLON', 'BROWNFIELD'* and *'B/100',* ie 1900: perhaps this particular jug's main claim to fame is that it was one of the last jugs to be produced before the firm went into liquidation in August 1900. The 'Exe' jug **(Fig 139)** was probably introduced in the years 1875-80, although there is neither an impressed date on this example, nor even an impressed Brownfield.

The illustration of three other mosaic patterned jugs — 'Adonis', 'Dunedin' and 'Stratford' **(Fig 140)** — is taken from the 1880 catalogue. All of these inexpensive jugs are likely to have been introduced between the years 1870-80. According to the 1880 Brownfield Catalogue, the 'Adonis' jug appears to have been produced on the same bodied shape as 'Clyde'.

There are three further engine turned mosaic jugs that are not identified from the salesman's 1880 catalogue and all were probably introduced in the same period 1875-1883. Identification of each proved possible because the firm's name is also impressed on the jug base. The first jug illustrated is called 'Gipsy' **(Fig 141)** and has the impressed date '1/84: the second is entitled 'Gypsy' and has an impressed date '5/84'. The third is 'Tiber' **(Col Pl. 142)** which is just impressed *'BROWNFIELD'* and *'TIBER'.*

In addition to these jugs, there were a further seven jugs in production by 1880 — as revealed in the 1880 Brownfield

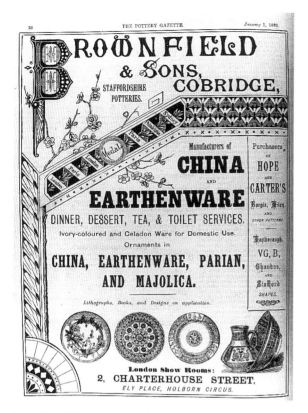

Fig 145A. WB. Brownfield Advertisement January 1881 —
Pottery Gazette.

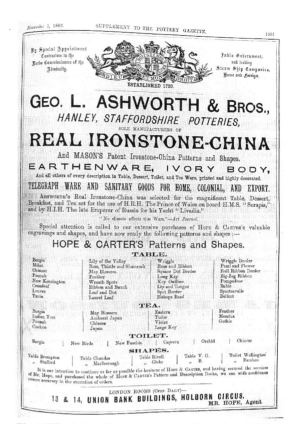

Fig 145B. Ashworth Advertisement November 1882 —
Pottery Gazette.

Catalogue. The first two of these are 'Dorking' I and II **(Fig 143),** found on pages 88 and 89 of the above book. Like 'Medieval', 'Sylvan' and 'Mandarin', the component parts of this dinner service illustrate several different wildlife scenes. The jugs might, therefore, show any one of the dozen or so scenes depicted on the plates, tureens, bowls, covered dishes etc. One of the transfer-printed scenes on the jugs is quite clear — it shows a swan searching for food in a lake. Others include two ducks drinking and a third shows a cockerel standing proudly on its perch. The markings on the jugs remain unknown.

Three further transfer printed jugs, 'Dartmouth', 'Taunton' and 'St. Germain' **(Fig 144)** were introduced by January 1880: all were component parts of a dinner service. The Brownfield 1880 catalogue shows that there were two versions of the 'Dartmouth jug', the same transfer-printed pattern being imposed on two different jug shapes.

The Melbourne Exhibition opened on 1st October 1880. Listed among those with displays were Minton, Worcester Royal Porcelain Co, William Brownfield & Sons, Moore Bros, Hammersley & Son and Pinder Bourne & Co. Brownfields had won a 2nd Order of Merit at Melbourne although it was not announced for what particular exhibit this was awarded. A Brownfield advertisement of January 1881 **(Fig 145A)** illustrates three plate patterns, the 'Sado' ewer and all the medals won at recent International Exhibitions. It also announces that Brownfields have purchased numerous Hope & Carter patterns. However, the next Ashworth advertisement states **(Fig 145B)** that they have acquired those self same patterns. Further research will be needed to clarify this issue.

'Neil' **(Col Pl. 146),** a bathroom water jug, is the first jug found from 1881, although it is possible that it was in production earlier. The second, 'Pastimes' **(Fig 147A),** was registered on 8th February although the design register shows that this was for a kettle. This, however, is misleading because at the same time a plain jug shape was registered and it was from this latter shape that both the 'Pastimes' and

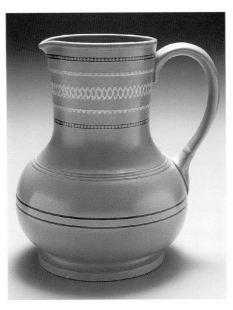

136. WB. 'Oxford' Jug. Impressed 'Oxford'/'Brownfield'. Private Collection. 7¼" — 18.5cm.

137. WB. 'Clyde' Jug. Impressed 'Clyde'/'Brownfield'. Pat No '799'. 5¾" — 14.5cm.

142. WB. 'Tiber' Jug. Impressed 'Brownfield'/'Tiber'. BM Collection. 6¾" — 17cm.

146. WB. 'Neil' Water Jug. Impressed date — 1881. Private Collection. 6" — 15cm. Courtesy Von Bulow Antiques, The Antique Centre, Dorking.

148. WB. 'Mistletoe' Jug. Moulded Twin globes, Moulded Cartouche and Reg D for 4th May 1881. Impressed '1/82'. DJ Collection. 8" — 20.5cm.

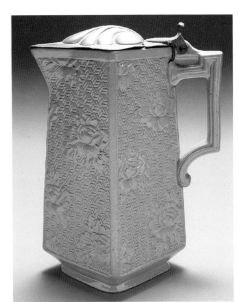

152. WB. 'Montana' jug. Moulded Twin globes, Reg D for 25th August 1883. Moulded Cartouche — 'Montana'/'12'/'4/84'/'M'. 7½" — 19cm.

"PASTIMES."

"WISCONSIN."

Fig 147A. WB. 'Pastimes' jug. Engravings from the Pottery Gazette 1884.

Fig 147B. WB. Wisconsin jug. Engraving from the Pottery Gazette 1884.

'Wisconsin' jugs (**Fig 147B**) were developed. It seems possible that a whole variety of scenes may be depicted on these jugs; the kettle design in the design register depicted a swallow flying towards a large leaf, while the 'Pastimes', illustrated by the Hampsons in 1980, showed a little boy sitting at a low table. No example of a jug impressed 'Pastimes' has yet been found, but an advertisement in the 1884 *Pottery Gazette* clearly shows the design and shape of the two jugs. The impressed markings on the 'Pastimes' kettle are *'BROWNFIELD', 'DUBLIN'*, a size number and *'9/81'*. The impressed 'Dublin' may be a mistake or it may be the firm's alternative name for the 'Pastimes' pattern.

The 'Mistletoe' jug (**Col Pl. 148**) was registered on 4th May 1881, a pattern name more easily understood than any other! The one illustrated has a brown enamelled band at both the top and bottom of the jug and also of the two uprights which divide the Mistletoe into separate panels. Another 'Mistletoe' jug has gilding instead of the brown enamel. For the first time, a new technique has been used to attach the Britannia metal lid to the top of the jug. Instead of the four tiny holes around the jug lip, there is now a hole in the very top of the jug handle, through which a pin secures the lid. The markings on this jug are moulded twin globes, a registration diamond, a size number, a cartouche containing *MISTLETOE* and an impressed date — *'1/82'*. A shape for another plain water jug was registered on 4th October 1881 (Reg No 370885), probably used for a range of different transfer prints with enamel decoration. A much more elaborately moulded jug, seemingly a 'Pumpkin' (?) design (**Fig 149**), was introduced six months later on 4th April 1882 (Reg No 379212) — although the engraving in the Design Register does not make clear identification easy. Unfortunately, the Design Register does not give Brownfields' name for this jug.

Further Minton patented ovens were opened in September 1882, increasing Brownfields' porcelain production capacity and two months later Brownfields displayed at Stafford four large figures manufactured in biscuit china representing the 'Four Seasons' (see Chapter 8). The unregistered 'Ayr' jug (**Fig 150**) was in production at least by April 1882. It is produced on the 'Merton' or 'Dublin' shape first introduced in the autumn of 1879. It has been found in a stippled grey stoneware, the only decoration being the application of white leaves just below the neck of the jug. The jug illustrated is only four inches tall and has the impressed marks of *'AYR'*, *'BROWNFIELD'* and the date *'10/82'*. The initial production of 'Ayr' may have begun somewhere between 1875-82.

William Brownfield and Son(s) appears to have been a thriving business during the years 1871-82 and more than holding its own with its competitors. Advertisements in 1876 and in the 1879 *Pottery*

Fig 149. WB. 'Pumpkin'? Jug. Registered 4th April 1882. Engraving from the Design Register — courtesy the PRO.

Fig 150. WB. 'Ayr' Jug. Impressed 'Ayr', 'Brownfield', '10/82'. 5" — 12.5cm.

Gazette show that it had an agent, a Mons. J L Tourton of 1 Rue de Rocroy, Paris, attending to its exports to France and Belgium: a Mr J Davison, 13 Barclay Street, was their representative in New York. The Centennial Exhibition Catalogue printed in Philadelphia in 1876 shows that Brownfields also had agents in Berlin and Vienna. Throughout 1881 and 1882 the firm funded a full page advertisement in the *Pottery Gazette* listing its recently awarded medals at International Exhibitions and illustrating some of its current products. Brownfields were still receiving major reviews in the trade journal; one in January 1881 reported on recently introduced dinner services made in both celadon and ivory bodies — a design known as 'Dayton'. Later in November 1883 a dinner service order was being made for Tiffany's, the well known New York importers: a new dinner service with an ivory body, entitled 'Ophelia', had also been just made and several new jug designs had been introduced. Trade statistics suggested that firms (like Brownfields), who depended on substantial exports, would enjoy a healthy future. Between 1880-83 china and earthenware exports were increasing to America, Canada, India, Australia and France.

However, July 1883 brought the first 'reported' news of the sudden departure of its managing director, William Etches Brownfield. A terse announcement was made of the dissolution of his partnership on 27th February, followed by an equally brief statement that he had 'retired' from the company. The Brownfield factory was one of the biggest employers in Cobridge and this lack of detail seems strange because every week the paper had a column entitled 'Local Intelligence' and much more inconsequential happenings were reported in Cobridge during the months of March to July. It has, however, proved impossible to find any further contemporary evidence to explain William Etches's departure.

Frederick Rhead, later Brownfield's Artistic Director in the 1890s, subsequently referred to 'disastrous speculations'. There is just a suspicion that they might have been personal financial speculations. When William Etches died in 1902, two of his sisters went to the trouble of proving his will even though their brother had died in Australia — to which he had emigrated in the 1890s. Their efforts revealed that he left less than £2 — a ludicrously small sum for a man who had inherited a one third share in a profitable family business. By comparison, his brother Arthur, was in the mid 1890s still worth on paper well over £25,000 at least, despite placing the long established family firm in voluntary liquidation in 1892. The immediate economic climate was bright in 1882-83 for the Staffordshire pottery industry in general, and for William Brownfield & Sons in particular, but William Etches' departure in February 1883 meant a reorganisation of its management and the future of William Brownfield and Son now lay in the hands of the second son Arthur.

CHAPTER 5
THE FINAL YEARS: 1883-1900

1. THE BEGINNING OF DECLINE: MARCH 1883-AUGUST 1892

Fig 151. WB. Relief-moulded Jug. Registered 18th June 1883. Engraving from the Design Register — courtesy the PRO.

Arthur Brownfield took over the firm from the end of February 1883. It seems that he inherited control at a rather inauspicious time; the three years 1880-82 had been prosperous years for pottery factories, but the economic climate began to turn sour towards the end of 1883. Four jugs were registered between June and November 1883: two of these were introduced on 18th June. The first **(Fig 151)** is a very unspectacular affair judging from its appearance in the Design Register (Reg No 399557); the second, the porcelain 'Gentleman' jug is illustrated in Chapter 8.

'Montana' **(Col Pl. 152)** is the third of the registered 1883 jugs, introduced on 25th August (Reg No 402839). The example shown in the Design Register clearly indicates a contrast between the colour of the background and the flowers. Its shape is most unusual, the jug having four straight sides rather than the normal rounded design. A number of flowers (possibly peonies) are set against a background panel of lattice work. The jug illustrated has the moulded twin globes trade mark, a registration diamond, a cartouche containing the title *'MONTANA'*, its size *'12'*, an impressed date *'4/84'* and a potter's mark *'M'*. The lid is attached by the recently introduced screw method, but has still had to be resoldered at least once on the underside. Clearly the new technique for attaching lids was not as successful as had been hoped. The last registered jug of 1883 is a strange 'Tree Trunk' jug **(Fig 153)** introduced on 13th October (Reg No 405364). No example of this has yet been found and the description here is taken from the Design Register.

Fig 153. WB. 'Tree Trunk' Jug. Registered 13th October 1883. Engraving from the Design Register — courtesy the PRO.

Only a dozen other newly registered jugs were introduced between 1884-93. The first of these was registered in February 1884. (To avoid confusion with the old pre 1884 pattern numbering system, we have to remember that a fresh start was made in January 1884. The new pattern numbers covered all categories of registered designs and not just ceramics — as had been the case until the end of 1883.)

These later Brownfield jugs have only been identified very recently and no examples have yet come to light. The first **(Fig 154)** is a plain stoneware jug introduced in February 1884 (Reg No 1629), the second **(Fig 155)** (Reg No 7627) was registered four months later in June, its shape being very similar to that of 'Montana', issued only the previous August. This jug registration is probably explained by 'Montana' being a relief moulded jug while this plain jug was for use with transfer prints. No example has yet come to light.

Fig 154. WB. Plain Water Jug. Registered February 1884: Reg No 1629. Engraving from the Design Register — courtesy the PRO.

Fig 155. WB. Plain 'Montana' shaped Jug. Registered June 1884. Reg No 7627. Engraving from the Design Register — courtesy the PRO.

Fig 156. WB. Transfer Printed Chinoiserie Jug. Registered July 1884. Reg No 9462. Engraving from the Design Register — courtesy the PRO.

The jug shape of February 1884 was re-issued six months later in July 1884 with a transfer print (**Fig 156**) (Reg No 9462). It seems surprising that the firm needed a fresh registration as both jugs were produced in the same shape.

A *Pottery Gazette* advertisement in October 1884 (**Fig 157**) publicised all the medals won by Brownfields at past Exhibitions, and illustrated the designs of eight new or recent products. Three jugs or water ewers, 'Wisconsin', 'Yesso' and a different transfer printed example of the 'Pastimes' shape are among these. Full identification of the first two is only possible from advertisements. The 'Yesso' jug shape is based on the registered shape of 9th January 1879 and the 'Pastimes' and 'Wisconsin' jugs are produced on the registered shape of 8th February 1881. Five other designs are shown, the first being a design called 'Niel' produced as a jug or water ewer as well as a plate and covered tureen. Other illustrated plate designs include 'Madras', 'Ningpo' and 'Laburnum'. The 'Niel' pattern also led to a jug and, therefore, these later three designs may have done, but none has so far been found. A new pattern in dinner ware was introduced in 1885 — this has an ivory body and the design represents the signs of the zodiac. The one new jug of 1885 (**Fig 158**), registered in January, has more relief-moulding than other recent jugs and harks back to the naturalistic designs of the 1850s and 60s.

In December 1886 Brownfields patented a jug (**Fig 159**) with a new self-balancing removable cover which meant that the cover lid could now be taken off, facilitating washing the inside of the jug. Brownfields advertised this innovation in the *Pottery Gazette* in December 1886 and again in January and February 1887, but then discontinued it for the rest of the year. The innovative lid is shown on a 'Merton' shaped jug, except that this jug has a floral transfer print and not one

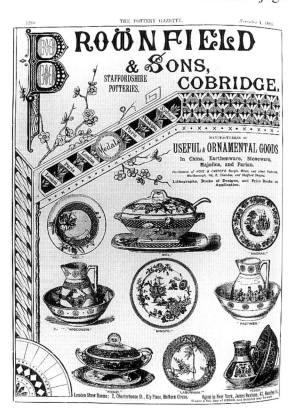

Fig 157. WB. William Brownfield & Sons Advertisement — October 1884 Pottery Gazette.

Fig 158. WB. Relief-moulded Jug — Registered January 1885. Regn No 20555. Engraving from the Design Register — courtesy the PRO.

Fig 159. WB. 'Merton' Jug with Innovative lid. Picture taken from the December 1886 Pottery Gazette.

of the normal range of 'Merton' designs introduced in 1879. A new registered jug **(Fig 160)** was introduced in March 1887, the first for two and a quarter years. Its shape and design is depicted in the artist's engraving in the Design Register. This is, seemingly, for a water jug as it is accompanied by a bowl with the same moulded pattern as the jug.

The *Pottery Gazette* announced late in 1887 that the presentation of the famous Gladstone vase **(Fig 161)** had been made to the distinguished politician in November. There is no evidence that William Brownfield's sons continued the political activity for which their father had been renowned,

Fig 160. WB. Relief-moulded Jug — Registered March 1887. Reg No 71415. Engraving from the Design Register. Courtesy the PRO.

Fig 161. WB. The 'Gladstone Vase'. November 1887. Reproduced courtesy The Gladstone Pottery Museum and A Jarrold & Son, Norwich.

Fig 162. WB. William Brownfield & Sons Advertisement — taken from the February 1888 Pottery Gazette.

but clearly the Liberal tradition remained strong, and accepting a commission from some Burslem townsfolk to manufacture a special vase, represented an astute public relations exercise. Apparently the idea of a Gladstone vase first arose in January 1887; by the autumn it had been finished and placed on display at the Wedgwood Institute in Hanley. The transcription under the vase read 'Designed and executed at Burslem for a few Liberals of that town as a slight expression of their admiration, affection and gratitude'. According to the Hampsons original article in 1980, the vase was presented at Hawarden, Gladstone's family home, on 20th August 1888.

A study of Gladstone's life and political career throws up no obvious anniversary for celebration. Indeed the only real cause for celebration that can be detected in 1887 is the fiftieth anniversary of William Brownfield's entry into the management of the old firm of Robinson, Wood and Brownfield! There appears to be nothing of note in Gladstone's career in 1837, 1847, 1857 etc. to explain this public presentation and even 1862 (a twenty-fifth anniversary) offers no special achievement. It does not even commemorate the Gladstones' golden wedding. However, F A Rhead argued in an article in *Pottery No 4* (1930) that it was presented mainly in appreciation of Gladstone's labours for Irish Home Rule. The Gladstone Vase was until recently kept at the Gladstone Pottery Museum in Longton, Stoke-on-Trent.

After ten months' abstention from advertising in the *Pottery Gazette* during 1887, a much reduced quarter page advert was included in January 1888 **(Fig 162)**. However, this only lasted until July 1888 and thereafter the firm appeared to be back operating on a very tight budget. No more advertising was placed after August 1888; indeed this was the very last time that William Brownfield and Sons advertised in the *Pottery Gazette*. Other firms were either more fortunate with their promotional budgets because of a better cash flow, or they took the positive and contrary policy of continuing advertising even in hard times. In early 1889, Doulton, Grimwade, Thos. Forrester & Sons and the Royal Worcester Porcelain Co each funded an expensive full page monthly advert in the Trade Journal. Many others like J Dimmock, Dudson, J Furnival, S Fielding, Brownhills, Robinson & Leadbetter and Edge & Malkin all continued either a half-page or a quarter-page monthly advert. Only one new item — a coffee pot **(Fig 163)** — was registered in 1888, in May (Reg No 100389).

Brownfields opted to take stand No 90 at the 1889 Paris International Exhibition, evidently a sizable one, for the company had decided to show their famous 'Earth Vase'. The vase reached Paris on 1st May 1889, but damage had occurred which the firm's Parisian agent tried to repair in order to facilitate

Fig 163. WB. Coffee Pot — registered May 1888. Reg No 100389 — May 1888. Engraving from the Design Register — courtesy the PRO.

Fig 164. WB. Water Jug — registered July 1889. Reg No 128561. Engraving from the Design Register — courtesy the PRO.

its display. The wares displayed at Paris included a number of plates revealing the firm's finest, most delicate and artistic decoration. One new registered jug **(Fig 164)** was introduced in 1889 and this appeared in July (Reg No 128561). This is a rather bulbous, fluted water jug designed to take different transfer printed scenes.

In March and June 1890, Brownfields registered two new designs for jugs (Reg Nos 146658 and 150706). Their illustration is taken from the Design Register **(Figs 165-166).** In June 1890 the long-established Anchor Pottery run by Sampson Bridgwood and Son, Longton failed — an indication of the downturn in the pottery industry. Despite the economic vicissitudes of the past few years, the workforce at Brownfields in 1891 was now up to 600 — seventy more than it had been in 1881. The production of china, majolica and pate-sur-pate might well have required some additional skilled workers, but it does seem surprising that no effort was made in the very difficult years 1885-90 to cut the wage bill by reducing the workforce. For two years or more (1888-90) Arthur Brownfield had been urging his fellow master potters to raise prices because pottery businesses' profit margins were seriously unsatisfactory. Despite this, he had done little or nothing to diminish his own workforce.

Fig 165. WB. Relief-moulded Jug — registered March 1890. Reg No 146658. Courtesy the PRO.

Fig 166. WB. Relief-moulded Jug — June 1890 Reg No 150706. Courtesy the PRO.

167. WB. 'Prunus' jug. Impressed 'Prunus'/ 'Brownfield'. BM Collection. 5¾" — 14.5cm.

172. WB. 'Shamrock' pattern for a Teapot. Registered 20th May 1859. Probable marks as on 'Shamrock' jug.

174. WB. 'Severn' Teapot. Reg D — 19th June 1868.

175. W P & G Phillips. Pattern for 'Westminster' Teapot. Registered 21st October 1868. Marks as on 'Westminster' jug. Made by WB.

176. WB. 'Nile' Teapot. Regd 10th June 1870. Marks as on 'Nile' jug. Courtesy Von Bulow Antiques, Dorking Antique Centre.

183. WB. 'Mistletoe' Teapot. Reg D for 8th Feb 1881. RH Collection.

189. WB. 'Argyll' Teapot. Moulded circular Trade Mark (no registration diamond). 'W Brownfield'/'Cobridge'/'Argyll'.

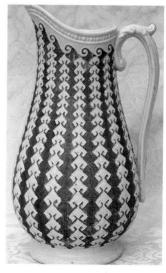

190. Dudson. 'Argyll' jug. Moulded circular Trade Mark — Argyll/Dudson.

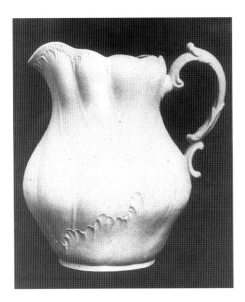

Fig 168. WB. Relief-moulded Jug — Registered March 1892. Reg No 190591. Courtesy the PRO.

Arthur Brownfield voiced his first public thoughts on the idea of a Pottery Guild in May 1891 — a brave course of action as it was a rather Utopian scheme: the commonest reactions were hostility and incredulity. The whole pottery industry was currently bedeviled by a pay dispute in which the workers were demanding an extra 10%; in response the bosses proposed a reduction of 10%! This was not a climate in which idealism was likely to receive a favourable or sympathetic hearing.

The 'Prunus' jug (**Col Pl. 167**) was introduced by October 1890, possibly earlier. This is an unusual shaped jug with more relief-moulding than for some considerable time. The examples discovered are produced in green or grey stoneware without any enamelling of the branches or leaves. A set of three jugs have recently been identified with the impressed date '–/84', indicating that production had started six years earlier than had hitherto been thought. The harsh trading climate of 1891-2 is illustrated by the bankruptcy of Ambrose Bevington's New Hall Works, Hanley, which occurred in April 1892 and this was followed a month later by the enforced closure of E J Bodley's Hill Pottery, Burslem. By the end of 1892, no less than twenty-two pottery firms had gone out of business and this appears to have included only those forced into bankruptcy rather than those who opted for voluntary liquidation. It was in this gloomy climate that Brownfields registered a new jug (**Fig 168**) in March 1892 (Reg No 190591). This was to be the last new registered jug manufactured by William Brownfield and Sons. We know nothing about the internal discussions that must have taken place among the Brownfield factory managers during the months of May, June and July 1892, but by August it had been decided that the factory could no longer pay its way. The decision was accordingly taken to place William Brownfield and Sons in voluntary liquidation. The Prospectus for its successor, the Brownfield Guild Pottery, was issued in October. After 42 years under the family management of father and sons, the Brownfield firm was closed down. Some honour was salvaged by the payment of all its outstanding debts.

2. CO-OPERATIVE AND ULTIMATE FAILURE: AUGUST 1892-AUGUST 1900

Arthur Brownfield propagated his ideas of a Co-operative throughout the months preceding May 1891. He had spent nearly three years trying in vain to persuade his fellow manufacturers to co-operate in finding a collective solution to the growing difficulties of the Staffordshire Pottery industry. The business fortunes of the Brownfield firm were almost certainly not rosy, but then this was true of a large portion of the industry. The Bo'ness Co-operative, launched in January 1892, was also experiencing serious difficulties and was still making a loss as the autumn of 1892 approached.

Arthur believed that the key to overcoming the great problems of the past was to introduce a joint committee of workers and managers (a committee that would be chosen by election); this body would manage the business by determining prices, the standard of wages and by regulating the apprenticeship system. Additionally, and of major importance to the workers, it would 'decide on any and every grievance'. All this was fine in theory but not in practice. There were likely to be, from the outset, major problems with the 'structure of the management team'. The committee was to consist of thirty individuals — fifteen from the former managers and fifteen from the workers. This would be unwieldy

Fig 169. Brownfield Co-operative Guild Devon Water Ewer. Printed monogram 'BGP', 'Devon'. Pat No '920'. c1892.

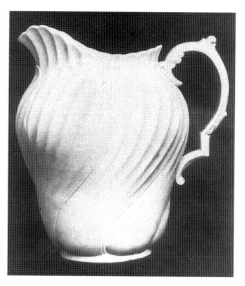

Fig 170. Brownfield Co-operative Guild. Jug — Reg November 1893. Reg No 223134. Engraving from the Design Register — Courtesy the PRO.

and make decision making more rather than less complicated. Remarkably, this committee was only to be in charge for one year, after which fresh elections would be held. This would lead to a serious lack of continuity in personnel (and perhaps in policy); it was also likely to aggravate the lack of experience among many of those elected to the management committee. Most hard headed observers concluded that the only realistic way to solve the industry's problems was 'to close at least 20% of the existing factories'. Others pointed out that the 1890s was the age of the machine and the producing power of the Potteries had doubled.

The Guild was fortunate enough to retain the services of Louis Jahn as Artistic Director for the immediate future and it is thought that he remained with the Co-operative until 1895. His successor, Frederick Rhead, writing in 1906, believed that the Guild started with good products, excellent business connections and a body of well-trained and capable craftsmen. The next jug illustrated is the 'Devon' water ewer (**Fig 169**) manufactured by the Guild and probably introduced in about 1892. Its marks include the printed monogram 'BGP', 'DEVON' and a pattern number '920'. Between December 1892-September 1893 only six new products were registered (see Appendix 2) and none of them were jugs. The next new registered jug (**Fig 170**) was not introduced until November 1893 (Reg No 223134). With a workforce of approximately 400, the Co-operative generated a business turnover of £19,000 in its first year. This had declined from the £29,000 of the previous year, but the workforce size had been trimmed by over 200. The Co-operative had survived its first daunting year.

The Guild submitted only five applications for new designs in 1894, and in the event only three were granted by the Design Register Office. Neither the applications of January and September 1894 were issued although the reason for this is not given. The first internal realisation that all was not well with the structure of the Guild's management came in July 1895 when it was announced that the rules of the Guild were to be changed. The original management body was to be converted into a departmental committee and a new group of thirteen men chosen by the major shareholders took over all management decisions.

1896 was a year of very mixed fortunes. Guild membership had now grown to 779, a quite remarkable number and over 150 larger than it had ever been in its old form as William Brownfield and Son: however, this figure of 779 would have included workers and Co-op members. Whether this meant that all were working efficiently to maximise output is another unknown matter. Turnover had been marginally increased to £21,379 (this represented about a 10% increase) and a gross (but NOT a net) profit of £1,137 had been achieved. Unfortunately for the Co-operative, all the other developments of 1896 were major setbacks. The first of two serious problems came in February 1896 when the Guild

196. RW&B. Transfer Printed 'Flowers and Urn ' Plate. Printed Cartouche with Crown — 'Opaque Stone China'/'No 24'/'RW&B' cJune 1837. Plate Diameter 23.6cm.

197. RW&B. Transfer Printed 'Flowers and Vase' Plate. Printed Cartouche and Crown — 'Stoneware'/'RW&B'/'No 31'. cJune 1837. Plate Diameter 22.8cm.

198. RW&B. 'Mansion' sugar bowl. Printed Circular Cartouche with foliage — 'Mansion'/'RW&B'. c1837. Diameter 14.6cm.

199. RW&B. 'Zoological plate. Printed Oval Cartouche with crown and with foliage. Printed 'Stoneware'/'RW&B'/'Zoological'. c1837. Plate Diameter 26.5cm.

200. W&B. 'Zoological Plate. Printed Oval Cartouche — 'Stoneware'/ 'W&B'. Impressed '7'. Printed 'Zoological'. Diameter 26.5cm. Courtesy Amanda Watt Antiques, Devon.

202. W&B. 'Amoy' plate. Printed Cartouche — Amoy/No 54/ W&B/cFebruary 1838. 'Higginbotham & Son, 17 Sackville Street, Dublin. Impressed Cartouche — 'W&B'/Pearl Ware Cobridge. Diameter 27cm.

Fig 171. Brownfield Pottery Ltd. 'Mimosa' and 'Stuart' Toilet Sets. Picture from the May 1899 Pottery Gazette.

was successfully sued by a Mr L Salomon, formerly the commission agent in Australia and India for the old Brownfield company and, more recently, for the Co-operative. Matters worsened when the Guild took the case to the Court of Appeal, only for judgement to go against the Guild.

By the beginning of 1897 the Co-operative had survived its first four and most difficult years. However, the economic climate was still extremely unfavourable and it was acknowledged by all within the industry that the domestic market was in a worse state than that overseas. By the late summer a cash flow problem seems to have developed within the Guild and payment of bills for necessary raw materials was falling well behind normal and acceptable schedule. The Sneyd Colliery and Brickworks Ltd petitioned for the compulsory winding up of the Co-operative Guild on November 16th 1897, alleging unpaid bills of £412 (over £10,000 in today's values). To make matters worse, Mr L Salomon now chose to claim a further £450 for unpaid commission. By the 26th of November, it had been agreed to proceed with the winding up of the Guild and Mr Charles Bullock of Hanley and Mr T Wood of Manchester were appointed as joint liquidators.

In December 1897 and early 1898, Mr L Salomon instituted further proceedings to bring about liquidation and this was carried out in the next few weeks. The winding up was to be a 'voluntary' one, implying that by some means all bills were being settled. In February 1898, it was announced that Mr. Salomon would be given notice of any contract for sale of the Guild — duly done when the Brownfield Guild Pottery was put up for sale in February 1898. Endeavours were still being made in the early autumn to sell the Guild's assets to a new company still in the process of formation — probably the Brownfield Pottery Ltd, for the latter was in operation with 300 workers by the late autumn of 1898 and was registering new designs in January 1899. It listed its London agents as Samuel Wood and Arthur Brownfield, and its London showroom as 1 Farringdon Avenue, EC.

Arthur Brownfield acted only in the capacity of joint London agent for the new firm. The new management was appointed by the co-operative societies' shareholders who were anxious to rescue as much as possible of their earlier investment in the Guild and to protect the jobs of the remaining 300 workers. In 1898 no less than thirty-two pottery companies in Staffordshire went bankrupt while a further thirty-four were terminated by a deed of arrangement. In 1899, a further twenty-one went bankrupt and twenty-eight were ended by a deed of arrangement. The prospects for the new company improved when it obtained orders from the White Star shipping line to replace their steerage tinware with crockery and for the complete outfitting of the new SS Oceanic with crockery. New wares in May 1899 included samples of dinner services and toilet ware. The 'Stuart' toilet set decorated with a new trellis pattern was one of the new designs; 'Mimosa' ware (**Fig 171**) exhibiting 'fanciful enamelled goods in natural colours' was another. This included a range of teapots, butters and covers, sardines, handled boxes, trays etc.

The new company made a profit of £514 for the last five months of 1899 but a loss for the year as a whole. Two new designs were registered in April 1900 — the last Brownfield products to be registered. The first signs of the approaching end came, perhaps, in May 1900 when Wood and Brownfield, the commission agents in London, took on a new agency — to act for the Royal Art Pottery Co, Waterloo Works, Longton. By August 4th 1900, the decision had been taken to wind up the Brownfield Pottery Co for good and by September 26th the works had been auctioned and sold. Sixty-three years of Brownfield pottery production had finally come to an end.

3. REASONS FOR DECLINE AND FALL

A partial explanation of the ultimate downfall of Brownfields lies in the general situation within the Staffordshire pottery industry in the years 1880-1900; the rest is found in inadequacies within the Brownfield firm itself. The demise of Davenports and a host of lesser known firms in the years 1885-1900 is a clear indication of the enormous problems within the pottery industry. The main one was the serious overproduction in relation to demand, both within the domestic and export market; this was partially explained by the growth in mechanised production in the last two decades of the nineteenth century. There was also a major increase in foreign competition, especially from France and Germany in the 1880s and 1890s.

However, many firms were able to withstand and survive that growing competition. The problems probably hit worst those companies that continued to assume that a ceramic product made in Staffordshire must therefore be best! Some British manufacturers were too unaware of the competition to react positively to it; there was sometimes a lack of awareness of the needs of overseas countries. Some pointed to a lack of innovation in design ideas, others to the excess of designs that made economies of production difficult to achieve. This was the general context in which Brownfields foundered. Other contributory factors might include the general lack of business acumen of Arthur Brownfield as managing director, the failure to prune the workforce in the late 1880s and the failure to advertise the company's goods throughout the period 1888 to 1899.

Arthur Brownfield was a very fine man with admirable principles and an acute social conscience, but these did not make him a successful business manager. His father William Brownfield possessed not only business acumen but also those crucial salesman's skills acquired in his early years. Arthur Brownfield was far more suited to the role of a clergyman (his original aspiration) than to the post of chief executive in the cut-throat environment of capitalist enterprise. William Etches' abrupt departure in 1883 seems to have had a very adverse effect; his continuation as managing director in the challenging period 1883-92 might possibly have saved the Brownfield factory.

CHAPTER 6

(A) TEA AND COFFEE SERVICES

It is not clear just how many tea or coffee pots designs (or services including a tea or coffee pot) Brownfields manufactured during the years 1837-1900. The design register reveals the relatively small number of about twenty. (See Appendix 9A.) The Brownfield 1880 Factory Catalogue confirms that many others were produced, adding another eighteen. About forty Brownfield teapots, tea or coffee services will be illustrated, those manufactured in porcelain being reviewed in Chapter 8. There may be many other unregistered ones .

No Wood and Brownfield teapots made during the years 1837-50 have come to light. 'Shamrock' **(Col Pl. 172),** introduced in May 1859, is the first teapot pattern illustrated, this being based on the relief-moulded jug of the same name: in this instance the teapot was not registered separately. Other teapot designs may have been based on other jug patterns like 'Jewel', 'Wicker' or 'Fern', the latter being an enormously popular design in the mid Victorian era. However, no such additional teapots have yet come to light. Somewhat unusually, Brownfields produced two teapots with the design title 'Shamrock' and the May 1859 example should not be confused with a second, transfer-printed one with enamel decoration introduced between 1870-80. (This second one based on a teacup and saucer is illustrated in the 1880 Brownfield Catalogue.)

The next registered teapot design was not introduced until 1868 and three were then recorded within the space of five months. 'Cone' **(Fig 173),** registered on 12th June 1868, is the first: its shape and pattern are illustrated on page 125 of the 1880 Factory Catalogue where it appears as a sugar box, bowl, coffee and teapot. 'Cone' has the kettle type handle and the spout, the handle and the lid-bob all enamelled in a bright red. 'Severn' **(Col Pl. 174)** followed a week later, based not on a design for a relief-moulded jug, but on a separate design just for a teapot. Collectors will have to be very wary about the 'Severn' design; some teapots were erroneously manufactured with the impressed title 'Westminster' — an error apparently stemming from a mistake in the Brownfield factory's own 1880 catalogue where on page 55 the wrong pattern name is listed. This wrongly marked 'Severn' might, therefore, be considered an unusual collector's item.

The 'Westminster' teapot **(Col Pl. 175)** was registered in October 1868 and is unique in the Brownfield firm's output. It was made for and registered by a London retailer W P & G Phillips and its markings are, therefore, different from those usually found on the firm's own teapots. The design follows that of the 'Westminster' jug and the teapot was not registered separately. 'Westminster' teapots, like the jug, may also be discovered dating from as early as 1864: pre-registration examples will have a pattern number about '140' or '151'. The 'Nile' teapot **(Col Pl. 176),** based on the relief-moulded jug, was introduced on 10th June 1870; it is known to have been manufactured in both plain white stoneware and in blue and white enamel decoration. On 27th

173. WB. 'Cone' Teapot. Moulded Circular Trade Mark — 'Cone'/'WB'/'Cobridge'.

Fig 177. WB. Teapot — Registered 27th March 1871 — No 251246. Engraving from the Design Register. Courtesy the PRO.

Fig 178. WB. Teapot — Registered 14th November 1872 — No 267894. Engraving from the Design Register — courtesy the PRO.

Fig 179. WB. 'Aston' Teapot. Registered 6th June 1874. Picture from the 1880 Brownfield Catalogue. Courtesy Spode Ltd and Keele University.

Fig 180. WB. Tea Service. Registered 20th January 1875 — No 288554. Courtesy Geoffrey Godden.

March 1871 and again on 14th November 1872 Brownfields introduced two more designs **(Figs 177, 178).** Unfortunately the Design Register gives no pattern name for either. The 'Aston' teapot **(Fig 179),** introduced on 6th June 1874, is illustrated from the 1880 Factory Catalogue as no actual teapot has so far been found. Its markings should include the moulded twin globes and registration diamond that were introduced in 1874. This was followed by the introduction of a tea service **(Fig 180)** on 20th January 1875.

On 31st October 1876, Brownfields registered three most unusual teapots — the 'Man and Gourd', the 'Face and Pigtail' and the 'Fish'. All known examples are produced in porcelain or majolica and these are illustrated in Chapter 8. Brownfields introduced a new tea service **(Fig 181)** on 26th October 1878 (Reg No 328320), and the 'Basket' teapot **(Fig 182)** was registered just over two years later on 26th January 1880 (Reg No 345719). 'Argyll', 'Aston', 'Butterfly', 'Cone' and 'Basket' all seem to have been produced only in teapot form.

Brownfields registered two teapot designs in February 1881, although surprisingly both were based on the same outline shape. The basic shape is that of the 'Mistletoe' jug, but the first of the teapots is produced in a plain body, facilitating the use of different enamel decorated transfer prints. Half a dozen quite different enamelled decorated teapots could, conceivably, be found on this shape. The second **(Col Pl 183)** is an orthodox relief-moulded 'Mistletoe' pattern.

The only coffee pot so far discovered is an unregistered design which was probably introduced in

Fig 181. WB. Tea Service. Registered 26th October 1878. Engraving from the Design Register. Courtesy the PRO.

Fig 182. WB. 'Basket' teapot. Registered 26th January 1880. Engraving from the Design Register. Courtesy the PRO.

Fig 184. WB. Coffee pot. Impressed 'Brownfield', '7/83'. 8¹/₂" — 21.5cm.

1883 **(Fig 184).** It is impressed 'Brownfield' and '7/83'. Its pattern name is not known. 'Clamshell', registered on 13th October (Reg No 405363) is the last of the teapots revealed by the old design register which ended in 1883. Like the three teapots of 1879, this was produced in porcelain (see Chapter 8). It is not yet known if it was produced in stoneware as well.

The New Design Register reveals five more teapot designs introduced between 1884 and 1888. The first of these **(Fig 185)** was registered in September 1884 (Reg No 12805): this, and the remaining four, are illustrated from the engravings in the register. The next two **(Fig 186)** were introduced in March 1886 (Reg No 45262-63) and the last ones **(Fig 187)** in October 1887 and June 1890 (Reg No 83253 and 150704). The last item to be shown in this section is a coffee pot registered in June 1890 (Reg No 150703) **(Fig 188).** A set of four 'Isle of Man' teapots (c1880) was also illustrated in Marilyn Karmason and Joan B Stacke's *Majolica: A Complete History and Illustrated Survey* (New York, 1989). Mention of the majolica 'Hotei' teapot, introduced in the mid 1870s, is included in Chapter 8. A rare collector's item, it fetched £1,200 at a Phillips west country auction in December 1994.

(B) TEA AND COFFEE SERVICES

In addition to these registered teapots, we know of at least five more tea or coffee services identified from the 1880 Factory Catalogue. The 'Argyll' coffee pot **(Col Pl. 189)** is very similar to the Dudson pattern. Its precise introduction date is not known although it would not have been before the 23rd of December 1868, the date when the three years legal protection for the Dudson 'Argyll' **(Col Pl. 190)** elapsed. Some Brownfield 'Argyll' teapots have the customary impressed circular mark on the base containing the pattern name, 'W Brownfield' and 'Cobridge'. There is, however, no registration diamond within this circle as the teapot was not registered **(Marks 26).**

'Rose Leaf' **(Fig 191)** is the second of the five tea services depicted in the 1880 Catalogue. Unfortunately the sepia photograph on page 50 is not very good and the pattern is rather difficult to see. The teapot itself is shown in the centre of the service. The date of manufacture is not known, but it was probably introduced in the years 1865-80. The teapot may have no attributive marks. The third and fourth sets are 'Richelieu' and 'Cambridge' **(Fig 192) (Fig 193),** illustrated on pages 117-118. The sepia photographs are again poor, but both look to be plain designs for transfer prints; very little relief-moulding can be discerned. The basic shape of the teapots can, however, be identified; apart from the tea-cups and sugar bowl, the basic shape of 'Richelieu' and 'Cambridge' appears to be the same. Their introduction date was probably c1865-80. 'Butterfly' **(Fig 194)** is the last of the five tea services found

Fig 185. WB. Teapot. Registered September 1884. (Reg No 12805) Engraving from the Design Register. Courtesy the PRO.

Fig 186A. WB. Teapots. (1) Registered March 1886. Reg No 45262.

Fif 186B. Reg No 45263. Engravings from the Design Register — courtesy the PRO.

Fig 187A. WB. Teapots. (1) Registered Oct 1887 (Reg No 83253).

Fig 187B. June 1890. (Reg No 150704). Courtesy the PRO.

Fig 188. WB. Coffee pot June 1890 (Reg No 150703) Courtesy the PRO.

in the 1880 catalogue, illustrated on page 55.

In 1972 Desmond Harrison illustrated a William Brownfield cabaret set (a teaset for two known as a 'tête-à-tête') **(Fig 195),** originally consisting of eight pieces, but reduced sadly to seven by the disappearance of the teapot. This elaborately enamelled set, decorated in rich shades of red, blue, turquoise, orange, pink and green, has much in common with many of the plates of the mid to late 1850s. No date was given for the manufacture of this cabaret set; teapot collectors may be able to identify the teapot from the cabaret set's design and colours.

Marks 26. WB. 'Argyll' Coffee Pot. Moulded Circular Trade Mark (without Reg Diamond) — 'Argyll'/'WB'/'Cobridge'. Potter's Marks 'RH'.

IDENTIFICATION

Collectors who have registration-marked but otherwise unidentified pots or plates can, by examining the data within the Registration Diamond, work out when and by whom it was manufactured. An explanation of how to do this can be found in many reference works including those by Geoffrey Godden and J P Cushion, but for collectors having no access to such works, a brief guide to 'reading' the Diamond is now provided. Sometimes, it is not possible to identify all the numbers and letters, but if you can see most of them clearly, it *may* still be possible to track down the maker, especially if there is a very unusual parcel number — see below. Both the above guides will show that the layout of the registration diamond changed in 1868.

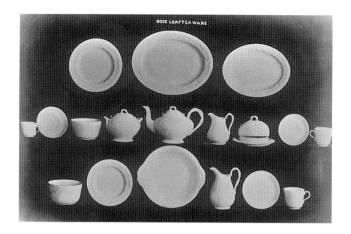

Fig 191. WB. 'Rose Leaf' Tea Service. c1865-80.

Fig 192. WB. 'Richelieu' Tea Service, 'Cambridge' Tea Service.

Fig 193. WB. 'Cambridge' Tea Service

Fig 194. WB. 'Butterfly' Tea Service — pictures from the 1880 Brownfield Catalogue, courtesy Spode Ltd and Keele University.

Fig 195. WB. Cabaret Service. c1855-65. Illustration courtesy Desmond Harrison.

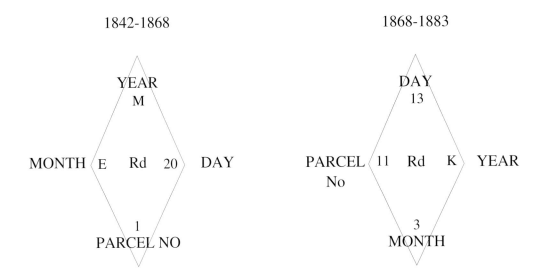

1842-1868

YEAR
M

MONTH ⟨E   Rd   20⟩ DAY

1
PARCEL NO

1868-1883

DAY
13

PARCEL ⟨11   Rd   K⟩ YEAR
No

3
MONTH

The first example on the left is the Brownfield 'Shamrock' teapot, registered on 20th May 1859: the second is the Brownfield 'Clamshell' teapot, registered on 13th October 1883. The moulded Registration Diamond with precise details of day, month and year was no longer employed after 1883 and a simple registration number (often inside a printed diamond shape) was used instead. If the maker's name is not given, then one has to go the Public Record Office at Kew and consult one of the massive leather bound tomes of the Design Register. The approximate age of a post 1883 teapot can be assessed from the number alone; a guide to this can be found in J P Cushion's *Pocket Guide to British Ceramic Marks* and in Geoffrey Godden's *Staffordshire Porcelain*.

CHAPTER 7
BROWNFIELD PLATE DESIGNS: 1837-1900

ROBINSON, WOOD AND BROWNFIELD: 1837-1837

Appendix 3 provides a complete inventory of all the known plate designs manufactured by the firm between 1837 and 1900. The first plate illustrated is a rare, marked Robinson, Wood and Brownfield plate made in about July 1837. The plate **(Col Pl. 196)** has no pattern name, but *'OPAQUE STONE CHINA'*, *No '24'* and *'RW&B'* are printed in an almost rectangular cartouche on the back **(Marks 27)**. The pattern is similar to that on the RW&B jug (Pattern Number 30), illustrated in Chapter 1, which it probably preceded by only a matter of days. This same pattern was also used for number '22', produced in a different colour combination; it may, too, have been used for '23'. The plate shows a collection of flowers, the stems of which protrude from a two handled urn. The enamel colours are very soft and restrained in comparison to the brighter ones used in the 1850s, but the enamelling here is of a high standard. Additional flower heads appear in the outer border with the edging enamelled in brown with intermittent yellow daisies. The '2' of the '24' is printed while the '4' is hand painted. Printed foliage and flowers surround the cartouche on both sides — a characteristic of the factory marks employed in the 1830s and 40s. This plate is probably one of the relatively few products to be marked 'RW&B' as Noah Robinson died just some two months later and (with one exception) the marks on goods after September 1838 only record 'W&B'.

This same No '24' plate is also found with different and rather misleading markings. Several different 'runs' of the product were made and the second or third (?) batch of this plate emerged with a different printed cartouche, probably in late 1837 or early 1838 **(Marks 28)**. The plate's only difference is that the 'outer' transfer print has been imposed differently in relation to the 'inner' print. The different marks *'Pat No 2'* are explained by the premature and untimely death of Noah Robinson in September 1837. Rather than create a new factory stamp immediately, the same one has been used probably for 1837 and 1838, the 'R' of 'RW&B' has been deleted, and a factory worker has forgotten to add the '4' of pattern number '24'. Another rare RW&B plate is the 'No 31' **(Col Pl. 197)**, probably introduced within a few days of No '24'. The transfer print with brown, yellow and green enamel decoration is very similar — an ewer and a bowl surrounded by an abundance of flowers and foliage.

Marks 27. RW&B. Pat No 24 Plate. Printed Cartouche with Crown and foliage — 'Opaque Stone China'/'No24'/ 'R.W&B'. cJuly 1837.

Marks 28. W&B. Pat No 24 Plate — Erroneous Printed marks 'No 2'. Printed Cartouche — 'Opaque Stone China'/ 'W&B'. c1838-39. Pat No 24 was produced by RW&B in 1837.

Marks 29. RW&B Plate Pat No 31 — Printed Cartouche with Crown and foliage — 'Stoneware'/'RW&B'/'No31'. cJuly 1837.

Fig 201. RW&B.'Canton' Plate. Printed 'Canton'/'RW&B'. c1837. Courtesy Geoffrey Godden.

The printed marks include an almost circular cartouche containing 'STONEWARE', 'RW&B' and the pattern number '31' (**Marks 29**). 'Mansion' (**Col Pl. 198**) is the next Robinson, Wood & Brownfield product to be illustrated. The sugar bowl is part of a tea service, but the patterns depicted on the other pieces are different from this one. The printed marks include 'STONEWARE'/'MANSION'/'ROBINSON, WOOD & BROWNFIELD'. There is unusually no pattern number inside the printed cartouche, but these marks indicate an introduction date in 1837, prior to Noah's death in September.

Another Wood & Brownfield plate pattern is 'Zoological' (**Col Pl. 199**) (**Col Pl. 200**), the title of a dinner service produced some time in 1837. This has no pattern number, but it has the usual printed circular cartouche surrounded by flowers — found on other 1837 products. Each of the dinner plates has a different transfer-printed picture and the same is probably true of the tureens, platters etc. The first one shows two enormous tigers in a cage being admired by a mother and her child and by another couple; the second a spoonbill and heron in a pond in front of a lake and a temple. There is a much more elaborate border pattern here than on any of the other known RW&B plates. The first transfer print is effected in light green, the second in blue and the markings on the first follow those found on the 'RW&B' plates, numbered 22 and 24, except that they do not have the pattern number. The marks on the second are 'W&B', the 'R' having been erased, and an impressed '7': this would suggest an introduction date of 1838-39. At present, the latest known Robinson, Wood & Brownfield plate pattern is 'Canton' (**Fig 201**), illustrated on page 245 of Geoffrey Godden's *British Pottery, An Illustrated Guide*. The plate illustrated has a transfer-printed chinoiserie scene, typical of the late 1830s and its marks are 'RW&B', dating it as c1837. Other 'Canton' plates may have 'W&B', dating their introduction as 1838-40.

WOOD AND BROWNFIELD: 1837-1850

'Amoy' (**Col Pl. 202**) is the earliest Wood and Brownfield plate shown, probably introduced in February 1838. This has a chinoiserie scene showing two men standing on a railed balcony, one with a fishing rod in his left hand, very similar to that on the 'Nankin' jug of 1843. To the side and in the rear are two pagodas with the customary trees and foliage. The scrolls in the plate border are most attractively enamelled in green and light brown, accompanied by four large flower heads and a multitude of smaller flowers and foliage. The detailed printed marks on the back are very interesting: there is a circular cartouche containing 'AMOY', the factory pattern 'No 54' and the letters 'W&B'. Just below this is another oval garter containing the name of a retailer — 'HIGGINBOTHAM AND SON, 17 SACKVILLE ST, DUBLIN'. There

Marks 30. W&B. 'Amoy' plate — cFebruary 1838. Printed Circular Cartouche with Crown, Oval printed Cartouche — 'Higginbotham, 17 Sackville St, Dublin'/ Impressed Cartouche — 'Pearl Ware'/ 'W&B'/'Cobridge'.

Marks 31. W&B. Chinoiserie plate — Printed Coat of Arms & Unicorn — 'Warranted Real Ironstone China'/'W&B'. Enameller's Painted 'v'. Pat No '303' — cMay 1842. cJun 1842.

Marks 32. Careys, Lane End (1823-1842). Chinoiserie plate with same Pat No '303'. Printed Coat of Arms/'Dieu et Mon Droit'/'Improved Ironstone China'. Impressed '7'. Pat No '303'.

Marks 33. W&B. Plate. Printed Coat of Arms — 'Warranted Real Ironstone China'. Printed Cartouche — 'Higginbotham & Son, 17 Sackville St, Dublin'. Pat No '328' — cJun 1842. (Note that there is no 'W&B'.)

is also an impressed rectangular mark containing 'W&B', 'PEARL WARE' and 'COBRIDGE' **(Marks 30)**. This fascinating detail provides us with considerable food for thought. Firstly, it is noticeable that the marks do not denote RW&B even though a Robinson was still technically a partner in the firm (until March 1841). This means that only items produced before Noah Robinson's death in September 1837 will contain the letters RW&B which will make it a rare collector's mark. Even more remarkable, perhaps, is the evidence denoting a Dublin retailer in this extremely early period — only a year after the new firm had been launched at the Cobridge works. In 1856, Higginbotham was at 102 Grafton Street, and was still Brownfields' retail outlet in Dublin. (See later in this chapter.)

Another 'Real Ironstone China' plate **(Col Pl. 203)** (Pat No 303), bearing clear Wood & Brownfield marks, was in production by about May 1842. Mason's Patent Ironstone China had been introduced in 1813 and had quickly become one of the most popular forms of earthenware — especially for dinner services. The plate's chinoiserie scene is typical of the 1840s and early 1850s — two oriental houses built on wooden pole supports, two pagodas in the left background and an abundance of dog roses, both in the plate centre and in the border. The rich deep enamel colours — blue, green and reddish-orange — are typical of those employed by the Wood and Brownfield firm (inter alia) in the 1840s. The plate has an elaborate printed mark containing a royal coat of arms incorporating a lion and unicorn, a crown heading a circular cartouche containing the motto *'HONI SOIT QUI MAL Y PENSE'* — identical to that found on the 'Grecian Statue' plate reviewed later in the chapter. *'WARRANTED REAL IRONSTONE CHINA'* is printed, partially above and below the coat of arms: underneath this is *'W&B'* and nearer the rim a pattern number *'303'* **(Marks 31)**. The same pattern was produced by Careys of Lane End and most unusually its pattern number is also '303'. **(Marks 32.)**

In June 1842 Wood & Brownfield introduced a further 'Real Ironstone China' plate **(Col Pl. 204)** (Pat No 328). The scene depicted shows a vase in blue and gold enamel decoration, surrounded by flowers and foliage, while on the right a little child stands on a platform holding what looks like a cake stand on his head. The plate border is dominated by the same three large dog roses enamelled in orange found on Pattern Number '303', interspersed here with geometric shapes and patterns. The blue and orange enamel colours and the glaze match almost exactly those used on the previous 'Real Ironstone' plate, manufactured only a month earlier. The plate marks include the lion and unicorn, the royal coat of arms headed by a crown and *'WARRANTED REAL IRONSTONE CHINA'*. Underneath this is the printed cartouche denoting 'HIGGINBOTHAM AND SONS, 17 SACKVILLE STREET, DUBLIN': there are also two gilded enamellers' marks — an '=' and a 'x' and a painted pattern number *'328'* —

Fig 205. WB. 'Palmyra'/'Inkerman' platter. Introduced c1850. Printed Scroll surrounded by trees, foliage and temple — 'Palmyra'/'WB'. Courtesy Fair Finds Antiques, Rait, Perth.

but no impressed potter's mark and no 'W&B' (**Marks 33**). Technically, there is no proof that this is a Wood & Brownfield product because the letters 'W&B' are missing, but its close similarities with the preceding plate (Pat No 303) in both enamel decoration and markings make it likely that it was made in the same factory.

A very attractive rose patterned dessert service was introduced in about November 1842. (Pat No 397' — but not illustrated here.) This was the first in a series of at least eight different patterns all produced between 1842 and 1865 on the same unregistered relief-moulded plate edging. Only the first two and last in this series have clearly recognised, currently known marks. Both the first and second (Pat No 428), have an impressed rectangular cartouche (as on 'Amoy') containing 'W&B', 'COBRIDGE' and 'PEARLWARE'. The last example of about 1855-60 has a moulded Staffordshire knot and 'WB'. Each component part of the 1842 dessert service has the same transfer printed rose, filled in with high quality enamel decoration — the best of any Wood & Brownfield plates identified so far. It was followed in this series by the chinoiserie dessert service of December 1842 (Pat No 428), by the 'Convolvulous' (sic) plate (Pat No '4142/7') and by another Floral Wreath design (Pat No 4150), both in July-August 1849. Others will probably be discovered.

The grey transfer printed 'Palmyra' plate (also produced by Brownfields as 'Navarro') was thought to have been introduced by Wood and Brownfield in 1845. In 1971, Desmond Harrison illustrated a commemorative dish 'Inkerman' in an article in *Antique Collecting* and its transfer printed scene is identical to that on the Palmyra plate. (See later in this chapter.) The Palmyra platter (**Fig 205**) is actually the William Brownfield product, also having an elaborate printed cartouche in the form of a scroll, containing 'PALMYRA' and underneath 'WB'. The Wood & Brownfield edition of the plate is likely to have very similar markings, but with 'W&B' instead.

The next plate (**Col Pl. 206**) (Pat Nos '642') is a Wood and Brownfield colour variation of a pattern that was later repeated by William Brownfield both in January 1856 and as the 'No 35' plate in about December 1856. A re-issue of successful designs was frequently done by most factories. The illustrated plate has no specific marks clearly indicating that it emanated from the Brownfield factory, but careful comparison of the pattern with that of plate 'No 35' strongly suggests that it did. This chapter will explain that all the numbered items discovered, including 'No 35', are Brownfield products. (See Appendix 6C.) Four plates, pattern numbers '642' and '2602', pattern number '8907' and the No '35', all show a vase containing flowers and what appears to be a little wrapped-up gift. The Wood and Brownfield plates have the same border as well as the same central picture. The first two of these four

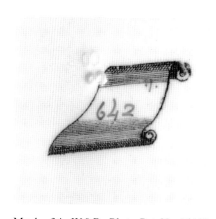

date from about June 1842 and January 1847 respectively. Both pattern numbers are contained within a printed scroll, closely similar (but not identical) to that printed on the back of the Brownfield 'Palmyra' plate **(Marks 34)**. Another firm could have produced their own copy of this unregistered design, but there are now sufficient examples of Brownfields re-using an old pattern to suggest that all four of these plates emanated from the same factory.

Marks 34. W&B. Plate Pat No '642'. Printed Scroll mark. Printed '3'. Painted Pat No '642'. cJune 1842.

Marks 35. W&B.'Grecian Statue' plate. Printed Rectangular Cartouche with Coat of arms — Lion & Unicorn. Printed '2'/'Grecian Statue'/'Stoneware'/'W&B' (c1840-45).

The style of the 'Grecian Statue' plate **(Fig 207)** suggests it was produced in the early 1840s rather than later in the decade. This is a Brownfield pattern name found in the liquidation sale list of 1900 when it was bought by W T Copeland. *(Pottery Gazette March 1902.)* This elaborate transfer printed plate has a wealth of detail in the border and a statue of a woman sitting on a horse placed on top of a memorial plinth. The markings include *'W&B'* and a rectangular cartouche headed by a lion and unicorn, each supporting the royal coat of arms containing the motto *'HONI SOIT QUI MAL Y PENSE'* **(Marks 35)**. It was still in production in the early 1890s, fifty years later. The only piece of blue and white to be illustrated is 'Venetian Scenery' **(Col Pl. 208)** which was introduced by Wood & Brownfield, also probably in the early 1840s. Confirmation of this is found in a copper plate owned by Spode Ltd which tell us that this pattern was bought by Copelands in 1900 and that it originated in the years 1841-50. The marks include an elaborate blue printed cartouche headed by a crown containing the pattern name *'STONE CHINA'* and *'W&B'*. This particular example is also impressed *'BROWNFIELD'* and *'4/86'*, indicating a production run of over forty years.

The 'Pomona' plate **(Col Pl. 209)** was introduced in about June 1845. (See Appendix 6A.) Its design is similar to a great number produced by a whole range of firms in the 1840s and early 1850s — a fruit and flower transfer printed pattern with gold enamel decoration. The markings include a printed floral cartouche containing the pattern name and a pattern number *'1676'*. Some plates are likely to have a printed 'W&B' below the printed cartouche although this particular example has none. Other designs were produced on the same outline shape, and in particular the edging of the plate. 'Oriental' **(Col Pl. 210),** pattern number '1690', was introduced in about June 1845. It seems highly likely that at least some of patterns numbered '1677-1689' (and post '2000') will be further designs produced on the same shaped plate: one such is 'Chiswick' manufactured in about 1844-46. 'Oriental' has a printed cartouche containing the pattern name and number and underneath *'W&B'*. Not every plate is

Fig 207. W&B. 'Grecian Statue' plate. Printed Cartouche and Coat of Arms. 'Grecian Statue'/ 'Stoneware'/'W&B'/ '2'. c1840-50. Plate Diameter 27cm.

Fig 216. W&B. 'Cable' platter. Printed Cartouche — 'Cable'/W&B'.

marked in this way (only one in five or ten may have been) and the key for plate collectors is its outline shape and the relief-moulded leaves on the border. 'Windsor Wreath' **(Col Pl. 211)** is the fourth produced on this shape, having the identical edging and depicting a range of flowers. Its pattern number '2030' indicates an introduction date of about January 1846. Its markings include a printed cartouche containing *WINDSOR WREATH, 'W&B'* and the pattern number.

The printed cartouche surrounded by foliage, containing the pattern name or number and sometimes 'W&B', seems to be a characteristic mark found on several plates in the years 1837-50. It appears that the firm clearly marked some of the enamelled wares manufactured in the early 1840s, but it must be remembered that only a tiny proportion has to date been discovered. However, a chinoiserie plate (Pat No '2768'), with an identical scene to that on the jug (Pat No '3008' — reviewed in Chapter 1) has no clearly identified marks at all. It has only a blue printed *'o'*, found on many other Wood and Brownfield wares in the late 1840s.

Wood & Brownfield introduced their first and only registered plate design on 20th March 1848. This merely registered a shape and, at most, a particular relief-moulded border. This design was used to produce at least six different plates, including 'Alma', 'Moultan', 'Blackberry', the very mundane 'Cable', and two unnamed patterns. The 'Alma' plates **(Col Pl. 212) (Col Pl. 213)** are two of the most attractive 'Brownfield' plates produced over a very long period. The central pattern is floral, exquisitely enamelled in green, yellow and gold with an equally attractive border. The marks include a printed cartouche containing *ALMA* and *'W&B'*. The two 'Alma' plates illustrated have William Brownfield pattern numbers *'7749'* and *'7750'*, dating them as about August 1854. Both have a transfer printed sunburst '*' on the back, a mark seen on a large number of products from the Brownfield factory in the late 1840s and 1850s.

The 'Moultan' plate **(Col Pl. 214)** bears almost no resemblance to the known relief-moulded edging of the 1848 registered design: the minimal relief-moulding is lost under the enamel decoration. The plate has a printed circular cartouche almost identical to that on 'Pomona', containing the design name, a pattern number *'3738'* and *'W&B'*. This number indicates an introduction date of about November 1848. There is also the registration diamond for 20th March 1848. 'Blackberry' **(Col Pl. 215)** is the third of the 1848 patterns, shown here on a platter; its marks include the registration diamond, and the printed sunburst '*'. The 'Cable' platter **(Fig 216)** is, by contrast, a dour black and white (or blue and white) transfer print of interlocking rope, linked by frequent Staffordshire knots around the plate border. Its marks include an oval printed cartouche containing *'CABLE'* and *'W&B'*. The 'Alma', 'Moultan', 'Blackberry' and 'Cable' plates have an impressed registration diamond for 20th March 1848 and their registration number was 50994. The 'Cable' mini-platter appears to be a pre 1848 product for it lacks the registration diamond. By May 1849 the factory was selling a 'Convolvulous' plate **(Col Pl. 217)** with a pattern number '4142/7'. It has no specific attributive marks, but it was the third of several manufactured on this shape. A 'Dog Rose' plate **(Col Pl. 218)**, then followed, the pattern number '4595/4' suggesting a date of about March 1850. The last plates registered in March 1848 **(Col Pl. 219-20)** have no pattern name and were produced with slight differences in enamel decoration; each plate has a registration diamond, but no printed or impressed W&B. One has a Pat No '4682', introduced in about June 1850.

Appendix 6B includes a few further plates that Wood and Brownfield *may* have produced, but no others can be proved to have emanated from the Wood & Brownfield factory. This indicates the difficulties found in attributing Wood & Brownfield products with certainty.

WILLIAM BROWNFIELD: 1850-1871

'Alba' **(Col Pl. 221) (Col Pl. 222)** is the name of the first plates attributed to William Brownfield, introduced in about December 1850. Attribution is based on very technical evidence, much of which relates to subsequent Brownfield products, especially the crucial 'No 46' wares. (See Appendix 6C.) The first 'Alba' plate shows a transfer printed floral sprig, with beautiful enamel decoration: the patterned border is also of a very high quality. The enamel colours are very similar to those on subsequent Brownfield plates, especially the 'No 7' plate (Pat No 6411) of August 1852. The markings on the first plate are an impressed 'ALBA', a pattern number '5146', and the painted enameller's mark '∴', unaccompanied by any potter's impressed letter or printed garter mark. This enameller's mark has been identified on over ten other early Brownfield products, including the 'Cuba' jug and the No '35' plate of December 1856. The second 'Alba' plate with a similar outline shape shows quite different flowers, but is very reminiscent of many Brownfield plates in the early 1850s. It has exactly the same impressed 'ALBA', an impressed '3', a pattern number '7646' and a printed mark '§', seen on several other Brownfield plates in the 1850s. This unusual '3' has also been found on several Wood & Brownfield plates. The introduction date of pattern '7646' was about June 1854.

The other supportive evidence for this Brownfield attribution comes from the discovery of an 'Alba' jug, without any factory mark, but with a painted pattern number '9660', an impressed 'Alba' and a printed 'No 46'. All the 'numbered' items from the years 1851-1870 can be shown to be Brownfield products. (See Appendix 6C.) The registration diamond on a 'No 46' 'Alba' Tureen indicates that it was probably produced by William Brownfield in about November 1856 (registered on 27th November). The pattern number '9660' on the 'No 46 Alba' jug shows that it was produced in about November or December 1856. These 'Alba' products were all probably manufactured by William Brownfield during the years 1850-57.

The 'Eureka' bowl **(Col Pl. 223)** and accompanying 'Eureka' water jug have a common pattern but different pattern numbers. The bowl is marked '5217/0', showing that it preceded the jug ('5272') by only a week or ten days. Unlike the 'Eureka' jug, it has no registration diamond, but its marks include a printed Brownfield garter mark, containing the pattern name and number. 'Bouquet' **(Col Pl. 224)** (Pat No '5436') is the first registered Brownfield plate design, introduced on 10th February 1851. This 'Bouquet' edging was probably first introduced in about February 1851. However, this cannot be certain because another 'Bouquet' edged plate has been identified with the pattern number '5160' and this may have been a pre-registration pattern number or the number for February 1851. William Brownfield's propensity to manufacture items for some time prior to registration suggests that the former is more likely. The 'Bouquet' edged design is produced in at least twelve different patterns between 1851 and 1855: there are probably others so far undetected. Its marks include a registration diamond, a pattern number, and the distinctive printed sunburst mark '*', denoting the Brownfield factory. (See Appendix 6B.) The second 'Bouquet' edged comport **(Col Pl. 225)** is Pat No '5590', while the third **(Col Pl. 226)** shows an example with a different pink border and centre. This, however, has no pattern number and its precise date cannot be established. It is likely to have been introduced in the years 1851-55. A fourth 'Bouquet' edged plate **(Col Pl. 227)** has a different design, a green border, but no pattern number. It, too, would have been introduced between 1851-55.

In December 1851, William Brownfield introduced an attractive plate pattern **(Col Pl. 228)** (Pat No '5915/4'). This, like all the plates produced in the 1850s, is a transfer printed design with enamel decoration, in this case attractively enamelled in green, yellow, red and violet, with additional gilding of the plate edging. It is this edging that facilitates attribution to the Brownfield factory. This particular example has no obvious marks linking the plate to William Brownfield, its only marks being the painted pattern number. Unusually, there are no enamellers' marks, no printed '*o', nor an impressed potter's mark. It is, however, the first in a sequence of eight Brownfield plates made on this plate edging although an earlier Wood & Brownfield example has recently been found with the pattern number '4210', dating its probable introduction as about September 1849. The 'Hibiscus' plate **(Col Pl. 229)** (Pat No '6055') was introduced in about June 1852; this too has no clear attributive marks other than the blue-printed factory mark '*', suggested by the author as being exclusive to Brownfield wares. A comport **(Col Pl. 230)** (Pat No '6370') was the second in the series produced on this unregistered relief-moulded edge: this has no clear impressed or printed marks, just a blue printed factory mark only recently identified. Later ones included Pat Nos '7449', '7459', '8940', '8947', '11,703', '11,707' — all having a variety of marks clearly linking them to the Brownfield factory.

A 'Bouquet' edged comport **(Col Pl. 231)** was probably introduced in late 1851 and this has quite a different floral pattern from its predecessors. It has a registration diamond for 10th February 1851, the customary printed sunburst mark '*' and an *'o'*. Close examination of the enamel decoration provides a lovely example of the inexperience (or tiredness) of the young girls in the paint shop. It was clearly intended that the yellow paint should be applied to the three shapes depicting roses. It appears that the three pear shapes were not to be coloured apart from a dab of crimson for the two leaves. What resulted, perhaps towards the end of a twelve hour shift, was the yellow being applied to one of the pear shaped motifs instead of to the last of the near crescent shaped rose patterns. Inadequate quality control may have allowed this to slip through, or the comport may have been sold off as a second.

The most likely explanation of the Brownfield 'numbered' items is that they were produced under a patent taken out by William Brownfield. All these 'numbered' items are transfer printed plates (or jugs) with enamel decoration. The first of the William Brownfield numbered plates to be found is 'No 7' **(Col Pl. 232)**, (Pat No '6411'). The attribution of this particular plate is beyond doubt; in addition to the *'No 7'*, it is clearly impressed *'BROWNFIELD'*. Three different colour combinations of the same pattern have been found, dating from the initial production of August 1852 to the last in February 1886. Another in the sequence of 'floral' plates, the quality of enamelling is extremely good and much superior to the later two examples. The second 'No 7' plate has the identical pattern, but it has no painted pattern number indicating its introduction date. Its only markings are *'No 7'* and the printed factory marks '*o'. This plate, like many Brownfield products, had a production run of at least 34 years.

The 'No 8' bowl (and dinner service) **(Col Pl. 233)** was produced about eight months later. The initial 'No 8' dinner service has the pattern number '6817', dating it at about May 1853, but it was still in production in October 1880 — pattern number '9417', an edition introduced in about September 1856. The patterned border of the 'No 8' bowl is identical to that on the 'No 7', but it has no specific marks attributing it to W Brownfield. The 'No 9' plate **(Col Pl. 234)** with a pattern number *'6510'* was

203. W&B. 'Real Ironstone' China plate. Pat No '303'. Printed Coat of Arms/Printed 'W&B'. Plate Diameter 26cm. Courtesy Morrison Antiques, Bromyard.

204. W&B. 'Real Ironstone' plate. Printed Royal Coat of Arms/ 'Warranted Real Ironstone China — Higginbotham & Son, 17 Sackville St, Dublin'. Pat No '328'. Plate Diameter 23.4cm.

206. W&B. Transfer printed 'Vase/Gift' plate. Pat No 642. Printed Scroll — '642'. cJune 1842. 21.8cm.

208. W&B. 'Venetian Scenery' plate. Printed Cartouche with Crown — 'Stone China'. Impressed 'Brownfield'/'4/86'. 26cm. Courtesy Amanda Watt Antiques, Devon.

209. W&B. 'Pomona' plate. Printed Cartouche — 'Pomona'/'No 1676'/ 'W&B'. cJune 1845. Plate Diameter 26.5cm.

210. W&B. 'Oriental' plate. Printed cartouche — 'Oriental'/ 'No 1690'/'W&B'. cJune 1845 Plate Diameter 24.5cm.

211. W&B. 'Windsor Wreath' bowl. Printed Cartouche — 'Windsor Wreath'/'W&B'. cJanuary 1846. Diameter 24.5cm.

212. W&B. 'Alma' plate. Printed Garter Mark — 'Alma'/'W&B' or 'WB'/Pat Nos '7749'. Painted Factory Marks */o/cAugust 1854. Impressed Reg D — 20/3/48. Diameter 24cm.

213. W&B. 'Alma' Plate. Printed Garter Mark — 'Alma'/'W&B' or 'WB'/Pat No '7750'. Painted Factory Marks '*'/'o'/cAugust 1854. Impressed Reg D — 20/3/48. Plate Diameter 24cm.

214. W&B. 'Moultan' plate. Reg D — 20/3/48. Printed circular cartouche with foliage — 'Moultan', Pat No '3738'/'W&B'. Diameter 24.7cm.

215. W&B. 'Blackberry' platter. Impressed Reg D— 20/3/48. Printed Factory Mark '*'. Impressed 'WB' Courtesy Joyce & Lindsay Newton Antiques, Rait, Perth.

217. W&B. 'Convolvulous' plate. Pat No '4142/7'. Factory Mark '*'. Diameter 23cm.

218. W&B. 'Dog Rose' plate. Pat No '4595/4'. cMarch 1850. Printed Factory Mark '*'. Diameter 22.5cm.

219. W&B. Unnamed plate. Impressed Reg D — 20/3/48. Plate Diameter 24cm.

220. W&B. Unnamed plate. Impressed Reg D — 20/3/48. Pat No '4682' — cJune 1850. Plate Diameter 24cm.

221. Attributed to WB. Alba plate. Pat No '5146' Impressed Alba/Painted mark '::'. cJan 1851 Diameter 25cm.

222. Attributed to WB. Alba plate. Pat No '7646'/Impressed 'Alba'/'3'. Painted mark ' '. cJune 1854. Diameter 25cm.

223. WB. 'Eureka' Bowl. Printed Garter Mark — 'Eureka'/'WB'/Pat No '5217/0' — cJan 1851.

224. WB. 'Bouquet' I edged plate. Impressed Reg D — 10/2/51. Pat No '5436'. Printed Factory Mark '*' cFeb 1851. Plate Diameter 22.8cm.

225. WB. 'Bouquet' II edged Comport. Impressed Reg D — 10/2/51. Pat No '5590'. cMay 1851. Length 28.4cm. Courtesy Hunt's Auctioneers, Taunton. Somerset.

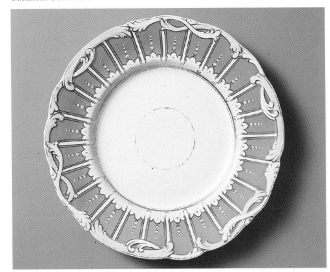

226. WB. 'Bouquet' III edged plate. Impressed Reg D — 10/2/51. Plate Diameter 22.8cm.

227. WB. 'Bouquet' IV edged plate. Impressed Reg D for 10/2/51. Impressed 'W'. Plate Diameter 22.8cm.

228. WB. Plate. Pat No '5915/4' — cDecember 1851. Printed Factory Marks '*'/'o'. Plate Diameter 22.5cm.

229. WB. 'Hibiscus' plate. Pat No '6055' Printed Factory Mark '*'. cNovember 1852. Diameter 22.5cm.

introduced in about October 1852. It, too, has many design characteristics in common with the 'No 7' plate. Additionally, the range of enamel colours used is typical of early Brownfield plates and there is the painted enameller's mark '§', found on several other Brownfield products in the early 1850s. Another example with different enamel decoration has been found with the pattern number '6514'. Pattern numbers '6511-6513' may well be other 'No 9' plates.

The 'No 12' plate **(Col Pl. 235)** and the 'No 13' Sweet Meat Dish **(Col Pl. 236)** both appeared before the end of 1853. The first of these is another floral design and like the 'No 8' it lacks any specific marks attributing it to William Brownfield. It has, however, the crucial printed factory marks '*' and 'o' found in the years 1845-60. The 'No 12' has no pattern number (only the customary printed '*' and 'o'), but it probably followed fairly soon after the 'No 9' and would have been produced by the end of 1853. (See Appendix 6C.) A separate 'No 13' plate has been found with the pattern number '6707', dating it as about February 1853. Confirmation that the 'No 13' dish is a Brownfield product comes in 1877 when this exact pattern was re-used on a marked Brownfield porcelain plate. The 'No 15' Platter **(Col Pl. 237)** is similar in style to the preceding 'Nos 7 and 9'. The example illustrated is the second largest the author has ever seen — over twenty inches across. (The largest, 'Gordon' c1856, measures twenty-six inches by twenty-one.) The same basic pattern is used for the plates **(Col Pl. 238)** in the accompanying 'No 15' dinner service. The only other markings on this are a pattern number '7148', dating it as cDecember 1853.

An attractive comport **(Col Pl. 239)** (Pat No '7447') was introduced in about April 1854. The only marks on this are the pattern number and the factory printed sunburst '*', insufficient evidence perhaps to persuade the sceptic of its Brownfield origins. However, cross reference shows that this mark is to be found on over twenty 'known' Brownfield products (see Appendix 6B), and this exact 'edging' was employed on six other Brownfield plates including those with pattern numbers '7459', '8940' and '8947', the latter two being the 'No 27' plates in the Brownfield numbered series. It was followed by the blue and purple plate with a geometric design **(Col Pl. 240),** (Pat No '7459'), introduced during the same week in April 1854. It also has the printed '*' and 'o', but no other clear attribution marks. Further versions, '11,703' and '11,707' appeared in January 1859. It is surprising that the firm did not register this relief-moulded plate shape as it was used at least once in the 1840s and seven times in the 1850s.

The very attractive 'Dog Rose' plate **(Col Pl. 241)** (Pat No '7589/1') was introduced in about June 1854. This has no specific Brownfield attribution, but it has the vital factory printed marks '*' and 'o'. Its Brownfield attribution is supported by the discovery of three plates with exactly the same relief-moulded 'edging', first the marked Wood & Brownfield plate (Pat No '397'), secondly Pat No 428, and thirdly one found with a Staffordshire knot and the letters 'WB'. It was followed in late July or early August 1854 by two more examples of the 'Bouquet' edged design **(Col Pl. 242) (Col Pl. 243)** (Pat Nos '7727' and '7732'). Both these have a much more elaborate pattern than previous 'Bouquet' designs. The first has a rich colour combination of crimson, gold and a soft yellow on a white background — used several times by Brownfields in the 1850s. The second has blue, yellow and additional gilding and a white central background. In both, the inner border is made up of three circles containing flower heads, interspersed with three crescent shaped curves containing further dog-rose heads. The enamelling is of a higher class than on some Brownfield plates, but even here, there is on the first plate one little section where the soft yellow colour has inadvertently been omitted. The marks include a registration diamond for 10th February 1851 and the factory printed marks '*' and 'o'. Many plates have no pattern number, but the accompanying comport in crimson, gold and white has '7727', while the blue, gold and white has '7732'. It has long been accepted that William Brownfield was one

230. WB. Plate. Pat No '6370'. Printed Factory Marks '<.'/'}'. cJuly 1852. Plate Diameter 23cm. Courtesy Chris Rawlins Antiques, The Antique Centre, Taunton.

231. WB. 'Bouquet' edged Comport. Impressed Reg D for 10/2/51. Pat No illegible. Printed Factory Marks ' *'/'o'cm. Length 24cm.

232. WB. 'No 7' plate. Pat No '6411' — cAugust 1852. Impressed 'Brownfield'. Printed 'No 7'. Plate Diameter 24cm.

233. WB. 'No 8' Bowl. Pat No '6817' — cMay 1853. Printed 'No 8'. Plate Diameter 26cm.

234. WB. 'No 9' plate. Printed 'No 9'/'. Pat No '6510' — cNovember 1852. Diameter 23cm. Courtesy Milverton Antiques, Somerset.

235. WB. 'No 12' plate. Printed 'No 12'. Printed Factory Marks '*'/'o'/c1853. Diameter 26.1cm.

236. WB. 'No 13' Sweet Dish. Printed 'No 13'. Date c1853. Pat No '6923' — cJul 1853. Courtesy Bits & Pieces Antiques, Ross- on-Wye.

237. WB. 'No 15' Platter. Printed 'No 15'. Pat No '7146' — cDecember 1853. Courtesy Young's Antiques, Edinburgh.

238. WB. 'No 15' plate. Printed. Pat No '8714'. cSeptember 1855. Plate Diameter 26cm.

239. WB. Comport. Pat No '7449' — cApril 1854. Printed Factory Marks '*'/'o'. Length 24.5cm.

240. WB. Plate. Pat No '7459' — cApril 1854. Printed Factory Marks '*'/'o'. Diameter 22.5cm.

241. WB. 'Dog Rose' plate. Pat No '7589/1' — cJune 1854. Printed Factory marks '*'/'o'/. Plate Diameter 24cm.

of the most prolific nineteenth century Staffordshire potters. The twelve different designs produced on the 'Bouquet' edged shape and the sixteen different examples on the plate design of 2nd October 1854, are beginning to show just how prolific.

Towards the very end of 1854, Brownfields introduced the 'Watford' plate pattern **(Col Pl. 244A)** (Pat No '8073'), which has a printed Garter Mark, *'WILLIAM BROWNFIELD'*, the factory sunburst '*' and an impressed *'WB'*. This was followed by another 'Bouquet' edged plate **(Col Pl. 244B)** (Pat No '8079') picked out in green, gold and yellow enamel: the introduction date of both would have been about December 1854. The second plate has an impressed registration diamond, an enameller's mark '#' and a potter's mark *'P'*. The quality of the enamelling on this example is much superior to that on its predecessor. The 'Sweaborg' dinner service **(Col Pl. 245)** (Pat No '8413'), introduced in the summer of 1855, was based on the design of 2nd October 1854. The quality of the whole service can be judged from the subtle and sophisticated enamel decoration of the dog roses and foliage. The plate markings include a registration diamond for 2nd October 1854, a printed garter mark topped by a crown, a pattern number *'8413'* and the printed sunburst mark '*'.

The pattern name of this service is most unusual and is explained by a recent military incident in the Crimean War of 1853-56. Hugh Seton-Watson's *The Russian Empire 1801-1917* explains that, on August 9th-10th 1855, a British naval squadron under Admiral Dundas was engaged in a bombardment of Sweaborg (adjacent to Helsinki) as part of the naval campaign against the Russians — albeit to no real effect. This bombardment was part of a new military plan to find a different way of attacking the Russians through Finland (controlled by Russia since 1808) because of the lack of success on the ground in the Crimea itself. Brownfields were commemorating this very recent Crimean War incident, an opinion confirmed by the introduction of 'Sweaborg' in about August 1855, just a few weeks after the naval bombardment had taken place. (Another Brownfield toilet set 'Anapa' (Pat No '8221') commemorated the allies intended landing there in June/July 1854, although this plan was substituted by another which focused on Sebastopol.)

The 'Blackberry and Rose' plate **(Col Pl. 246)** (Pat No '8500') has been attributed to William Brownfield, partly on the impressed *'ALBA'* on the back (see the earlier Alba plates with pattern numbers '5146' and '7646') and partly on the pattern number and the painted enameller's mark ':..'. Both the pattern and the enamelling are very 'Brownfield' and this example would date from about June 1855. This enameller's mark has been found on over ten other Brownfield products made initially between 1850 and 1857. This design has also much in common with the Wood & Brownfield 'Blackberry' plate of 1848. In August 1855 Brownfields produced another floral plate **(Col Pl. 247)** (Pat No '8649'), this one showing five large dog roses, accompanied by a multitude of smaller ones. The enamel decoration is done in deep blue, orange, red, yellow and pink with additional gilding. Its only markings include the blue printed *'o'* and *'/'*, an enameller's mark ':..' and a pattern number. Its enamel decoration is very similar to that on the 'No 15' plate of September 1855.

The 'No 26' plate **(Col Pl. 248)** (Pat No '8755/0') was probably introduced in about October 1855. Another in the sequence of 'floral' plates, this one is more attractive because it has a more elaborately designed border. Some elements of the design are similar to those on the blue and purple plate (Pat No '7459'). There are the usual printed marks '*'/'o' and an impressed (illegible) letter. The pattern number suggests that this was not a production run, but a specimen example made for assessment by a potential retail customer. The identity of this customer is not known. On the 2nd of October 1854 Brownfields had registered a design which led to at least sixteen different editions during the space of the next five years. The first of this sequence probably had a pattern number about 7870-7890 (see Appendix 6B), but no example of this has yet been found. 'Eupatoria' **(Col Pl. 249)** (Pat No '8829') was produced on this registered shape. The example illustrated has a central geometric motif and the whole pattern is most attractively enamelled in yellow and crimson with additional gilding. Its markings include a registration diamond, the printed garter mark containing the pattern name, the factory printed sunburst '*', a painted pattern number '8829' and 'WB'. The plate is another in the sequence issued to commemorate recent events in the Crimean War 1853-56. Eupatoria was where the allied troops, commanded by Lords Raglan and Cardigan, landed in the summer of 1854 on the western coast of the Crimean peninsula, after their arduous sea journey. It should be possible to build up a Crimean War collection of Brownfield plates, including 'Anapa', 'Azoff', 'Inkerman', 'Kars', 'Moldavia', 'Sweaborg', among others.

Fig 255. WB. 'Bude' plate. Printed 'Bude'/'WB'. Impressed Oval Cartouche — 'Brownfield'/'Crown'. c1855. Diameter 24cm.

Two editions of the 'No 27' plate followed in about January 1856, the first Pat No '8940' (**Col Pl. 250**), the second '8947' (**Col Pl. 251**). The first of these has a red border with an inner wreath of pink and blue flowers, while the second has a green border and a gilded edging and an inner ring of pink and orange flower heads. This same design has been found on several other Brownfield plates of this period. Pattern numbers '8941-8946' may well include others. Another 'Dog Rose plate (**Col Pl. 252**) based on the same 'edging', with dog roses enamelled in green and yellow has the common Brownfield printed marks '*'/'o' and an impressed 'W'. This plate has no pattern number, but its introduction date was probably early 1856. The overall plate design is enhanced by the central geometric pattern. This exact design was later produced in crimson, blue, green and yellow in about January 1859, but it has no obvious marks attributing it to the Brownfield factory.

In January 1857, Brownfields introduced a most attractive 'Fruit and Flower' plate. The first example is a plate (**Col Pl. 253**) (Pat No '9695'), followed almost immediately by '9706' (**Col Pl. 254**) — dating both at about December 1856/January 1857. Each has the factory printed marks '*' and 'o' while '9705' is another colour combination produced in green, yellow and gold. Pat No '9706', based on the same registered design of 2nd October 1854, shows honeysuckle, dog rose, fuchsia, passion flower and convolvulus and its markings include a registration diamond. Some of the pattern numbers 9696-9705 may be different colour combinations of the same design.

The 'Inkerman' plate was introduced in about 1855 and the list of Brownfield patterns printed in 1902 tells us that this was also produced by Brownfields as 'Bude'. The original 'Inkerman' plate was almost certainly made to commemorate the battle during the siege of Sebastopol (November 1854) in the recent Crimean War. 'Bude' (**Fig 255**) has 'BROWNFIELD' impressed, a printed pattern name, but no registration diamond. However, the scene depicted on this plate differs from that on 'Inkerman', illustrated by Desmond Harrison. The exact dating of 'Ascot' (**Col Pl. 256**) and 'Pekin (**Col Pl. 257**) is not known, but the printed garter marks on the back suggest that they originated in the period 1850-60, the years during which this form of marking was most common. The attributive marks on 'Ascot' are clear on some but not all plates — the one shown has a clear 'WB' under the printed garter mark, while others have no markings at all. The marking on the 'Pekin' plate is an elaborate leafy cartouche similar

242. WB. 'Bouquet' Edged plate. Pat No '7727' — cAugust 1854. Impressed Reg D — 10/2/51. Printed Factory Marks '*'/'o'/. Diameter 22.5cm.

243. WB. 'Bouquet' Edged plate. Pat No '7732'. Reg D — 10/2/51. Printed Factory Marks '*'/'o'/Diameter 22.5cm.

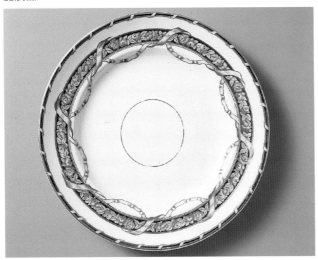

244A. WB. 'Watford' plate. Pat No ' 8073' cDecember 1854. Printed Garter Mark 'WB'. Impressed 'WB'/'E'. Printed Factory Mark '*'. 26.4cm.

244B. WB. 'Bouquet' Edged plate. Pat No '8079' — cDecember 1854. Impressed Reg D — 10/2/51. Painted Mark '#'. Impressed P. Diameter 23cm.

245. WB. 'Sweaborg' Dinner Service. Printed Garter Mark — 'Sweaborg'/'WB'. Pat No '8413' cAugust 1855. Printed Factory Marks '*'/'o'. Impressed Reg D for 2/10/54. Diameter 30.5cm.

246. WB? 'Alba' Blackberry and Rose plate. Painted Pat No '8500'/'::'. cJune 1856. Impressed 'Alba'. Diameter 23.4cm.

247. WB. Floral Plate. Pat No '8649' — cAugust 1855. Plate Diameter 25.5cm.

248. WB. 'No 26' plate. Pat No '8755/0' — cOctober 1855. Printed Factory Marks '*'/'o'. Plate Diameter 23.8cm.

249. WB. 'Eupatoria' plate. Pat No '8829' — cNovember 1855. Printed Factory Marks '*'/'o'. Plate Diameter 24cm.

250. WB. 'No 27' plate. Pat No '8940' — cJanuary 1856. Printed Factory Marks '*'/'0'. Plate Diameter 23cm.

251. WB. 'No 27' plate. Pat No '8947'. cJanuary 1856. Printed Factory Marks '*'/'o'/Painted Mark '::'. Diameter 23cm.

252. WB. Green, Yellow and White Dog Rose plate. c1856. Printed Factory Marks *'/'o'/Impressed W. Diameter 23cm.

Marks 36. WB. 'Pekin' plate. Printed oval Cartouche with flowers and Crown 'WB'/'Pekin'. Pat No. '55/6' — c1864.

Marks 37. WB. 'Kars' plate. Printed Garter Mark with Crown/'Kars', 'WB'/'*'/'o'. Painted '9146/6'. cApril 1856.

Marks 38. WB. 'No 28' plate — Impressed Reg Diamond for 10/2/51/ Printed Factory marks '*'/'o'. Pat No '9234' — Printed 'No 28'. cJune 1856.

to that on 'Pomona' (1845), suggesting that this design may well have been introduced by Wood and Brownfield in the years 1841-50 (**Marks 36).**

The portrait of the vase, flowers and gift box on Brownfield's pattern '8907' (**Col Pl. 258**) is identical to that on the Wood & Brownfield plates of 1842 and 1846. (Pat Nos '642' and '2602'); the border is also identical to these earlier versions, although the enamel colours used here are much softer. The markings on the back include the partially unfolded scroll (left blank), a pattern number '8907' and a painted 'v'. This edition of the plate dates from about January 1856 — only ten months before the pattern was re-used for the 'No 35' plate, manufactured in December 1856. The 'Kars' plate (**Col Pl. 259**) (Pat No '9146/6') was probably introduced in April 1856. The same pattern name was used by Minton for a plate of a quite different design and both manufacturers were probably commemorating another location involved in the Crimean war. The Brownfield edition is based on the registered design of October 2nd 1854, has a printed garter mark containing 'KARS' and underneath the letters 'WB'. It also has an impressed 'W' and the printed marks '*' '/o' (**Marks 37**). The 'No 34' plate (**Col Pl. 260**) (Pat No '9202') and a second edition of the 'No 28 Bouquet' edged plate (**Col Pl. 261**) (Pat No '9234') were both introduced in about June 1856. The first of these follows closely the design of the 'No 7' plate, but there are different flowers in the plate centre, accompanied by the same border design. It has the printed sunburst mark '*' and an impressed 'o'. The pattern number of this 'No 28' plate shows that it was not the first edition, but it is one of Brownfield's most attractive. The pattern follows that found on the neck of the 'No 28' water ewer illustrated in Chapter 2. It has an impressed registration diamond for February 10th 1851, the printed marks '*' '/o' and an impressed 'B' (**Marks 38**).

The 'Thrace' dinner service (**Col Pl. 262**) (Pat No '9568') was introduced in about November 1856. The dinner plates show a motto 'A CRUCE SALUS' (Salvation from the Cross) and two family coats of arms. The dinner service was ordered through Brownfield's Dublin retailers, 'HIGGINBOTHAM, 102 GRAFTON STREET, DUBLIN', this being printed on the back. This suggests an Irish customer, possibly a member of the Bourke family who held the title of Earl of Mayo in Southern Ireland. The Bourke's family motto was 'A Cruce Salus', but the left hand coat of arms does not belong to the main line of the Mayo earldom. The most likely customer is The Right Honourable Richard Southwell, a member of the Bourke family who was MP for Kildare, south-west of Dublin, from 1847-52. He was later MP for Coleraine 1852-57 and for Cockermouth 1857-68. He was appointed Chief Secretary for Ireland in 1852, 1858 and 1866 and in 1868 he was made Governor-General of India, where he remained for the next four years until he was assassinated in the Andaman Islands. The other marks on

253. WB. Fruit and Flower Plate. Pat Nos '9695'. cDecember 1856. Impressed Reg D — 2/10/54. Printed Factory Marks '*'/'o'. Pat No '9695'. Diameter 28.3cm.

254. WB. 'Passion Flower' plate. Pat No 9706' — cJanuary 1857. Printed Factory Marks '*'/'o'. Plate Diameter 23.3cm.

256. WB. 'Ascot' plate. Printed Garter Mark and Crown. c1855. 'Ascot'/'WB'. Diameter 26.5cm.

257. WB. 'Pekin' Bowl. Printed Oval Cartouche with Crown. 'Pekin'/'WB'. Pat No '55/6'. c1864. Plate Diameter 26cm.

258 WB? 'Vase and Gift' plate. Pat No '8907' — cJanuary 1856. Printed Scroll. Painted '8907' and mark 'v'. Diameter 21.4cm.

259. WB. 'Kars' plate. Pat No '9146/6' — cApril 1856. Printed Garter Mark with Crown. 'Kars'/'WB'./Painted '9146/6'. Printed Factory Marks '8'/'o'/. Plate Diameter 24.1cm.

260. WB. 'No 34' plate. Pat No '9202' — cJune 1856. Printed Factory Marks '*'/'o'. Painted '9202'. Diameter 24cm.

261. WB. 'No 28' plate. Pat No '9234' — cJune 1856. Printed factory marks '*'/'o'. Impressed Reg D for 10/2/51. Plate Diameter 23cm.

262. WB. 'Thrace' plate. Printed Garter Mark — 'Thrace/'No'/'WB'/ Printed Higginbotham & Son, 102 Grafton St, Dublin. Printed Factory Marks '*'/'o'/c1855. Plate Diameter 23.5cm.

263. WB. 'No 35' plate. Pat No '9632' — cDecember 1856. Painted mark '::'. Painted '9632'. Plate Diameter 23.6cm.

264. WB. 'No 40' plate. Pat No '10,108' — cMay 1857. Printed Factory Marks '*'/'o'/Impressed B. Painted '10,108'. Diameter 23.3cm.

265. WB. 'No 46' Plate. Pat No '10,414', cSeptember 1857. Staffordshire Knot 'WB'. Diameter 24cm.

266. WB. 'Wreath of Fruit and Flower' plate. Pat No '10,585' — cDecember 1857. Impressed Reg D — 2/10/54. Printed Factory Marks '*'/'o'. Impressed W. Plate Diameter 23.3cm.

267. WB. 'Wreath of Fruit and Flower' plate. Pat No '10,592' — cDecember 1857. Impressed Reg D for 2/10/54. Printed Factory Marks '*'/o. Plate Diameter 23.3cm.

268. WB. 'Wreath of Fruit and Flower' plate. Pat No '10, 597' — cDecember 1857. Impressed Reg D — 2/10/54. Printed Factory Marks '*'/'v'. Painted Pat No '10,587'. Diameter 23.3cm.

269. WB. 'Melbourne' Tureen Base. Impressed Reg D — 10/2/51. Printed Factory Marks '*'/'§'. Impressed x.

270. WB. Crimson, Gold and White plate. Impressed Staffordshire knot — 'WB'. Otherwise unmarked. Diameter 26cm.

271. WB. 'No 47' plate. Pat No '10,949' — cMarch 1858. Printed Factory Marks '*'/'o'. Impressed !. Painted '10,949'. Printed 'No 47' Diameter 25.8cm.

272. WB. 'No 48' plate. Pat No '10,910' — cMarch 1858. Impressed W. Printed 'No 48'. Painted '10,910'. Diameter 26.1cm.

273. WB. 'Crimson Border' plate. Pat No '10,979' — cMay 1858. Impressed Reg Diamond — 2/6/58. Impressed W. Painted '10,979'. Diameter 23cm.

274. WB' No 60' Cherry and Flower plate. Pat No '11,047/1'. cJune 1858. Impressed Reg D — 2/10/54. Printed Factory marks '*'/'o'/. Painted 11,047. Plate Diameter 23cm.

275. WB. 'Crimson Border Flower' plate. Pat No '11,703' — cJanuary 1859. Printed Factory Mark 'o'. Impressed B. Painted '11,703'. Plate Diameter 23cm.

276. WB. 'No 61' plate. Pat No '11,728' — cJanuary 1859. Impressed Reg D for 2/10/54. Printed Factory Marks '*'/'o'. Plate Diameter 23cm.

277. WB. No '53' plate printed No '53'. Pat No '12.068'. cApril 1859. Plate Diameter 22.5cm.

Marks 39. WB. 'Thrace', Printed Garter Mark with Crown/'WB'/ 'Thrace'. Retailer's Mark, 'Higginbotham & Son, 102 Grafton St, Dublin'. Printed factory marks '*'/'o'. c1856. 1858.

the plates include a printed garter mark containing the pattern name and 'WB' and the printed marks '*'/'o' **(Marks 39)**.

The 'No 35' plate **(Col Pl. 263)** (Pat No '9632') was introduced in about December 1856, a floral plate with a slight difference, there being an octagonal shape in the plate centre, containing a vase with yet more flowers. Its markings are minimal — 'No 35', a pattern number and the painted mark '::' — found on other Brownfield products in the 1850s,

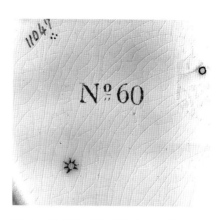

Marks 40. WB. 'No 60' plate — Impressed Reg D for 2/10/54/Painted Pat No '11,047/1' — Printed Factory marks '*'/'o'/'No 60'. cMay 1858.

including the 'Alba' plate. This plate was a fourth edition of the pattern (introduced by Wood and Brownfield in June 1842 and January 1847). The 'No 40' plate (Pat No '10,108') **(Col Pl. 264)** is a further edition based on the registered design of 2nd October 1854: this was introduced in about May 1857. It has the printed marks '*' '/o' and an impressed 'B'. The 'No 46' tureen (Pat No '10,414') followed shortly afterwards. The tureen's marks include an impressed 'ALBA', a painted pattern number and a registration diamond for 27th November 1856. Pat No '10,714' is another example of the No 46 (not so marked), but this has rather poor enamelling (more seconds), the centre piece being unfinished. The marks on this plate **(Col Pl. 265)** include a moulded Staffordshire knot containing 'WB', and a painted pattern number — indicating an introduction date of about January 1858

Three further editions of the registered 'Flower and Fruit Wreath' plate of 2/10/54 **(Col Pl. 266) (Col Pl. 267) (Col Pl. 268)** were introduced in about December 1857. These have an enamel coloured border, and inside this a circular wreath of fruit and flowers. The first has a pattern number '10,585', the second '10,592' and the third '10,597'. Their marks include a registration diamond, the printed marks '*' '/o' and an impressed 'W'. The 'Melbourne' tureen base **(Col Pl. 269)** has a registration diamond for February 10th 1851, the plate edging showing that it was based on the 'Bouquet' design. The markings include a printed garter mark containing the pattern name, 'WB', the printed marks '*' '/', a registration diamond and an impressed 'x'. This example has no pattern number, but it probably dates from about 1855-60. The crimson, gold and white plate **(Col Pl. 270)** has an identical border to that of the 'Dog Rose' plate (Pat No '7589/1') of 1854, but while it has no pattern number, it does have an impressed Staffordshire knot containing 'WB'. Other unmarked editions will probably be found.

The 'No 47' plate **(Col Pl. 271)** (Pat No '10,949') was introduced in about March 1858. Identification comes from the printed factory marks '*' '/o'. The first edition of the 'No 47' plate would have had a pattern number about '10,900-10,910'. The 'No 48' plate **(Col Pl. 272)** (Pat No '10,910'), also introduced in about March 1858, is in a somewhat distressed condition, but it is the only example discovered. The pattern follows quite closely the one used for 'No 47'; its only markings are the printed 'No 48', a pattern number and an impressed 'W'.

A crimson bordered plate **(Col Pl. 273)** (Pat No '10,979/7'), registered on 2nd June 1858, is much less elaborate than its predecessors, and appears to be a cheap selling line. The colour combination of crimson and gold on a white background is attractive, and if the central geometric pattern were enamelled in a more solid colour the plate might have a greater overall attraction. Its marks include a

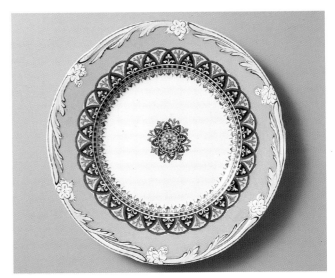

278. WB. 'No 54' plate. Pat No '12,552' — cAugust 1859. Impressed B/!. Printed Factory Mark '*'. Diameter 26.2cm.

279. WB. 'Turkish Design' plate. Pat No '12,630' — cSeptember 1859. Printed Factory Mark 'v'. Impressed B. Diameter 23cm.

280. WB. 'No 55' plate. Pat No '13,167'. cFebruary 1860. Impressed M. Diameter 26cm.

281. WB. 'No 56' plate. Painted Pat No '13,173'. cMarch 1860. Plate Diameter 26cm.

282. WB. 'No 58' plate. Printed 'No 58'. Otherwise unmarked. cMay 1858. Plate Diameter 25.5cm.

283. WB. Vegetable Dish. Pat No '13,457'. cJune 1860. Impressed Reg D — 6/6/80. Moulded Staffordshire Knot — 'WB'. Length 29.5cm.

286. Attributable to WB? 'No 68' plate. Printed 'No 68'. Otherwise unmarked. Diameter 23.5cm.

287. WB. 'No 73' Gravy Dish and Base. Pat No '166' — c1864. Impressed Reg D for 5/1/64. Printed 'No 73'. Impressed EL.

288. WB. 'No 74' Bowl. Printed Coronet and 'No 74'. c1860-64.

289. WB? 'No 76' Cake Dish. Printed 'No 76'. Otherwise unmarked.

290. WB. Plate. Pat No '14,399' — cMay 1861. Impressed Reg D — 2/10/54. Printed Factory Marks '*'/'v'. Diameter 23cm.

291. WB 'Compiegne' plate. Pat No. '14,847' — cNovember 1861. Printed Garter Mark with Crown — 'Compiegne'/'WB'. Impressed Reg D — 14/3/62. Factory mark '*'. Diameter 26cm.

registration diamond, a pattern number and an impressed 'W'. This suggests an initial introduction date of about April/May 1858, shortly ahead of its registration. The 'No 60' **(Col Pl. 274)** (Pat No '11,047'), based on the registered design of October 2nd 1854, is, perhaps, the most attractive of all the numbered plates. This shows a collection of fruit and flowers, a small cluster of three cherries taking centre stage, while the border is full of beautiful, enamelled flowers. Its pattern number suggests an introduction date of about June 1858, and it has the printed marks '*' '/o', and a registration diamond **(Marks 40).**

The next floral plate from early 1859 **(Col Pl. 275)** (Pat No '11,703') has a crimson border, but a more elaborate and attractive one than that of 2nd June 1858. Six groups of flowers are shown, but they have a less dominant role than on the No 60 plate. This is a later edition of the same relief-moulded plate edging first introduced in late 1850 and also produced in about January 1856 — enamelled in green and yellow with additional gilding of the relief-moulded edging. This plate has a pattern number, a printed 'o' and an impressed 'B'. It is the sixth example of a plate based on this relief-moulded border (used earlier for the No 27 plates): '11,707' is the seventh and there may be others still to be found. The 'No 61' **(Col Pl. 276)** is also very attractive, but in a different way: this is the ninth example of the design registered on October 2nd 1854. The purple colouring of the border is unusual on a Brownfield plate; flowers have disappeared and have been replaced by a mixture of geometric patterns. Its marks include the printed '*' '/o', the pattern number '11,728' and an impressed 'B'. Its date of introduction was about January 1859.

The 'No 53' plate **(Col Pl. 277)** (Pat No '12,068') has a geometric pattern at its centre and five large floral groups around the border, interspersed with five smaller single enamelled flowers. Its overall design is very similar to that of the 'No 54' plate which followed soon afterwards. The 'No 54' plate **(Col Pl. 278)** (Pat No '12,552'), seemingly issued out of order, was introduced in about August 1859. This is a re-issue of the original 'No 54' in a different enamel decoration — in the same way that the No 7 was manufactured in three separate editions over a twenty year period. An earlier 'No 54' with a pattern number nearer '10,975' will eventually be found. Its other marks include an impressed 'B' and '!'. Other examples of the 'No 54' plate have been found with the printed Brownfield sunburst mark '*'. The 'Turkish' plate illustrated from 1859 **(Col Pl. 279)** (Pat No '12,630') is yet another edition based on the shape registered on October 2nd 1854. This time a green border envelops a circular ring of geometric shapes, while the centre is focused on another geometric pattern. It has a printed '>' and an impressed 'B'. The original 'No 55' plate **(Col Pl. 280)** (Pat No '13,167') was very possibly introduced in the 1850s or early 1860s. This particular example is likely to be a second or third edition of a pattern introduced in about March-April 1859. The plate has little in the way of markings — 'No 55', a pattern number and an impressed 'M' — this example dates from about February 1860. The No 56 plate **(Col Pl. 281)** (Pat No '13,173') would have originated in about April 1858 although this example dates from about February 1860.

The 'No 57' (not illustrated here), also introduced in 1858, was still being produced on a newly registered shape (No 7044) in November 1887. The flowers have much in common with those on the 'No 7' plate issued in 1852, but the inner banding has been removed. The two tone colour combination of orange and blue, augmented by a little gilding of the outside border, is one Brownfields frequently used. It has a Brownfield registration number to confirm its attribution. (See Appendix 6C.) The 'No 58' plate **(Col Pl. 282)** is yet another in the long sequence of 'floral' plates, but this one has no pattern number facilitating precise dating. It was probably introduced in about April-May 1858. The covered vegetable dish **(Col Pl. 283)** (Pat No '13,457') originated in about June 1860, but this piece gives no indication of its pattern name. The cover has an impressed Staffordshire knot and 'WB', while the dish has a registration diamond for 6th June 1860, accompanied by a pattern number.

Fig 284. WB. 'Mother and Child' plate. Printed Reg D for 14/3/62. Printed Cartouche 'PHIZ', 'H K Browne'.

Fig 285. WB. 'Mother and Child' plate. Printed Reg D for 14/3/62. Printed Cartouche 'PHIZ', 'H K Browne'.

The 'Mother and Child' dinner service **(Fig 284)** was registered on the 14th March 1862, the same outline shape being used for at least four if not more different plate designs. The first shows the same Bacchanal scene found on the registered jug illustrated in Chapter 3. The second **(Fig 285)** is a variation on the same Bacchanal theme. These may well have been issued in a set and others are likely to be found. A third oval plate and a fourth platter have been identified with other Bacchanal scenes **(Marks 41)**.

The most enigmatic of over thirty 'numbered' plates is the 'No 68' **(Col Pl. 286),** the first in this series to cause the author anxiety over correct attribution. The type of print used to denote the *'No 68'* is different from that used on *all* the remaining numbered Brownfield plates. Secondly, the range of colours used is markedly different from those on the No 7-61 plates. The 'No 73' dinner service **(Col Pl. 287)** (Pat No '166') was initially registered on 5th January 1864 — the only item available for illustration being a gravy bowl and its stand. Its marks include a pattern number, a registration diamond and the impressed potter's letters *'EL'*. The new pattern numbering system was only introduced in 1864 and this particular product was probably introduced in that year. The pattern of the 'No 74' soup bowl **(Col Pl. 288)** follows very closely that on the 'No 73' gravy bowl, but the plate centre shows a group of flowers typical of dozens of Brownfield plates in the 1850s. The quality of enamel decoration is much better than on many Brownfield products. The only markings on this example are the printed *'No 74'*, and a printed coronet, unaccompanied by any pattern number or printed enamellers' marks. Its introduction date was probably about 1860-64. The range of colours used in the enamel decoration on the 'No 76' cake plate **(Col Pl. 289)** is rather different from that found on earlier Brownfield pieces, but the type of blue print used for the *'No 76'* is exactly the same. This print suggests that it also originated in the same factory, but a more elaborately marked example is needed to confirm this. This particular example has no other markings — no pattern number, no potter's mark and not even an impressed date. The introduction dates of 'Nos 73 and 74' suggest that this 'No 76' dates from about 1864.

Marks 41. WB. 'Mother and Child' plates — Printed Reg Diamond for 14th Mar 1862. Printed Cartouche, 'PHIZ' Printed 'H K Browne' — c1862.

Another 'Wreath' design, pattern number '14,399' **(Col Pl. 290),**

292. WB. Dinner plate. Impressed Reg D for 5/12/62. Impressed 'W'. Pat No '16,423'. cJuly 1863. Diameter 23cm.

293. WB. 'Magenta' plate. Printed Garter Mark — 'WB'/'Magenta'. Printed Factory Mark '*'/'<'. c1850-65. Plate Diameter 26cm.

294. WB. 'Geneva' Comport. Impressed Reg D for 30th June 1864. Printed Garter Mark — 'Geneva'/'WB'. Factory Marks '*'/'#'. Diameter 23.5cm.

295. WB. 'No 79' Tureen Base. Impressed Reg D — 26/11/63. Printed 'No 79'.

296. WB. 'No 92' Plate. Impressed Reg D — 5/1/64 (not on this example). Pat No 'T2671' — c1864-70. Diameter 24cm.

297. WB. 'Denmark' plate. Printed Garter Mark with Crown — 'Denmark/WB'/Impressed Reg D for 5/12/62. Printed Factory Mark '*'. Impressed G. Plate Diameter 24.1cm.

299. WB. 'No 115' Platter. Printed Twin Globe Factory Trade Mark. Impressed 'Brownfield'/'1/76'. Printed 'WB & Sons'. Length 30cm.

300. WB. 'No 131' plate. Moulded Staffordshire knot — 'WB'. Impressed Reg D — 10/11/70. Pat No 'T 5970/2'. Diameter 26.2cm.

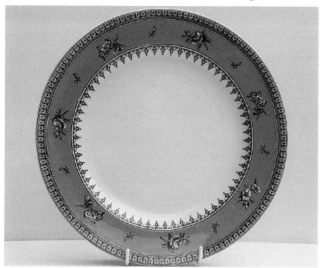

301. WB. 'Smyrna' plate. Impressed Reg D — 10/11/70. Pat No '7497'. Plate Diameter 26.3cm.

302. WB. 'Cressy' plate. Printed Garter Mark with Crown — 'Cressy'/WB' Pat No 'T2081'. c1870-75. Diameter 26cm.

303. WB. 'Shakespeare' plate. Pat No '1790'. c1870-75. Printed Garter Mark with Crown — 'Shakespeare'/'WB' Diameter 26cm —

308. WB. Sylvan — 'The Woodland Fountain' plate. Printed Reg D for 10/6/74. Impressed 'Brownfield'. Printed 'No 2'. Diameter 24cm.

originally introduced in about May 1861, has attractive enamel decoration in green, orange, pink and blue. This was based on the registered plate edging of 2nd October 1854 and follows the pattern on the crimson bordered flower plate of about January 1859 (Pat No '11,703'). 'Compiegne' **(Col Pl. 291)** (Pat No '14,847') was registered on 14th March 1862 and used the same outline shape as the 'Mother and Child' plate. The pattern of fruit and foliage is much less dominant here than on the plates of the early 1850s. Its marks include a printed garter mark headed by a crown, an impressed *'WB'*, the printed sunburst mark '*' and an impressed *'E'*. Its introduction dates from late October or early November 1861.

On 5th December 1862 Brownfields registered a dinner service, all the plates of which have the same relief-moulded edging, but are produced in different enamelled colours. One of these is illustrated **(Col Pl. 292)** (Pat No '16,423'). Each plate has a moulded registration diamond and one has a pattern number. This set was issued in about August 1864. Next to be illustrated is the 'Magenta' plate **(Col Pl. 293)** which probably dates from the years 1860-65. Its only markings are a printed garter mark containing the pattern title and *'WB'*, and the factory blue printed starburst '*'. The 'Geneva' comport **(Col Pl. 294)** was registered on 30th June 1864 and it too has a printed garter mark, the pattern name and *'WB'*. The 'No 79' dinner service **(Col Pl. 295)** was introduced in late 1863 or early 1864, but the tureen base illustrated is of poor quality. It has a registration diamond for 26th November 1863, but no pattern number: others may well have one.

From 1864 until 1893, Brownfields operated at least two parallel pattern numbering systems, one or possibly two being used for earthenware goods and another for porcelain. (See Appendix 6A.) The remaining plates illustrated will be accompanied by their actual date of production (as and when found impressed on the back), but it may not be impossible to pinpoint their introduction date with any accuracy. The first plate **(Col Pl. 296)** (Pat No 'T2671') was initially registered on 5th January 1864, but this example has no markings other than a pattern number: others are clearly marked *'WB'* and have the appropriate registration diamond. The same design was re-issued later in about 1869-70 as the 'No 92' plate: its only marks are a printed 'No 92', unaccompanied by any registration diamond or pattern number.

The 'Denmark' plates **(Col Pl. 297)** were based on a design initially registered on 5th December 1862, but the only design element registered was the relief-moulded edging. The centre of the first illustrated plate shows a printed oval containing a leopard passant, with the motto *'VERITÉ SANS PEUR'* (Truth without fear.) The second plate shows a printed circle containing a lion rampant: this one has no family motto in the circular band. Both plates were probably part of a dinner service commissioned from Brownfields by some affluent family. Debrett's *Peerage, Burke's General Armoury and Fairbairn's Crests* show that while three or four families had the motto *'Verité Sans Peur',* only one had this in conjunction with the coat of arms shown on the first illustrated plate — a lion passant, guard. This was George Willoughby Hemans, the son of an Irish soldier Capt Alfred Hemans and Felicia Dorothea Hemans (née Browne) who married in 1812. Felicia had five sons between 1812-18, at which juncture her husband decided to go to Italy from which he never returned. Felicia subsequently became quite a celebrated poetess and novelist and ultimately settled in Dublin in 1831, where she lived with her brother.

Little is known about George Willoughby Hemans, for whom the dinner service was made; he was born between 1812-16 and is thought subsequently to have been engaged in ordnance survey work. The printed garter mark and others on the back suggest it was probably commissioned between 1862-65. These others include the pattern name *'WB'*, a registration diamond for 5th December 1862, the printed sunburst mark '*' and an impressed potter's mark *'G'*. Hemans may have chosen the pattern name

'Denmark' because of his original links with that region. The registered 'Denmark' pattern had three years' legal protection, preventing copying until 1865. Interestingly, in February 1870 Brown-Westhead, Moore & Co produced a very similar design **(Fig 298)** to Denmark (and even closer to a registered Brownfield plate design of 6th June 1860). There are marginal alterations both in the moulded edging and in the circular wavy band, but the essential theme follows the earlier Brownfield designs. Many factories borrowed their competitors' ideas, but this imitation of Brownfield's patterns helps to explain why in the late 1870s Brownfields were considered by the *Pottery Gazette* to be 'trend setters' in the sphere of dinner service designs.

Fig 298. Brown-Westhead Moore. Dessert Service plate. Reg 1st February 1870. Courtesy Geoffrey Godden.

The 'No 115' platter **(Col Pl. 299)** has the printed twin globes trade mark, *BROWNFIELD & SON* in a cartouche and an impressed *'BROWNFIELD'*. This particular example also has *'7/76'*. The 'No 131' plate **(Col Pl. 300)** (Pat No 'T5970/2) and 'Smyrna' **(Col Pl. 301)** (Pat No '7497') were both based on the registered shape of 10th November 1870; the first bears little or no resemblance to the other. The 'No 131' plate can be attributed to William Brownfield because of its registration, but it also has a Staffordshire knot and *'WB'*. The 'Smyrna' plate has no Staffordshire knot, just the registration diamond and a pattern number. The 'Cressy' plate **(Col Pl. 302)** (Pat No 'T2081') probably originated in the early 1860s as it has the printed garter mark topped by a crown. However, the pattern number suggests an introduction date in the early 1870s. The outer border consists of heart-shapes with enamel decoration in green, red and brown, while the inner border contains acanthus leaves alternating with rope type loops.

WILLIAM BROWNFIELD AND SONS: 1871-1893

The 'Shakespeare' plate **(Col Pl. 303)** (Pat No '1790T') was probably introduced in the 1870s. However, there is a printed garter mark containing *'SHAKESPEARE'* headed by a crown and *'WB'*, which was a style of marking much more associable with the early 1850s. This is probably a second or subsequent edition of a design introduced many years earlier. The 'Audley' dinner service **(Fig 304)** was introduced on 10th September 1874, the design being available in the form of a transfer printed jug, a covered dish, a toilet pot and a dinner plate. The jug itself was one of several

Fig 304. WB. 'Audley' Dinner Service plate. Registered 10th September 1874. Courtesy Spode Ltd and Keele University.

Fig 305. WB. 'Dorking' Dinner plate. Registered 10th September 1874. Courtesy Spode Ltd & Keele University.

309. WB. Sylvan — 'The Australian Bush' plate. Printed Reg D — 10/6/74. Printed Twin Globes Factory Mark. Printed 'No 4'. Impressed Brownfield. Painted Pat No '927'. Diameter 24cm.

310. WB. 'Sylvan' — 'Monarch of the Glen' plate. Printed Reg D — 10/6/74. Printed Twin Globes Factory Mark. Impressed 'Brownfield'. Printed 'No 5'/Alfred Shaw, Brisbane. Diameter 23cm.

311. WB. 'Sylvan' — 'Retrieving'. Printed Reg D for 10/6/74. Printed 'No 6'. Diameter 23cm

312. WB. 'Medieval' plate. Impressed Reg D for 7/2/77. Pat No '8403'. Plates Diameter 26.7cm.

313. WB. 'Medieval' plate. Impressed Reg D for 7/2/77. Pat No '8403'. Plates Diameter 26.7cm.

314. WB. Bird plate I. Impressed 'Brownfield'/'2/78'. Plate Diameter 23cm.

315. WB. Bird plate II. Impressed 'Brownfield'/'2/78'. Plate Diameter 23cm.

316. WB. Bird plate III. Impressed 'Brownfield'/'2/78'. Plate Diameter 23cm.

317. WB. 'Denver' plate. Pat No '9191/2'. Impressed 'Brownfield'/'1/80'. Diameter 25cm.

318. WB. 'Texas' plate. Pat No '7050'. Printed Twin Globes Trade Mark. Impressed 'Brownfield'/'Ivory'. Impressed '4/80'. Diameter 25cm.

319. WB. 'Young Girl' Wall Plaque. Impressed 'Brownfield'. Signed W Bourne. Dated 1882. Impressed '9/81'. 23cm.

321. WB. 'Pastimes' plate. Impressed 'Brownfield'/'10/83'. Pat No 'a922/1'. Diameter 26.5cm.

Fig 306. WB. 'Mandarin' Dinner Service. Pattern illustrated from Jewitt's Ceramic Art of Great Britain (1877).

Fig 307. WB. 'Hong Kong' Dinner Service plate. Coourtesy Spode Ltd and Keele University.

editions of the 'Bangor' jug registered on the same date. One dinner plate shows three storks flying above some water lilies.

The 'Dorking' design (Fig 305) depicts various wild life scenes — including a cockerel and a swan — but it is likely that a much wider range will eventually be found. The 'Mandarin' design (Fig 306) follows the patterns to be found on the jug of the same name — reviewed in Chapter 4. This toilet set pattern (along with Dorking) is shown on page 476 of Jewitt's *Ceramic Art of Great Britain* (1883). 'Hong Kong' (Fig 307) is the last of the four designs of September 1874, showing a whole range of scenes, most of which depict flowers and birds — and, in one known jug pattern, a stork.

On 10th June 1875 Brownfields issued the 'Sylvan' dinner service. The pieces depict no less than thirteen different wildlife scenes, ten of which are individually named. Four of these are illustrated here, the first being 'Woodland Fountain' (Col Pl. 308) — 'No 2' in the series — indicated on the back of the plate. The second is 'Australian Bush' — 'No 4' (Col Pl. 309) — the various transfer prints for this set being done in blue, brown or black, with one superior porcelain set done in enamelled colours. The third is 'Monarch of the Glen' — 'No 5' (Col Pl. 310) — and the last is 'Retrieving' — No 6 (Col Pl. 311). All 'Sylvan' items have a registration diamond for 10th June 1874 and are impressed *'BROWNFIELD'*. Other pattern names in the same dinner service include 'The Partridge Family', 'The Timid Hare', 'Wild Ducks at Home' and 'Spring with the Pheasants': these latter patterns only seem to appear on side plates. ('Wild Life in the Alps — No 1 — and 'The Haunt of the Snipe' — 'No 3' — are both illustrated in Chapter 8.) One example of 'Sylvan' has also been found with printed details of what would appear to be a retailer — 'Alfred Shaw, Brisbane' — indicating that the series was exported to Australia.

In February 1877, Brownfields produced the 'Medieval' dinner service (Col Pl. 312-313) (Pat No '8403'), containing almost certainly their largest series of patterns based on a single theme — that of 'Medieval' life. There are no less than twenty-two different scenes depicted in this set. (See Appendix 3.) Only two can be illustrated — both from the group showing 'Activities in the Countryside'. These both have a pattern number and the first, unusually, has both an impressed and printed registration diamond. They lack the sophistication of earlier plates, but a whole series would look most impressive. A series of bird plates (Col Pl. 314-316) followed, probably towards the end of the 1870s. Just how many there are in this set is not yet known — they are not a registered design and they do not feature in the 1880 catalogue. Four different ones have been identified: all are impressed *'BROWNFIELD'* and three have the impressed date *'2/78'*, suggesting that these may have survived from a single service produced in February 1878. These might be thought to depict specific types of non-British birds, but examination of the first two suggests that artistic licence was given even in the drawing and painting of the same bird. All these bird plates were also manufactured in porcelain.

Marks 42. WB. 'Pastimes' plate — Printed Twin Globes Trade Mark, Printed Cartouche — Impressed Circular Cartouche — 'Brownfield'/'Cobridge'. Impressed 'Ivory'/'2/85'.

'Denver' **(Col Pl. 317)** (Pat No '9191/12') and 'Texas' **(Col Pl. 318)** (Pat No '7050') were both in production by 1880. The first has elaborate foliage covering the whole plate and three birds and three butterflies can be picked out among the foliage. The markings include an impressed *'BROWNFIELD'*, a pattern number and *'1/80'*. The 'Texas' plate is probably a second, third or fourth edition of an 1850s style floral plate. This one, however, has printed twin globes, is impressed *'IVORY'* and *'BROWNFIELD'*, is dated *'4/80'* and has a pattern number. The pattern name suggests that they may have been made principally for the American market.

In the years 1870-1882 Brownfields produced a series of wall plaques and the first of these to be discovered originates in 1881. This hand painted portrait of a young girl **(Col Pl. 319)** was the work of W Bourne for it is signed and dated at the bottom right by the artist. The marks include an impressed *'BROWNFIELD'* and *'9/81'*. Later examples, illustrated by Desmond Harrison in *Antique Collecting* in February 1971, included a pair of Art Nouveau plaques in blue and white. The first depicts a young maiden holding two small birds to her exposed bosom, the second shows a young child in her mother's arms, clasping her hands round her mother's neck: both were said to be manufactured in 1897. A second article in *Art & Antiques* in 1972 included another nine and a half inch plaque showing a richly coloured parrot, probably introduced in the mid 1870s: this had an impressed *BROWNFIELD* mark and was hand painted by George Hassall. The last known plaque is a country cottage scene, signed by F Holloway and dated 1882. This was also impressed *'BROWNFIELD'*.

The 'Pastimes' pattern **(Fig 320)** (Pat No '922/1') was registered on 8th February 1881, but it had already been used for a transfer printed jug probably made in about 1879 (see Chapter 5). The first example shows four children playing in a field of corn. The second **(Col Pl. 321)** depicts four children playing in the countryside. The markings on the first are very clear — a circular impressed cartouche containing *'W BROWNFIELD AND SONS'*, *'CROWN'*, *'2/85'* and also twin printed globes with *'W BROWNFIELD & SON'* **(Marks 42)**. The discrepancy between the printed and impressed marks may be explained by the hasty departure of William Etches in early 1883. The marks on the second include an impressed *'10/83'*. A third plate shows four children playing on a beach, two sitting with their backs to a sandcastle while two are making sandpies. This plate has the printed twin globes trade mark, *'W BROWNFIELD & SONS'*, a cartouche containing *'PASTIMES'*, an impressed *'IVORY'* and *'3/82'*: it also has a pattern number *'a702/1'*. It is likely that a variety of other scenes is available with this design. (See also Chapter 8.)

There then followed a separate issue of different bird plates, the first called 'Merton' **(Col Pl. 322)** and the second 'Spring' **(Col Pl. 323)**. The date of initial manufacture appears to have been about 1879-80. However, the detailed marks on two 'Merton' plates suggest otherwise. The printed registration number is given as *'7044'* — an item registered in May 1884. Both have printed twin

322. WB. 'Merton' plate. Impressed Reg No '7044'. Printed Twin Globes — W Brownfield & Son/Merton. Impressed — 'W Brownfield & Sons'/9/85. Plate Diameter 24cm.

323. WB. 'Spring' plates. Printed Twin Globes Trade Mark. Printed Cartouche — 'Spring'/'W Brownfield & Son'. Impressed Twin Globes. Impressed '12/83'. Plate Diameter 24cm.

325. WB. 'Cyprus plate. c1878-83. Printed Twin Globes Trade Mark. William Brownfield & Sons/Cyprus. Pat No. '8899/'10. 26cm.

330. WB. 'Cockatoo' Jug. Impressed Twin Globes. 'Brownfield'/'7/78'. Courtesy 'Britannia' Antiques, Chelsea.

331. WB. 'Boy and Goat ' Vase. c1879. Impressed 'Brownfield'. Courtesy 'Britannia' Antiques, 58 Davies St, London W1.

332. WB. 'Swirling fish' Jug. Regd 9th January 1879. Impressed 'Brownfield'. Courtesy N Boston Antiques, Chenil Galleries.

333. WB. Majolica Vase. Moulded (erroneous) Reg D — 30th October 1875. Impressed 'Brownfield'/'122'. RH Collection.

334. WB. 'Monkey and Goose Jug. Unmarked example. Some jugs are impressed 'Brownfield'. Height 14" — 35.5cm. BM Collection.

335. WB. 'Cockatoo' Jug. Unmarked example. (Some may be impressed 'Brownfield'.) 10¾" — 27.5cm.

338. WB. Dinner Service Plate. Pat No '650' cSeptember 1877. Diameter 23.5cm.

341. WB. 'Cockerel' Dessert plate. Registered 6/11/74. Illegible Reg D. Otherwise unmarked. Width 8¾" — 22cm.

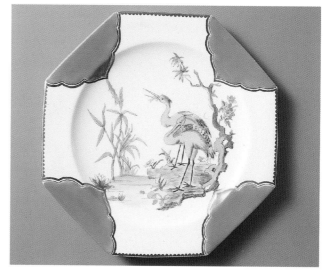

342. WB. 'Heron' Dessert plate. Registered 6/11/74. Impressed 'Brownfield'. Width 8¾" — 22cm.

Fig 320. WB 'Pastimes' plate. Impressed Circular Cartouche *'W Brownfield & Son'*. Printed Twin Globes — *'W Brownfield & Son'*. Printed *'Pastimes'*. Impressed '2/85'. Plate Diameter 23cm.

Fig 324. WB. 'Woodland' plate. Printed Twin Globes — 'Woodland'/Reg No. 14058. Impressed Cartouche 'W Brownfield & Sons'/'Crown'/Reg No '7044'/3. 24cm.

globes with the pattern name contained in a cartouche underneath and both have the circular impressed factory mark found commonly at this time. The printed version says *'W BROWNFIELD AND SON'*, the impressed *'W BROWNFIELD AND SONS'*. One 'Merton' plate is dated *'9/85'*. The 'Spring' plate, however, has an impressed *'12/83'* and appears to be a variation on 'Merton' rather than the reverse.

If this is so, then an unregistered 'Merton' plate may have been in production earlier in 1883 and its registration was possibly delayed because of the internal disruption caused by William Etches' departure in March 1883. 'Woodland' **(Fig 324)** was in production by 1885. The plate shows two people walking by a canal, with lock gates to their left and a big country mansion to the rear. In the forefront of the inner margin is a group of birds, possibly pigeons, and in the outer margin foliage and flowers. There is a plethora of contradictory marks on the back; there are printed twin globes denoting *'BROWNFIELD AND SON'* and underneath a cartouche with the design title. There is also a printed registration number *'14058'* taken out in October 1884. However, to complicate matters, there is also an impressed circular cartouche denoting *'W BROWNFIELD AND SONS'*, *'CROWN'*, an impressed registration number *'7044'* and the date *'9/85'*. These impressed marks would have been made when the glazed blank plate was ready for firing; the printed when the transfer print was effected. It could therefore be that when it was time to manufacture a further number of 'Woodland' plates, a worker erroneously fetched a pile of 'Merton' blanks.

Fig 326. WB. 'Niel', 'Madras', 'Rienzi' and 'Ningpo' plates. Picture from the Brownfield 1880 Catalogue — courtesy Spode Ltd and Keele University.

Fig 327. WB. Suez plate — from the 1880 Brownfield Catalogue — Courtesy Spode Ltd and Keele University.

Fig 328. WB. 'St. Germain' Dinner Service plates — from the 1880 Brownfield Catalogue — courtesy Spode Ltd and Keele University.

William Brownfield's own advertising material gives us details of another sixteen plate patterns. The first six of these were publicised in the *Pottery Gazette* between 1881 and 1885 and this suggests that all were relatively new creations at that time — initial production of each beginning somewhere between 1878-83. The first three, all advertised in 1881-82, had no pattern name given, but 'Texas' and 'Cyprus' **(Col Pl. 325)** have been identified from another source, namely the firm's own 1880 catalogue. By January 1885 Brownfields had improved their advertising layout and detail to include four named plate designs — 'Niel', 'Madras', 'Rienzi' and 'Ningpo' **(Fig 326).**

The remaining designs are all found in the Brownfield 1880 catalogue. 'Rose Leaf', 'Cambridge' and 'Richelieu' are all dinner services or tea sets introduced in about 1882-85. 'Suez' **(Fig 327),** 'Olympus' and

Fig 329. WB. 'Taunton' Dinner plates. Picture from the 1880 Brownfield Catalogue — courtesy Spode Ltd and Keele University.

'Harlech' are also dinner service designs probably introduced between 1870-80. 'St.Germain' **(Fig 328)** 'Taunton' **(Fig 329)** and 'Dartmouth' are much simpler designs — the only decoration being found in the plate border.

There is a further range of porcelain plate patterns in Chapter 8, but this selection covers over one hundred and thirty different Brownfield designs, a considerable number of which have not, hitherto, been attributed to a particular factory.

343. WB. Sylvan — 'Wild Life in the Alps' plate. Printed Reg D — 10/6/74. Printed 'WB. & Son', 'No 1'. Pat No'927/H'. Diameter 25cm.

344. WB. Sylvan — 'The Haunt of the Snipe' plate. Printed Reg D — 10/6/74. Impressed 'Brownfield'/'5/78'. Pat No'927'. Printed 'No 3'. Diameter 25cm.

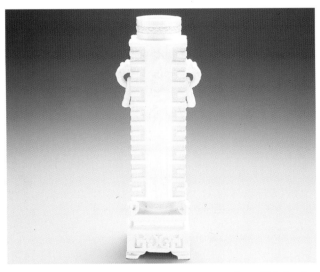

350. WB. Porcelain Vase. Moulded (erroneous) Reg D — 30th October 1875. Impressed 'Brownfield'. Impressed Size No '122'.

351. WB. 'Man and Gourd' Teapot. Regd 31st October 1876. Impressed 'Brownfield'. Courtesy Dowlishwake Antiques, Ilminster. Somerset.

354. WB. 'Clamshell' Teapot. Printed Registration D for 13th October 1883. Length 9" — 23cm.

357. WB? Mama & Papa Figures. Unmarked except for Pattern Number '21'. 7½"' — 19cm.

128

359. WB. 'Swallows and Gull' plate. Impressed 'Brownfield'. Impressed '9/78'. Diameter 23.3cm.

360. WB. 'Swallows and Mountain Lake' plate. Impressed 'Brownfield'/ '1/80'. Diameter 23.3cm.

361. WB. 'Swallows and Waterfall' plate. Impressed 'Brownfield'/'10/80'. Diameter 23.3cm.

362. WB. 'Swallows and Sailing Boat' Comport. Impressed 'Brownfield'/'11/80'. Diameter 23.7cm.

363. WB. 'Swallows and Windmill' Cake stand. Impressed 'Brownfield'. Diameter 23.3cm (359-63). Courtesy Oaks & Partners, Auctioneers, Whimple, Devon.

364. WB. 'Tulip' plate. Impressed 'Brownfield'. c1871-77. Plate Diameter 23.6cm.

CHAPTER 8
MAJOLICA AND PORCELAIN — 1871-1900

It was not until the autumn of 1871 that Brownfields installed ovens to manufacture porcelain, the production of parian and majolica commencing at the same date. Prior to this time, the firm had only manufactured earthenware and stoneware, although some jugs with a porcelain-like body can give an impression to the contrary. There is less scope for providing historical background to many of the porcelain pieces reviewed in this chapter and it will mainly serve as reference material for the identification and attribution of many items, previously unknown as Brownfields to many collectors and dealers. This is especially true as the markings on Brownfield porcelain are invariably minimal: sometimes there is only an impressed 'Brownfield', just occasionally accompanied by an impressed date (ie 11/72) or an impressed size number. However, many attributed pieces have no markings at all and even some items which were registered have no registration diamond. Only a small number of majolica wares can be shown here, but over a hundred and forty different porcelain items are illustrated and these represent only a proportion of the factory's output. A good number of these are shown from printed and photographic illustrations in factory advertisements for the 1876 Philadelphia Exhibition and from Brownfields' 1880 catalogue, now kept in the Spode Manuscripts in Keele University library.

The firm may have been hoping that its four new china producing ovens would have been brought on stream in time to exhibit their first china wares at the London Exhibition of 1871, but a delay seemingly prevented this. However, in October-November, the firm did display its first china wares at an exhibition in Stafford. Brownfields also produced their first wares in majolica in late 1871, and these were displayed at the same Stafford exhibition. These included the Majolica 'Cockatoo' jug (**Col Pl. 330**), later exhibited in Australia and possibly made primarily for that market. The superior example illustrated first is enamelled in white, yellow, brown and green: another has been found in green and brown. Both have the impressed twin globes trade mark, an impressed *'BROWNFIELD'* and a date, in both instances *7/78*. Other relief moulded jugs known to have been manufactured in majolica include 'Swiss' and 'Bangor'.

The 'Boy and Goat' vase (**Col Pl. 331**) emanated from about 1879, about the same time as a majolica 'Swirling Fish' jug (**Col Pl. 332**) (Reg No 330997), which was introduced on 9th January 1879. This example is enamelled in bright yellow, green, red and brown. Its markings should include the twin globes, a cartouche, a month and year date and 'W Brownfield & Son'. Another jug, in more sophisticated and subtle colours, can be seen in the Hanley Museum, Stoke-on-Trent. The earthenware vase with a majolica glaze (**Col Pl. 333**) was first illustrated by Desmond Harrison in the 1970s and again by the Hampsons in 1980. The example illustrated is 10½" tall, is filled in with brown and yellow majolica glazes, and is designed in the then popular Japanese style. It is impressed *'BROWNFIELD'* and has an erroneous moulded registration diamond for 30th October 1875: the Design Register clearly shows that it was registered on 1st December 1875. Desmond Harrison stated that his example of the vase was made in 1887 and so an impressed date (and Brownfield) must have been found. His example is finished in salmon pink, picked out with gilding and there are two hand-painted sprays on the sides.

The 'Monkey and Goose' jug (**Col Pl. 334**) was probably introduced in the years 1874-80, attribution being confirmed by the 1880 Brownfield catalogue. This is hardly the most attractive jug produced by Brownfields; some would be even less polite than that. Two examples have been found: the one illustrated is fourteen inches tall and produced in a deep reddish-brown majolica, while the

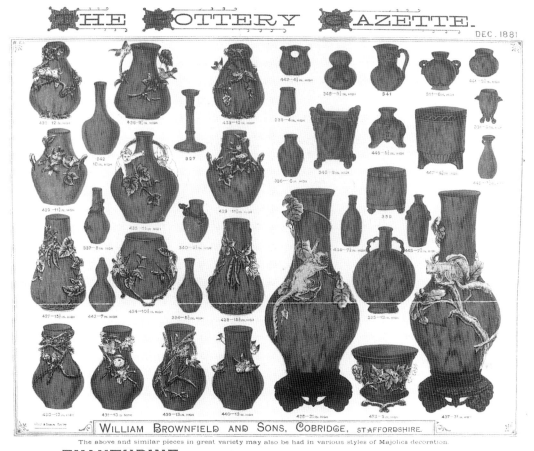

WILLIAM BROWNFIELD AND SONS, COBRIDGE, STAFFORDSHIRE.

The above and similar pieces in great variety may also be had in various styles of Majolica decoration.

EVANTURINE, NOVEL EFFECT IN IMITATION OF GOLD.

Fig 336. WB. Full page Advertisement for Majolica products — Pottery Gazette 1881.

second is about four inches and produced in porcelain. The jug is in the shape of a goose with its mouth stretched wide open while the handle takes the form of the monkey. The overall result is not attractive. Somewhat surprisingly, there are no moulded or impressed marks on some jugs to attribute them to William Brownfield and Son, but an identical one sold at a Christie's auction in London in 1990 was impressed 'Brownfield'.

The Cockatoo jug (**Col Pl. 335**) has also been discovered in the same bright reddish- brown majolica finish, and it too has no identifying marks. In comparison to the sophisticated and subtle coloured jug in the Hanley museum and the one illustrated earlier, this majolica finish is not very attractive. It was towards the middle of the 1870s that Brownfields introduced a majolica 'Hotei' teapot: one such five and three quarter inch teapot appeared in a Phillips west country auction in December 1994 and realised £1,200. The illustration in Phillips' catalogue reveals that this was the same teapot as the one called 'Man and Gourd' in the Brownfield 1880 catalogue. It should, therefore, have a registration diamond for 31st October 1874. Hotei was one of seven Japanese gods of good luck.

The next full page advertisement of Brownfield majolica ware (**Fig 336**) appeared in the *Pottery Gazette* in December 1881. These include two vases 31" tall, the first having a monkey sprigged on to the vase, the second a squirrel. Other smaller 13" versions have a variety of birds and foliage. In September 1880, Brownfields registered no less than ten different majolica vases (Reg Nos 355091-335100), including several of those illustrated in the *Pottery Gazette* advert. Among these designs are two birds among vine leaves, three birds on a branch, a squirrel on a branch with acorns and leaves, a

365. WB. 'Rose' plate. Impressed 'Brownfield'. c1871-77. Plate Diameter 23.6cm.

366. WB. Sultan Massoud Mirza Floral plate. Impressed 'Brownfield' (under Arabic script) and '2/79'. Diameter 23.5cm.

367. WB. Original pattern-Sultan Massoud dinner service. Impressed 'Brownfield'. Diameter 23.5cm.

369. WB. 'Pastimes' plate. Pat No '2213', Impressed 'Brownfield'/ '10/80'. Diameter 24cm.

370. WB' Pastimes' Comport. Pat No '1448'. Diameter 22.3cm.

372. WB. Dessert Service plate. Illegible Reg D for 4/5/81. Pat No '1780'. Impressed 'Brownfield/'2/82'.Diameter 21.5cm.

132

373. WB. Dessert Service plate. Reg D for 4/5/81. Impressed 'Brownfield. Diameter 21.5cm.

374. WB. Stylised 'Laburnum' plate. Impressed 'Brownfield'/'10/81'. Plate Diameter 26cm.

377. WB. Dessert Service plate. Pat No '2533'. Printed Reg D '10361' — Aug 1884. Impressed 'Brownfield'/'7/86'. Diameter 22cm.

378. WB. Dessert Service plate. Pat No '2533'. Printed Reg D '10361' — Aug 1884. Impressed 'Brownfield'/'7/86'. Diameter 22cm.

379. WB. Dessert Comport. Pat No '2533'. Printed Reg D '10361' — Aug 1884. Diameter 23.5cm.

380. WB. Dessert Comport. Pat No '2533. Printed Reg D '10361'. Diameter 23.5cm.

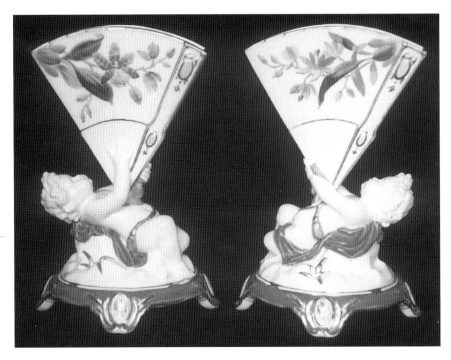

Fig 337. WB. Pair of Flower or Spill-holders. Reg D for 5/12/73. 6" high (16.5cm).
Courtesy Beagle Antiques.

monkey with a nut in its paws, a bird with hazel nuts and leaves, two little birds sitting on twigs, two birds with grapes, and two (cavorting) cherubs set among vines. Page 51 of the 1880 Factory Catalogue also indicates that the 'Barlaston', Passion Flower', 'Argos', 'Gothic', and 'Glenny' jardinières were produced in majolica.

PORCELAIN: 1871-1900

The first pieces of porcelain are a pair of Flower or Spill-holders **(Fig 337)**, previously illustrated in Geoffrey Godden's *Staffordshire Porcelain* (1983). Each is 6½" high and has a registration diamond for 5th December 1873: these impressed diamond are relatively uncommon on the Brownfield porcelain that the author has seen. They may also have a shape number '69': these pieces are likely to have been manufactured between 1873-76.

A dinner service (Pat No '650') **(Col Pl. 338)** was probably introduced in 1874. The pattern used on the illustrated plate is one first employed on the 'No 13' Sweet Dish of c1853. The plate marks indicate a manufacture date of September 1877, but there is no registration diamond and it is possible that another enamelled colour combination could have preceded it some time between 1871-74. The pattern also has much in common with the 1837 plate of Robinson, Wood and Brownfield — in that both show flowers in a two handled urn surrounded by a border of further flower heads. The quality of enamelling is an improvement on some of the earlier earthenware plates: the Brownfield management must have been aware that enamelling by lowly paid, inexperienced girls in the paint shop would not be acceptable on better quality porcelain. The marks on this plate include an impressed *'BROWNFIELD'* and a pattern number — in the post 1871 porcelain series.

The very attractive Brownfield porcelain dessert service **(Fig 339)** (Pat No '662') was introduced on a registered shape of 6th November 1874: this was also illustrated in Geoffrey Godden's *Staffordshire Porcelain* (1983). The official pattern name is not known, but it might well be 'Oriental Ladies'. At least six different scenes are shown and the full dessert service will probably contain even more. The

Fig 339. WB. 'Oriental Ladies' plate. Impressed Reg D for 6/11/74. Pat No '662'. Impressed 'Brownfield'. c1874-77. Courtesy Geoffrey Godden.

markings include an impressed *'BROWNFIELD',* a registration diamond and a pattern number. The same registered design was also used for a floral dessert service **(Fig 340),** shown in the same Geoffrey Godden book. This latter set does not appear to have had a pattern number, but it is likely to have been about 660-750 — c1874-75. Two further patterns were employed on the same registered relief-moulded plate shape — the first being a series of 'Pastimes' dessert plates and comport, one of which is illustrated later in the chapter, The second is another dessert service depicting a series of birds or fowl, the two here showing a cockerel **(Col Pl. 341)** and (despite their colouring) two herons **(Col Pl. 342).** One of these has an illegible registration diamond and the other a nearly illegible impressed *'BROWNFIELD':* neither has an impressed date nor a pattern number, although this is also likely to have been around 660-750.

The 'Sylvan' dinner service introduced in June 1874 (Pat No '927') was manufactured in porcelain as well as in earthenware. Two of the six different scenes can be shown here, the first being 'Wild Life in the Alps' **(Col Pl. 343)** ('No 1' in the series) and the second 'The Haunt of the Snipe' **(Col Pl. 344),** which is 'No 3'. The marks on each include a printed *'WB & SON',* a printed registration diamond for 10/6/74 and a pattern number *'927'.*

The two 8" figures carrying container baskets **(Fig 345-6)** were introduced in September 1874, each having a registration diamond for 30th September 1874. Both could have an impressed shape number '86'. The first is a cherub holding a rabbit while carrying a wicker basket on his back, the second has a net swung over its right shoulder and a basket in its left hand. The Satyr holding a shell **(Fig 347)** was first illustrated by Desmond Harrison in 1971, a design supposedly

Fig 340. WB. Floral Dessert service. Registered 6/11/74. Impressed 'Brownfield'. c1874-77. Courtesy Geoffrey Godden.

381. WB. Dessert Service plate. Pat No '2533'. Printed Reg D '10361' Impressed 'Brownfield'/'9/88'. Pat No illegible. Diameter 22cm.

382. WB. Dessert Service plate. Pat No '2533'. Printed Reg D '10361'. Impressed 'Brownfield'/'9/88'. Diameter 22cm.

383. WB. Dessert Service plate. Pat No '2533'. Printed Reg D '10361' Printed Twin Globes — 'Brownfield & Son'. Impressed 'Brownfield'/'9/87'. Pat No ' 2533x '. Diameter 22cm.

384. WB. Dessert Service plate. Pat No '2533'. Printed Twin Globes Mark — 'Brownfield & Son'. Printed Reg D '10361'. Impressed 'Brownfield'. Pat No '2533x'.

385. WB. Dessert Service plate. Pat No '2533'. Printed Twin Globes Mark — 'Brownfield & Son.' Printed Reg D '10361'. Impressed 'Brownfield'/ '9/87'. Pat No '2533x'. Diameter 22cm.

386. WB. Dessert Service plate. Pat No '2533'. Printed Reg D — '10361'. Printed Twin Globes — 'Brownfield & Son'. Impressed 'Brownfield'/ '9/87'. Pat No '2533x'. 381-386. Courtesy Pear Tree Antiques.

387. WB. Stylised Prunus plate. Impressed 'Brownfield'/'6/83'. Pat No '2613'. Plate Diameter 24.5cm.

390. WB. Statuette of Cherub with Wicker Basket. Impressed '130'/'Brownfield'. Courtesy Morton Antiques, Bournemouth.

391. WB. Statuette of Cherub with Wicker Basket. Impressed '130'/'Brownfield'. Courtesy Morton Antiques, Bournemouth.

453. WB. Cup and Saucer. Pat No '249'. Impressed –/79.

454. WB. 'Dragonfly and Hawthorn' Cup/Saucer. Impressed 'Brownfield'/'7/82'. Pat Nos '2336' and '1346'.

455. WB. 'Stork Christening' Cup/Saucer. Pat No '1428'. Impressed 'Brownfield'.

Fig 347. WB. Satyr and Shell. Registered 22 June 1872. Impressed 'Brownfield'. '–/76'.

Figs 345-346. WB. Flower or Spill Holders. Reg D for 30/9/74. 8" high. Impressed '86'. Courtesy Geoffrey Godden.

registered in 1874 (precise date not given) and it should therefore have a registration diamond. However, the only registration discovered of such a piece is 22nd June 1872 (shape number 40). The illustrated Satyr also has an impressed date — in this instance '-/76'. The same item is shown on page 16 of the 1880 Brownfield Factory catalogue, alongside two other similar designs. Its function is described in the Catalogue as a fruit dish. The height of the central strawberry dish piece on the same page is given as 6½" and the others in the set would appear to be the same height.

The Ornamental dish (**Fig 348**) and the Celadon and white glazed container (**Fig 349**) both originated in 1875, each having an impressed registration diamond for 31st March 1875. Both were illustrated in Geoffrey Godden's *Staffordshire Porcelain* (1983). The former was one of many 'Bird' themes employed by Brownfields on both earthenware and porcelain in the 1870s.

Fig 348. WB. Ornamental Dish. Reg D for 31/3/75. Impressed '108'. Courtesy Geoffrey Godden.

Fig 349. WB. Ornamental Celadon and white glazed container. Reg D for 31/3/75. Courtesy Geoffrey Godden.

The majolica vase illustrated earlier was also manufactured in porcelain. The vase shown (Col Pl. 350) is filled in with a very soft green enamel, and both have the marks found on the Rodney Hampson example: each is impressed 'BROWNFIELD' and '122'. It also has an applied registration diamond for 30th October 1875, a registration taken out not by Brownfields but by W P & G Phillips of Bond Street, London. However, this impressed diamond is an erroneous one and the vase was in fact registered by Brownfields on 1st December 1875. Examination of the design register shows that those for 30th October 1875 were of two boy and girl statuettes.

Fig 352. WB. 'Fish' Teapot. Registered 31st October 1876. Probable mark — Impressed Brownfield — from the Design Register — courtesy the PRO.

Three most unusual teapots were introduced in October 1876, the first, a porcelain 'Man and Gourd' teapot (Col Pl. 351), was illustrated by Desmond Harrison in *Art and Antiques* in 1972. That teapot was five inches high and seven and a half inches long and it was produced mainly in white with a pink ribbon below the lid and down the handle. Others have the ribbon in blue. Strange though this teapot looks, it appears to be a real collector's item: its provincial retail price is now over £200. The 'Fish' teapot (Fig 352) is the second of the three teapots introduced on 31st October 1874, hardly an attractive design, but doubtless no less a collector's item; the 'Face and Pigtail' (Fig 353) is the third. The latter two illustrations are also found in the 1880 Factory Catalogue, in which these unusual teapot names are found.

Another unusual 'Clamshell' teapot (Col Pl. 354) was introduced in 1883, its registration being effected on 13th October. The only example discovered by the author has a printed registration diamond for this date and a pattern number '6157'.

A Brownfield advertisement for their 1876 Philadelphia Exhibition display showed four other porcelain pieces. The first of these is a 'Cherub' cake stand (Fig 355) — also illustrated on page 9 of

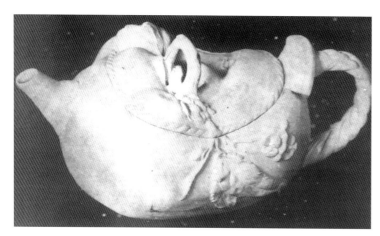

Fig 353. WB. 'Face and Pigtail' Teapot. Regd 31st October 1876. Impressed 'Brownfield' — from the Design Register — courtesy the PRO.

Fig 355. WB. Cherubim Cake Stand. Impressed '21'. Exhibited at the Philadelphia Exhibition 1876.

456. WB. 'Stork Christening' Coffee cup/Saucer. Pat No '1428'. Impressed 'Brownfield'/'5/79'.

457. WB. 'Stork Muffin Dish. Impressed 'Brownfield.

458. WB. 'Storks' Christening plate. Pat No '1529' — c1870-75. Impressed 'Brownfield'/'1/83'. Plate Diameter 23cm.

460. WB. Bird, Butterfly and Foliage Cup/Saucer. Impressed 'Brownfield'/'12/79'. Printed Reg D — 26 October 1878.

473. WB. Jenettte Jones Teacup, Saucer and plate. Impressed 'Brownfield'/'–/83'. Painted Monogram 'JJ'. Courtesy House Antiques, Weymouth.

474. WB. Acorn Leaf Trembler. Impressed 'Brownfield'/'11/80'. Pat No '2437'.

475. WB. Flowerheads Cup and Saucer. Pat No '2622'. Impressed 'Brownfield'/'7/82'.

477. WB. Silver and Gold Tree Cup/Saucer. Impressed 'Brownfield'/'1/83'.

478. WB Orange, Brown and Silver Flowerheads Cup/Saucer. Impressed 'Brownfield'/'6/86'.

479. WB. Celadon green bone china Teacup/Saucer. Impressed 'Brownfield'/'3/87'. Courtesy Rodney Hampson.

480. WB. Pink and Brown Flower Cup/Saucer. Impressed 'Brownfield'/'5/91'.

481. WB. Blue Foliage and Brown Edged Cup/Saucer. Impressed 'Brownfield'/'8/93'.

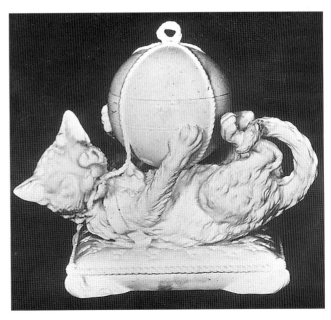

Fig 356. WB. Mama & Papa Figures. Impressed '112'. Exhibited at Philadelphia 1876. Courtesy Desmond Harrison.

Fig 358. WB. Cat and Globe Ornament. Exhibited at the Philadelphia Exhibition 1876.

the 1880 Catalogue. This had been registered by Brownfields on 14th November 1872 and its shape number is indicated by an impressed '21'. Its height is given as 12" and its width as 16½".

This is accompanied by ten and a half inch figures of 'Mama' and 'Papa' (**Fig 356**). Many Staffordshire firms produced this pair of figures, but the Brownfield versions include Mama wearing a very elaborate hat and full length gown, while the Papa has a distinctive top hat and an umbrella under his right arm. The ten and a half inch examples have shape numbers '*112*' and '*113*', but they were also manufactured in a seven and a half inch size (**Col Pl. 357**). Papa's smock is enamelled in a soft pink, his umbrella in green while his top hat is in a soft orange. Mama's dress is in blue and her gown in a soft pink: her flamboyant headdress is in pale green, blue and orange. Identical to the figures in the 1876 advertisement in all respects bar one, these have no impressed Brownfield nor an impressed size number. The one difference lies in the absence of the base circular plinth on which the taller and heavier ten and a half inch figures stand. Each, however, has a painted '*21*' which is more likely to be a pattern number than a shape number. This might suggest that they were among the very first Brownfield porcelain creations of 1871, an opinion supported by their lack of sophistication compared with later pieces. They could also be later continental imitations. They are, perhaps, a typical example of Victorian sentimentality. The fourth piece included in the Philadelphia advertisement is a 'Cat and Globe' ornament (**Fig 358**), which had been registered on 5th March 1875 as a flower stand or scent ornament: this is nine inches tall and may have an impressed shape number '99'.

The hand painted 'Swallows and Gull' plate (**Col Pl. 359**) (Pat No '1145') is part of a dessert service, first introduced in about 1877. It is likely that the other component parts of this set will show different kinds of birds in the bamboo rectangular inset: this is what happened when the same shape was used again soon afterwards. This later service (Pat No '1192') used the inset to depict four different scenes, the first (**Col Pl. 360**) a lake in the mountains, the second (**Col Pl. 361**) a waterfall. The third (**Col Pl. 362**), which is a comport, shows a sailing ship and the fourth (**Col Pl. 363**) a windmill. There may well be others still to be found. Each is hand painted and has an impressed '*BROWNFIELD*' and various dates from 1880 — '*1/80, 10/80*' and '*11/80*'.

The 'Tulip' plate (**Col Pl. 364**) (Pat No '1450'), introduced in the late 1870s, is part of an attractive dinner service. Only two plates have been discovered, the second depicting a rose **(Col Pl. 365)**; others are likely to have further flowers on them. Most manufacturers tended to choose a selection of flowers and Brownfields was probably no exception. The other plates will have the same edging and almost certainly the same ring of motifs inside the rim of the plate. The plate has a transfer printed pattern, but the enameller has not in fact used it, or certainly not the whole of it; instead the tulip, stalk and leaves appear to be hand painted: unused parts of the transfer print can be detected. The first porcelain plate mark is simply an impressed *'BROWNFIELD'* and the second has an impressed date *'5/79'*. Unfortunately the impressed year letter on the first is missing, but it is likely to have been 1879. The '1450' porcelain pattern number suggests an introduction date of 1879.

Fig 368. WB. 'Pastimes' Tea and Coffee Service. Impressed 'Brownfield' and '1/81'. Diameter 6" — 16.5cm. Courtesy Geoffrey Godden.

The beautifully hand-painted porcelain 'Roses' plate **(Col Pl. 366)** (Pat No '769') is based on a design probably first introduced in about 1874-5, but this one is part of a dinner service specially commissioned from William Brownfield and Son in February 1879 by Sultan Massood Mirza. Mr J R Smart of the Department of Arabic and Islamic Studies, Exeter University, kindly provided the information that he was the second son of Shah Naser -od-din, hereditary ruler of the Persian Empire until 1896. His full title was Soltan Masud Mirza Yamin Od-Doula Zell Os- Soltan and the Arabic script at the top of the plate says 'Zell os-Soltan', meaning 'shadow of the Soltan'. We know that Masud Mirza was three times appointed Governor of the large province of Fars (in the south of the current state of Iran). In 1881 he was given enlarged responsibility not only for Fars province but also nine other ones including Kurdistan. His elder brother Mozaffer-od-Din became Shah in 1896.

Such an order from the royal house of Persia must have been a major coup for the Brownfield firm and this is the first evidence we have of their exporting to the Middle East — a fourteenth country to which the firm is known to have exported. Interestingly, 1879 was the year that the *Pottery Gazettte* commented that 'many manufacturers were introducing dinner sets 'a la Brownfield'. The firm of William Brownfield & Son had clearly established a prominent name in recent years, both at home and abroad. The markings on the back of the 'Sultan Masud Mirza' dinner plate are very faint, but they include an impressed *'BROWNFIELD'* and *'2/79'* (legibility is impaired by the overprinted Arabic script). The comport **(Col Pl. 367)** shows what was probably the original design, but without the roses and the gilded Sultan's name. This is just impressed *'BROWNFIELD'*, and it probably originated in about 1874-75.

The 'Pastimes' tea and coffee service **(Fig 368)**, done in the style of Kate Greenaway, was produced in porcelain and earthenware. Several pieces of this were shown by Geoffrey Godden in his *Staffordshire Porcelain* (1983). There may be as many as a dozen or more different scenes depicted on the various Pastimes sets, but the three plates in this set show a couple of children blowing bubbles, a young boy riding an old penny farthing bicycle watched by two little girls, and two older children playing with rackets and shuttlecock. Two of the bowls in the set show two older children playing a racket and ball game over a net, the second depicting a girl playing with a hoop and a boy with a toy.

Fig 371. WB. Dessert plates. Reg D for 4/5/81. Impressed 'Brownfield'/'11/81'. Courtesy Geoffrey Godden.

The marks on some, if not all, pieces include an impressed 'BROWNFIELD' and '1/81', but some earthenware 'Pastimes' plates have been found emanating from 1879-80. Porcelain editions do not carry the 'Pastimes' pattern name, but this is printed on the earthenware edition. A 'Pastimes' dessert service was also manufactured in the late 1870s (Col Pl. 369). The plate illustrated shows two adults supervising six children carrying an assortment of hoop, kite, skipping rope, fishing rod and tennis racket. This example has an impressed 'BROWNFIELD' and '10/80' and a pattern number '2213'. Yet another superior edition of 'Pastimes' (Col Pl. 370) was made on the registered plate shape of 6th November 1874: this comport shows two young children sitting or standing on a fence, one fishing, one watching. Each of the corner segments contains a beautifully enamelled pink rose set amid leaves. This has no impressed marks at all, only a pattern number '1448', suggesting an introduction date of about 1876. A set of six plates in this set has recently been identified, each with a different transfer-printed picture: the scenes portrayed on these include a boy and girl on a seesaw, a boy on a penny farthing bicycle, a boy under a tree painting a picture of a yacht, a girl and boy with a hoop, a boy fishing with a girl standing watching, and lastly a boy and girl skipping. A red earthenware tea kettle with a 'Pastimes' pattern was also illustrated by the Hampsons in 1980. This was impressed 'BROWNFIELD', '9/81', had a registration diamond for 8th February 1881 and an erroneous pattern name 'DUBLIN'.

Another dessert service from the late 1870s (Fig 371) was also illustrated in Geoffrey Godden's *Staffordshire Porcelain* (1983). The pieces depicted there had a floral pattern, while the author has seen three other different floral examples on this same registered shape — the first with a pattern number '1584', the second '1780', the third without any pattern number. The last is likely to have a number between 1550 and 1850 and dates from December 1881 (Col Pl. 372) (Col Pl. 373). The registration diamonds on the last set are predominantly illegible, but the year is 1881 and the design register shows that the only dessert plate registered in 1881 was on 4th May. The first plate has an impressed '10/81', the second '2/82', the third '12/81' and each piece is impressed 'BROWNFIELD'.

The stylised 'Laburnum' plate (Col Pl. 374) was in production at least by October 1881: this is impressed 'BROWNFIELD' and '10/81'. This dinner service was produced in earthenware and porcelain. The Gentleman

Fig 375. WB. 'Gentleman' Jug. Impressed Reg D for 18th June 1883. Impressed 'W. Gallimore'. From the Design Register — courtesy the PRO.

144

jug **(Fig 375)** of 13th June 1883 (Reg No 399557) is flamboyant to say the least. The *Pottery Gazette* reviewed it on 1st November 1883 and described it as grotesque! The jug represents a distorted figure of an old English gentleman, with the frills of his shirt forming the spout of the jug. The only example of this known to the author is in a brightly glazed white porcelain with gilding of the various folds in the man's attire. It looks impressive if not attractive. Unusual impressed marks on the base indicate that it was designed by *'W GALLIMORE'* and it has a printed registration diamond for 18th June 1883.

A 'Roses and Butterfly' plate (Pat No '2074') was probably introduced in about 1879, although the example found is impressed '–/88'. The large spray of roses and yellow flowers is hand painted and there is a gilt dentil border. The marks on the back are particularly interesting — these include an impressed *'BROWNFIELD'*, a pattern number and a printed retailer's mark for *'GARDNER,*

Fig 376. WB. Dessert Service plate. Pat No '2402'. Impressed 'Brownfield'. Impressed '5/84'. Courtesy Geoffrey Godden.

CHARING CROSS, LONDON'. This is the only evidence discovered linking this retail outlet with William Brownfield. Another dessert service (Pat No '2402') **(Fig 376)** was illustrated by Geoffrey Godden in *Staffordshire Porcelain* (1983), its additional impressed marks indicating production in June 1884. The same dentil border suggests that this is a parallel dessert service to that of the 'Roses and Butterfly' plate.

The next illustrated plates and comports, part of a dessert service registered in August 1884 (Reg No 10361), are of exquisite quality and show Brownfield porcelain at its best. All the different patterns are of flowers, but considerable licence has been employed both by the artist and the painters. The first plate illustrated **(Col Pl. 377)** shows daisy-like flowers enamelled in pink, mauve and purple, the second **(Col Pl. 378)** old-fashioned roses in yellow and pink, the third **(Col Pl. 379)** yellow chrysanthemum and the fourth **(Col Pl. 380)** a yellow rose with brown foliage. The first three have a printed registration diamond for August 1884, and two are impressed *'BROWNFIELD'* and *'7/86'*: all have the pattern number *'2553'*. Six further plates in the same service have recently been found, each depicting a different flower. The first of these **(Col Pl. 381)** shows laburnum enamelled in yellow and brown, the second **(Col Pl. 382)** apple blossom in mauve, yellow and purple and the third **(Col Pl. 383)** is probably forsythia, hand painted in yellow, brown and green. Perhaps, the most difficult to identify is the next **(Col Pl. 384)**, which is most likely fruit blossom; the penultimate example **(Col Pl. 385)** shows a dog rose enamelled in yellow, mauve and brown, and the last piece **(Col Pl. 386)**, a comport, has hypericum or rose of sharon. It could well be that the

Fig 388. WB. Floral Rose Vase. 9" high. Impressed 'Brownfield'. Undated. c1875-84. Courtesy Geoffrey Godden

Fig 389. WB. Goat pulling a Perambulator. Reg D for 7th October 1875. Impressed '150'/'Brownfield'. Courtesy B Waters, Wellington, Salop.

range of colours used to paint these plates reflects a wish to have an attractive range across the dessert service rather than the appropriate natural colours of the flowers themselves.

The marks on all these plates include a printed twin globes factory mark including *BROWNFIELD & SON*, an impressed *BROWNFIELD* and a date — in three instances *'9/87'* and in the others *'9/88'*. All have the pattern number *'2533'*. The same registered edging was used for a floral patterned dinner service ordered by Tiffany's of New York in late 1883. This particular service has a pattern number '2234', a printed registration number '10361' and a printed mark Tiffany & Co, New York. A third series has also been found, again depicting a series of hand painted flowers, but with a brown patterned border rather than the dentil edging. This set also has the registration number 10361. In a somewhat less expensive style is a stylised Prunus tree plate **(Col Pl. 387)** with a pattern number *'2613'* which has an impressed *'6/83'* and *'BROWNFIELD'*.

Two vases, each with a lavender blue tinted body and applied flowers **(Fig 388)** were introduced probably between 1875-84. Neither of the 9½" vases has an impressed date, only an impressed *BROWNFIELD*, but manufacture was probably c1875-84. The applied flowers are very similar to those used on another pair of Brownfield vases (see Illustration 444), although the latter have neither the base plinth nor the vase lid of this more extravagant example.

In 1876 Brownfields introduced two goat ornaments, the first carrying a couple of panniers on its back, the second pulling a perambulator **(Fig 389)**. An example of the latter has been found and this has an impressed *'BROWNFIELD'*, *'150'* — its shape number and a registration diamond for 7th October 1876. In the same year, the firm was manufacturing two small ornamental figures, the first of a boy **(Col Pl. 390)**, the second of a girl **(Col Pl. 391)**: each is standing next to a wicker basket. They are shown with a sophisticated soft pink enamel finish. Both are impressed *'BROWNFIELD'* and *'130'* — their shape number. They could also have an impressed registration diamond for 1st February 1876, although this is missing on both of the illustrated figures. The quality of each is extremely fine and their current market price (£400+) places them on a par with some of the best small porcelain figures produced in this period.

PORCELAIN ITEMS DISCOVERED FROM THE 1880 FACTORY CATALOGUE

This section serves to provide a visual guide to many Brownfield porcelain pieces, all of which are illustrated in the 1880 factory Catalogue, kept in Keele University Library. The first illustration **(Fig 392)** is a cake stand supported by two cherubs: it may have an impressed shape number '31' and it is 20" tall and 13" wide. This is similar to the more elaborate cake dish with additional bon-bon tray exhibited at Philadelphia in 1876. This is one of three similar designs illustrated on page 13, accompanied by two other cake stands and a plate design for a tea service. The second example **(Fig 393)** shows the cherubs in reclining position under a stand 5½" high and 8½" wide: its shape number is '32'. The last in this group of three is an 11" wide cake dish **(Fig 394)** with a seated cherub at both sides: its shape number is '33'. It seems likely that all these were in production by 1876.

Page 21 reveals a fourth cake stand, this time supported by a bear **(Fig 395)**: 13" tall and 17" across,

  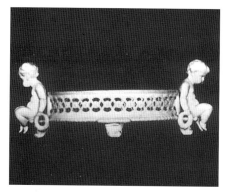

Figs 392-393-394. WB. Cherubim Cake Stands and Bon-bon dish. Shape Nos 31, 32, and 33.

Fig 395. WB. Bear Cake Stand. Shape No 48.

Fig 396. WB. Cake Dish with Bon-Bon Dish. Shape No 131.

Figs 397-398. WB. Ceres with a Sheaf of Corn and with a bunch of grapes. Both Shape Nos –34.

Figs 392-397 courtesy of Spode Ltd and Keele University.

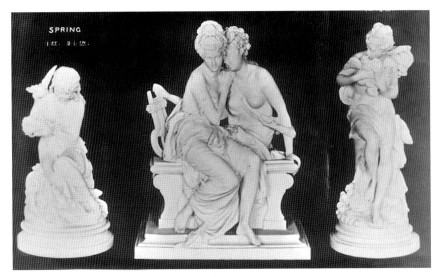

Figs 399-400-401. WB. Figures representing 'Spring', Confidence and Love — shape Nos 144, 142 and 143. Courtesy Spode Ltd and Keele University.

it has four moulded bears' heads around the lower rim and a shape number '48'. It may also have a registration diamond for 3rd May 1873. The fifth and last in this series **(Fig 396)** is illustrated on page 31, a really elaborate piece, 15½" high and 16½" wide, with both a cake stand and an adjoining 'bon-bon dish': its impressed shape number is '131'

The next group of illustrations from the factory catalogue are all substantial figures of goddesses, women or children. The first two, which appear on page 14, include an eleven and a half inch Ceres and a Bacchanal figure, the first holding a sheaf of corn **(Fig 397)**, the second some grapes **(Fig 398)**: their impressed shape numbers are '34'.

Three beautifully moulded figures, representing 'Spring', 'Confidence' and 'Love' respectively **(Figs 399-401)**, appear on page 30 of the 1880 Catalogue. The centre piece, 18" high, is the most elaborate of the three ornaments and depicts two of the graces. The markings are likely to include an

Figs 402-403-404. WB. Statuettes of a girl, A Woman holding a bird next to a Nautilus Shell and a Statuette of a boy — shape Nos 176, 178 and 176. Figs 402-4 courtesy Spode Ltd and Keele University.

Figs 405-406. WB. Tyrolean (?) Girls with Water Fowl. Shape Nos 193. Courtesy Spode Ltd and Keele University.

impressed 'Brownfield', and impressed shape numbers '144', '142' and '143' respectively.

Page 140 shows one large statue of a nymph holding a bird **(Fig 402)** standing in front of a nautilus shell. On her left-hand side is a young girl **(Fig 403)** holding a bowl and pinning her hand to her bonnet, and on the right a boy holding a rabbit in his hands **(Fig 404).** The first of these will have an impressed shape number '178' and the latter two '176'. The next illustration shows two figures of a Tyrolean (?) girl **(Figs 405-6)** accompanied by water fowl: these will have an impressed shape number '193'.

The two Japanese ladies **(Figs 407-408)** were first illustrated by Desmond Harrison in *'Art &*

Antiques' in 1972: both appear on page 149 of the 1880 Catalogue. The figures are 11¹/₂" and 10¹/₂" tall respectively. The taller of the two figures carries a fan in her left hand and a parasol under her right. 'The first lady's kimono is a pale pink embroidered with white flowers and her skirt is a deep olive green with gilding. The second lady's kimono is a pale turquoise embroidered with flowers and her full length skirt is pale mauve'. Both were dated as 1899 and so presumably had impressed date marks for that year; their shape numbers are '198' and '199'. Desmond Harrison's examples must be among the last of Brownfields' porcelain creations although they had been in production from at least 1880, if not a little earlier.

Figs 407-408. WB. Japanese Ladies in Kimonos. Shape No 197 and 198. Illustration courtesy Desmond Harrison.

Figs 409-410-411. WB. Cherubs and Nautilus Shells — shape Nos 208, 210 and 209. Courtesy Spode Ltd and Keele University.

In fact, these were the products not of the Brownfield Co-operative Guild which had failed in late 1898 but of the Brownfield Pottery Ltd, only created in 1899 and due to end in 1900.

The last in this group are cherubim holding on to nautilus shells **(Fig 409-411):** these appear on pages 162-3 of the catalogue and have shape numbers '208', '209' and '210'.

The next group of porcelain pieces are all of animals or birds. Page 49 of the Catalogue shows two cockerels **(Fig 412-413),** the first 22$^{1}/_{2}$" tall, the second 19$^{1}/_{2}$". As yet, their enamel colouring and markings remain unknown, but the latter may include an impressed '91' and '92' — their shape numbers.

On page 59 there is a parrot **(Fig 414),** with its wings unfolded and clutching a piece of bamboo cane in its claws: this is 24" tall and there may be an impressed '2050'; **(Fig 415)** is an exotic pheasant, with a shape number '2074'.

Much less grandiose are the two Elephants supporting Flower Holders **(Figs 416-17)** shown on page 57 (shape numbers '157' and '158'). The first of these, with a square rather than a circular flower holder, was registered on 8th

Figs 412-413. WB. Cockerels. Height 22$^{1}/_{2}$" and 19$^{1}/_{4}$" — shape Nos 91 and 92. Courtesy Spode Ltd and Keele University.

November 1876. These are shown alongside a Rustic scene **(Fig 418)** depicting a fox hunting chickens (shape number '154') and a parrot **(Fig 419)** (shape number '153') which was registered on 7th October 1876.

The Victorians seem to have been as devoted to their cats as the present generation and there are a number of porcelain figures showing cats or kittens in various poses. The first of these, which had been exhibited at Philadelphia, appears on page 18 of the catalogue and shows a cat lying on its back, holding a ball. The second,

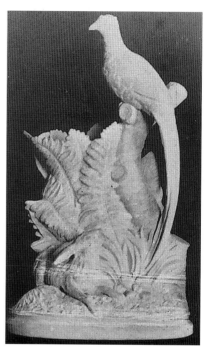

Fig 414-415. WB. Parrot. Height 24" — shape No 2050. Exotic Pheasant — shape No 2074. Courtesy Spode Ltd and Keele University.

on page 28, showing two kittens playing on an ornamental container has already been illustrated, and the third is a kitten lying playfully at the side of a container bowl **(Fig 420).** The bowl is eleven inches wide and the piece may have a shape number '138'. Page 136 shows another kitten **(Fig 421)** demonstrating customary curiosity about the contents of a wicker basket (shape number '171').

The last in this group **(Fig 422)** appears on page 165 and is very similar in design to Illustration 349, except that there are two additional circular plant pot containers on each side of the centre (shape number '110'). A 9½" chained bear candlestick **(Fig 423)** will have an impressed shape number '96' and may have a registration diamond for 9th April 1875.

The second goat figure in the catalogue **(Fig 424)** has the same marks as the goat and perambulator: this one will have a shape number '151' and a registration diamond for 7th October 1876. The final piece in this group is of two small Cockerels standing next to a wicker basket **(Fig 425):** its shape number is '171'.

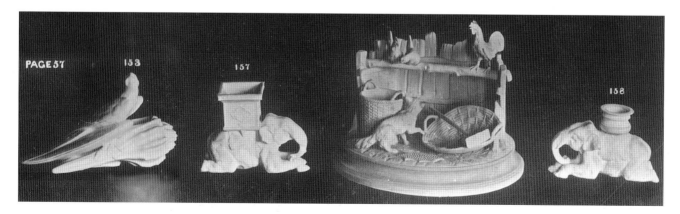

Figs 416-417-418-419. WB. Elephant Flower Holder. Shape No 157. Elephant Flower Holder. Shape No 158. Rustic Scene — Fox and chicken. Shape No 154. Parrot — twin flower pot holder. Shape No 153. Courtesy Spode Ltd and Keele University.

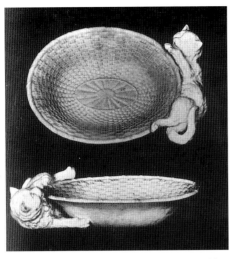

Fig 420. WB. Kitten and bowl. Shape No 138.

Fig 421. WB. Kitten investigates wicker basket. Shape No 171.

Figs 422-423. WB. Kittens & Triple flower stand — Shape No '110'. Chained Bear Candlestick — Shape No 96.

Fig 424. WB. Goat and Panniers. Reg D 7/10/75. Shape No 151

Fig 425. WB. Two Cockerels near a Wicker Basket. Shape No 171.

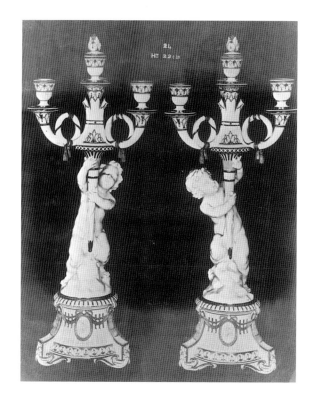

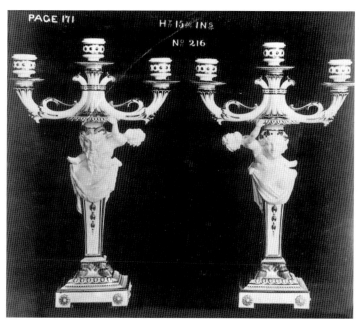

Figs 428-429.WB. Triple Candlesticks. Shape Nos 216.

Figs 426-427. WB. Triple Candlesticks. Shape No 24.
Triple Candlesticks. Shape No 24.

Fig 430. WB. Elaborate Paraffin Lamp. Shape No 71.

Figs 431-432. Paraffin Lamp supported by Child. Shape
No 43. Paraffin Lamp supported by Woman. Height 34"
— Shape No 73.

Figs 420-432 courtesy Spode Ltd and Keele University Library.

Fig 433. WB. Cherubs carrying netting hammock. Shape No 120. Courtesy Spode Ltd and Keele University.

Among the most impressive Brownfield porcelain pieces in the 1880 Catalogue are the candlesticks shown on pages 10 and 171 and the paraffin lamps illustrated on pages 38 and 41.

The first two candlesticks **(Figs 426-27)** each 22¼" tall, have a cherub holding on to the main pedestal which supports the triple candlestick holders: these have shape numbers '24' and both were registered on 14th November 1872. One of these was illustrated in Jewitt's *Ceramic Art of Great Britain* (1883) The second pair **(Figs 428-29)** are 15" tall and have the figure of a man's head just at the support for the triple candle holders: their shape number is '216' and each may have a registration diamond for 9th September 1878.

The first pair of paraffin lamps **(Fig 430)** are 24" tall (shape number '71'), the second pair **(Figs 431-432)** are 29½" (shape number '43') and 34½" respectively (shape number '73'). The first of these has a cherub clinging to the pillar of the lamp, the second has a graceful woman supporting the lamp on her head.

In addition to the animal ornaments, the catalogue shows a number of porcelain figures of cherubs and little children. The first of these appear on page 33 where two cherubs **(Fig 433)** are carrying what appears to be a fishing net which is designed to act as a fruit and flower basket. One example of this has been found with a light green enamelling, impressed *'BROWNFIELD'* and *'120'* — its shape number: it has neither a registration diamond nor an impressed date which is surprising since the piece was registered by Brownfields on 5th July 1875.

A much larger figure of a startled cherub **(Fig 434)** seeking to avoid a lobster pinching its hand, has a

Fig 434. WB. Startled Cherub avoiding Lobster. Shape No 41. Courtesy Spode Ltd and Keele University.

Fig 435. WB. Cherub and Triple Shell Dishes. Shape No '52'. Regd 3rd May 1873. Courtesy Spode Ltd and Keele University,.

shape number '41'. This is 14½" tall and 14½" wide. A cherub Strawberry dish **(Fig 435)** with triple shell dishes is illustrated on page 16 of the 1880 Catalogue. Its shape number is '52' and it may have a registration diamond for 3rd May 1873.

Two statuettes appear on page 56, the first a young boy **(Fig 436)** carrying a wicker box perhaps of fresh wrapped up loaves of bread, the second a girl **(Fig 437)** carrying what might be a bundle of washing. These will have shape numbers '148' and '149'. (The same two figures also appear on page 139, the boy carrying a basket of fruit on his head, the girl a bundle of flowers: the

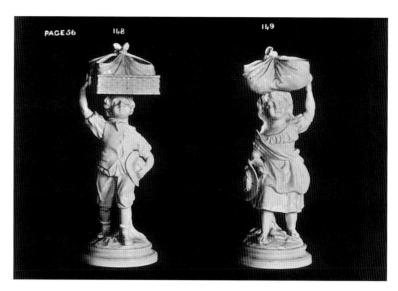

Figs 436-437. WB. Boy with Wicker Box on his head — Shape No 148. Girl with Bundle of washing — shape No 149. Courtesy Spode Ltd and Keele University,.

shape numbers of these are '66' and '65'.) The last in this group are four cherubs illustrated on page 168, the first two winged cherubs **(Figs 438-39)** standing sideways over a plant pot (shape numbers '211' and '212').

The second pair **(Figs 440-41)** are kneeling besides a sheaf of corn. (shape numbers '213' and '214') Three other very similar pieces are found on page 20, two cherubs seen full-face next to a basket and barrel respectively, while the third is a seated cherub carrying a quiver on its back. Their shape numbers are '59', '60' and '47'.

Perhaps two of the most elaborate pieces of Brownfield porcelain are found on pages 128 and 167 of the 1880 Catalogue. Both are sophisticated Flower Vases, the first **(Fig 442)** 46 inches tall, with a width of handle 22" (shape number '186'): three cherubim figures are shown clasping at the elaborately applied flowers and branches. The second **(Fig 443)** is 36" tall and has two cherubs supporting a large vase (shape number '200'). This was illustrated as Figure 1378 in Jewitt's *Ceramic Art of Great Britain*

Figs 438-439. WB. Winged Cherub standing on plant pot — Shape No 211. Winged Cherub standing on plant pot — shape No 212. Courtesy Spode Ltd and Keele University,.

Figs 440-441. WB. Kneeling Cherubs, each with a sheaf of corn — shape Nos 213 and 214. Courtesy Geoffrey Godden.

Fig 443. WB. Sophisticated Flower Vase. Shape No 200. Courtesy Spode Ltd and Keele University,.

Fig 442. WB. Sophisticated Flower Vase. Shape No 186. Courtesy Spode Ltd and Keele University,.

(1883). Two versions of this were offered, the second having a transfer print filled in with enamel decoration. This example has the same shape number '200'.

The pair of vases with applied roses **(Fig 444)** follow quite closely the style of the more ambitiously designed vase shown in Illustration 388. Like a number of Brownfield porcelain products, these are unmarked, but the nature of the applied flowers strongly suggests that they were made in the Brownfield factory, probably in the late 1870s.

Figures of dogs appear to have been a little less popular than cats with the Victorian public: the only two are found on page 18 of the 1880 catalogue. The first **(Fig 445)** is sitting in the begging pose holding a wicker basket in its mouth: this has an impressed BROWNFIELD, an illegible registration diamond for 6th June 1874 and might also have a shape number '83', although this example does not. The 1880 catalogue

Fig 444. WB. Pair of Floral Vases. Unmarked examples. Courtesy Ellie Downer Antiques, Devon.

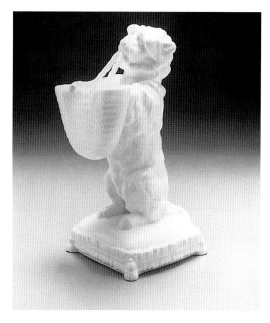

Fig 446. WB. Poodle — Basket in mouth. Shape No 44. Courtesy Mrs F Edwards, Devon.

Fig 445. WB. Poodle begging — Basket in its teeth. Illegible Reg D for 6th June 1874. Shape No 83 (not impressed on this example). Height 6¹/₂" — 16.5cm.

describes its function as a menu holder. The second, a poodle **(Fig 446)** is walking along also with a basket in its teeth (shape number '44'): it is also impressed *BROWNFIELD* and its date of introduction is likely to have been 1874-80.

The 'Dove' vase **(Fig 447)** is only six inches tall, but is beautifully moulded. Like the preceding piece, it has only an impressed *'BROWNFIELD'*. The same is true of the small monkey figure **(Fig 448)** and the tiny Satyr ornament **(Fig 449).**

BROWNFIELD'S MOST AMBITIOUS PORCELAIN PIECE

The most prestigious piece of porcelain ever manufactured by Brownfields was the eleven feet high bone china Earth Vase **(Fig 450)** this venture being the personal dream of Louis Jahn, the firm's artistic director. Massive publicity for the Brownfield factory was doubtless one of Louis Jahn's aims: the 20,000 plus people who visited the factory to see it on the one day allocated for public viewing indicates that this was successfully achieved. The vase was of celadon green china and had been modelled by A Carrier Belleuse: it was originally intended to exhibit it at the

Fig 447. WB. 'Dove' Vase. Impressed 'Brownfield'. Courtesy Mrs D Tipper, Devon.

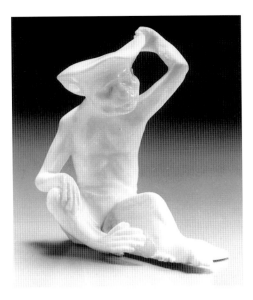

Fig 448. WB. Monkey. Impressed 'Brownfield'.
Courtesy Ellie Downer Antiques, Devon.

Fig 449. WB. Monkey and Bowl. Impressed RD for
22nd May 1877. Shape No '178'. Courtesy Spode
Ltd and Keele University.

Fig 450. WB. The 'Earth Vase' 1889. Courtesy Keele
University.

1879 Paris Exhibition. Manufacturing problems seemingly prevented this, the factory admitting that technical difficulties had at times seemed insurmountable, and it was not until 1884 that it was eventually displayed at the Crystal Palace Exhibition. The official description read as follows: 'On the summit stands Ceres, the goddess of fruitfulness and plenty, surrounded with attendant sprites. These are scattering from their horns of abundance the goddess' gifts of increase on the earth below, while the goddess herself is clasping to her breast a slumbering infant. The Earth is encircled by a zone reposing on four brackets, on which are seated four groups, typifying the four seasons of the year, Spring, Summer, Autumn and Winter.' The scale of the project is difficult to appreciate, but the pedestal frieze contained no less than sixty cupids engaged in hunting, fishing, harvesting etc.

'The globe is of a delicate green, known as celadon and upon it are traced the lines of latitude and longitude, and certain geographical outlines representing the seas and the continents. The Pedestal, from which spring the ornamental supports to the globe, is encircled by a frieze of numerous figures forming an endless procession, and all are engaged in the never-ceasing pursuits in which mankind are forever busy during the changing round of the years.' In 1889 the Earth Vase was displayed at the Paris Exhibition, although it suffered some damage en route to its display and had to be quickly repaired. Sadly

Fig 452. WB. Pheasant Vase (by Micklewright.)
Illustration Courtesy Desmond Harrison.

Fig 451. WB. 'Ceres' Figure. Courtesy Keele University.

Fig 459. WB. 'Swallow' Cup and Trembler. Pat No '2072'.
Impressed 'Brownfield '8/79'.

Marks 43. WB. Porcelain Cup Pat No '2195'. Printed Reg D on Cup — 26/10/78. Registration — 26th October 1878. Pat No '2195'.

its designer Carrier-Belleuse did not live to see its display in the French capital, he having died in 1887. The Vase was destroyed in a factory fire in 1894. The Ceres Figure **(Fig 451)** can also be illustrated: this is 25" tall and survived the factory fire of 1894. It remained in the Sadler Collection until February 1972 when it was sold at Sotheby's in London for the amazingly low figure of £24.

The last piece of porcelain illustrated is a beautiful 15½" vase **(Fig 452)**, decorated with pheasants and hand painted to a very high standard by F Micklewright. This was illustrated by Desmond Harrison in *'Art & Antiques'* in 1972, but no mention was made of any impressed marks or date. Presumably the piece is signed by the artist in the same way as the wall plaque painted by W Bourne in 1882. The quality of this vase stands very favourable comparison with those manufactured by Mintons, Davenport etc.

PORCELAIN TEA AND COFFEE SERVICES

The first cup and saucer illustrated **(Col Pl. 453)** has a pattern number *'249'* and an impressed date *'8/78'*. The pattern of roses, filled in with enamel decoration in yellow and brown with additional gilding was probably introduced in about 1873-74. The 'Dragonfly and Hawthorn' cup and saucer (Pat No '1346') **(Col Pl. 454)** was introduced in late 1878 or early 1879, although the impressed marks on this example show that it was manufactured in July 1882. (See end of Appendix 2.) The enamel

Figs 461-472. WB. 'Lubeck', Three Lines Under Glaze', 'Band and Line Under Glaze', 'Princes Ribbon', 'Bismarck', 'Shamrock', 'Moltke', 'Denmark', 'Marsala', 'Bethoor', 'Sicily', 'Durham' Tea cups. Courtesy Spode Ltd and Keele University.

Fig 476. WB. Pink Flowerheads and Foliage Cup/Saucer.
Impressed 'Brownfield'/'12/82'. Pat No '2194'.

decoration appears to be identical, but the pattern number on the teacup is *'2336'*, while that on the saucer is *'1346'*. Close examination shows that the transfer printing of the dragonflies is much better on the saucer than on the cup. This must therefore be a Victorian example of matching up a damaged piece, purchasing the nearest identical cup to go with the original saucer. The next 'Storks Christening' plate, teacup and saucer (Pat No '1428') **(Col Pl. 455)** and its parallel coffee cup and saucer (Pat No '1428') **(Col Pl. 456)** would both have been introduced in early 1879. This same theme was used for the muffin dish **(Col Pl. 457)** and again for another plate '1529'. The 'Storks' christening plate (Pat No '1529') **(Col Pl. 458)** probably first appeared in the late 1870s, but this example was produced in January 1883. The marks on '1528' have both *'BROWNFIELD'* and *'5/79'* impressed: '1529' includes an impressed *'BROWNFIELD'* and *'1/83'*, but there are neither impressed date marks nor Brownfield on many examples in the '1428' version.

The 'Swallow' cup and saucer (Pat No '2072') **(Fig 459)** is impressed *'BROWNFIELD, '8/79'* and has a pattern number. The transfer print used on this is of poorer quality than on most porcelain wares. More attractive is the 'Bird, Butterfly and Foliage' teacup (Pat No '2145') **(Col Pl. 460)** impressed *'BROWNFIELD'* and *'12/79'*. This example has a pattern number and a printed registration diamond for 26th October 1878. It is one of only two porcelain teacups and saucers so far found with such a registration diamond **(Marks 43).**

Page 124 of the 1880 Catalogue shows no less than twelve different designs — all for porcelain cups and saucers. The precise date of introduction of all these designs is unknown. The top group of four **(Figs 461-64)** includes 'Lubeck', 'Three lines under Glaze', 'Band and Line under Glaze' and 'Princes Ribbon'. The centre two are very plain while even the 'Lubeck' and 'Princes Ribbon' have a minimum of pattern. The middle group **(Figs 465-68)** includes 'Bismark', 'Shamrock', 'Moltke' and 'Denmark'. It seems likely that they were component parts of a tea service including a teapot. No actual specimens of the remaining four teacups have been seen and 'Marsala', 'Bethoor', 'Sicily' and 'Durham' **(Figs 469-72)** can only be identified from their appearance in the 1880 Catalogue. The 'Bethoor' pattern is much more elaborate than on any of the others in this group and 'Sicily' has a larger transfer printed pattern.

The next 'Jenette Jones' porcelain teacup, saucer and side plate **(Col Pl. 473)** is part of a most interesting and unusual teaset from 1883-4. This trio has a hand painted chinoiserie scene, while each of the other sets has a different hand painted picture. These items do not have the normal transfer print with enamel decoration because they were in fact bought as blanks from the Brownfield factory and, consequently, have no factory pattern number on them at all. There is, however, an unresolved enigma about the set: only the teaplate has an impressed *BROWNFIELD* and this is true of each trio. The registration diamond mark on the milk jug reveals another complication because it indicates that it came from the Brown Westhead-Moore factory. This latter piece dated from 6th October 1873 which might suggest that it (and other pieces) were bought in cheaply from factories' leftover stock.

The most likely explanation seems to be that all the various blanks were bought from a mixture of factories by a Jenette Jones of Tynyuheal House, Tona, near Neath in South Wales. A piece of family writing paper with the above address did in fact accompany the tea service. The Cardiff City Library confirms that a Jones family did live here throughout the second half of the nineteenth century and that there was a school for young ladies based there in the 1880s. It is possible that decorating teasets was one of the activities pursued in this school, for there was probably a minimum quantity of blank pieces that had to be ordered from any one Staffordshire factory. Each item has a hand painted monogram '*JJ*', and the date marks *11/83* and *11/84* found on various pieces indicate the years of manufacture.

The rather unusual 'Acorn Leaf' trembler (Pat No '2437') **(Col Pl. 474)** has an impressed '*BROWNFIELD*' and '*11/80*'. The 'Flowerheads' pattern teacup **(Col Pl. 475)** (Pat No '2622') enamelled here in rust, green and blue is impressed '*BROWNFIELD*' and *7/82*. This suggests an introduction date probably a little earlier in late 1881. The next 'Pink Flowerheads' teacup and saucer **(Fig 476)** was made in December 1882: this has no pattern number, but is impressed '*BROWNFIELD*' and '*12/82*'. The silver and gold tree pattern found on the next cup and saucer **(Col Pl. 477)** is impressed '*1/83*' and '*BROWNFIELD*', but without any pattern number. The orange, brown and silver flowerheads cup **(Col Pl. 478)** dated '*6/86*' and impressed '*BROWNFIELD*' is the first example to have a patterned border.

The next green celadon bone china cup and saucer (Reg No '43302') **(Col Pl. 479)** was manufactured in March 1887, and was first illustrated by the Hampsons in 1980. This is two and a half inches high and is printed in brown, gilded rims. It is impressed '*BROWNFIELD*' and '*3/87*' and its printed registration number indicates introduction in February 1886. Celadon was a special, delicate green body employed in the making of anything from teacups to the enormous Earth Vase. Both the last examples from the early 1890s are two cups and saucers **(Col Pl. 480)** which have a floral pattern, this time with a much wider border. The first, enamelled in pink and brown, is impressed '*5/91*' and '*BROWNFIELD*': the last **(Col Pl. 481)**, enamelled in brown and blue, is '*8/93*'. Neither of the last two items has any painted pattern number to indicate their date of introduction.

POSTSCRIPT

In late 1994, when this book had already been completed, the author took four pieces of unmarked Brownfield porcelain to the Antiques Roadshow in his locality. The quality of the three plates and a comport was considered excellent, the hand painting was thought to be extremely good and overall the pieces were very much admired although the identity of the manufacturer had not yet been revealed. In due course, this was divulged. The subsequent brief discussion of value was set in this context of the factory name. IF only they had been Minton, they would have been worth several hundred pounds each, but being Brownfield, one was valued at only £300 and the remaining three at £125 each.

This would imply that there is considered to be an established 'hierarchy' of manufacturers. Top quality and the appropriate 'cachet' to go with that, can only come from the established big names — Chelsea, Minton, Worcester etc. The author believes that quality should speak for itself regardless of the name and reputation of the manufacturer. The quality of the hand painting on Brownfield pieces cannot rival that on Royal Worcester, Chelsea etc, but it is sometimes as good as on some Minton, Davenport, Ridgway and Copeland pieces.

In 1989 the author discovered a Brownfield 'Gothic' jardinière on sale in the King's Road, London, advertised as Minton and offered at £650, a not inconsiderable price in those days. The jardinière had no markings at all and clearly the dealer was so impressed by the quality that he deduced that it must be (or very probably was) Minton. The quality of the jardinière supported a Minton label and this endorses the view that Brownfield could, sometimes, be every bit as good as Minton. Moreover, over the last ten years, this has hardly been an isolated occurrence. In August 1995 a Brownfield flower stand with virtually illegible marks was on sale at the NEC: described as Minton, it was priced at £975. Its superb quality matched that of Minton.

The Brownfield firm has remained in virtual obscurity since its demise in 1900, and it has, therefore, little or no reputation for excellence in the current ceramic circle of the 1990s. Some Brownfield products were of a rather mediocre standard, some were good and (dare it be said?) some were excellent and every bit as good as some Minton. It is to be hoped that this book will have done something to re-establish the reputation of Brownfields for excellence, a reputation which evidence from the 1860s, 1870s and 1880s, clearly shows it held over a hundred years ago.

Appendix 1A

BROWNFIELD REGISTRATIONS: 1842-1883

The initial table shows the number and frequency of Brownfield registrations taken out during the years 1842-1883 in order to obtain three years' protection (from fraudulent copying) for either a design or a shape. The subsequent analysis seeks to throw additional light on the use of the Design Register in London and to illustrate how misleading 'bare statistics' can be — in terms of the total number of products that were manufactured with legal protection from imitation.

1848	1		1860	2	(4)	1872	5	(9)
1849	–		1861	3	(4)	1873	3	(7)
1850	–		1862	4	(5)	1874	6	(10)
1851	3	(4)	1863	5		1875	7	(12)
1852	2	(3)	1864	4		1876	6	(14)
1853	–		1865	2	(3)	1877	8	(15)
1854	3		1866	1	(2)	1878	5	(8)
1855	2	(4)	1867	2	(6)	1879	4	(7)
1856	2	(3)	1868	3	(4)	1880	6	(23)
1857	2	(3)	1869	4	(5)	1881	4	(9)
1858	3	(4)	1870	6	(9)	1882	5	(8)
1859	2		1871	2	(5)	1883	11	(23)

The first recorded figure indicates the number of times each year that Wm Brownfield (& Son) registered products. The second bracketed figure shows the number of different items that were registered in each year. Initially most submissions to the London Register Office contained just a single item but gradually two or more products were registered on each occasion presumably for administrative convenience to the firm or to the 'agent' making the application on Brownfield's behalf. It is interesting to break down the number of applications into three different periods.

1842-1861	35	1861-1873	64	1873-1883	129

In common with most of the leading manufacturers, Wood & Brownfield and Wm Brownfield were very reluctant to make use of the Register at all in the years 1842-1852. As suggested in Chapter One this was probably due, in part, to the intimidation thought to have been brought about by the leading London wholesalers and retailers. It has also to be remembered that in the early years 1842-52 pottery firms could and did register their products under an older law of 1811. This was done in the case of the jugs produced in 1839 and 1841 — Vertical Columns (1839), Willie (1841) and the Judgement of Solomon (1841).

Only one item was registered by Wood & Brownfield under the new 1842 system and that was in 1848. Why this was so remains a complete enigma. Even in this instance the registered plate shape was used to produce at least five totally different designs and future discoveries may well reveal others. The misleading nature of these bare statistics is first apparent in February 1851 when the registration of the 'Bouquet' plate design (2/10/51) was subsequently used to produce at least thirteen different patterns. Another of 2/10/54 produced sixteen, each plate having in common just the same relief-moulded border design. Each and every one of these had legal protection against imitation. So while the number of individual registrations in the early years seems few in number, this is highly misleading when we count the total number of articles manufactured under the same registration.

The figures in the first table shows a marked increase in the number of items registered from about 1870-71: prior to that, no more than six items had ever been registered in any one year. Even that number had only resulted once — in 1867 and this was very probably due to the occurrence of the Paris Universal Exhibition held in that year. For the rest of the decade 1872-1879 an average of ten items a year were registered and again we have to remember that each one of these was almost certainly used to produce five, six, seven or more individual products. Why the number should have begun to rise at this time remains unknown although it is possibly attributable to the influence of William Etches who joined his father on the management board in 1871. There is still enormous scope for detailed research into the use of the Design Register in this period and of the 'background' factors that might help to explain why major Staffordshire pottery firms began to make much more intensive use of it in the early 1870s.

The use of the Register by Wm Brownfield and Son(s) reached its peak in the years 1880-83. In those four years alone sixty-three separate products were registered, representing probably no less than 300-350 individual items manufactured in the factory. By the time that the new registration system was introduced in 1883, Brownfields' decline was possibly not far away; in any case we have to remember that to some extent there was perhaps less need to register new products because so many earlier ones had extensive 'production periods' of twenty years or more. Although only 228 items were individually registered during the whole of the years 1842-1883, it is much more likely that this represented over 1350 products emerging from the Brownfield factory with legal protection from fraudulent copying. It is debatable just how worthwhile this protection was, for it is clear from the prosecution of Samuel Bevington over the imitation of the Fern jug (inter alia) that many people connected with the pottery industry considered the enforcement of the law to be highly suspect and deficient.

APPENDIX 1B

INDEX OF ALL REGISTERED BROWNFIELD DESIGNS: 1842-83

WOOD AND BROWNFIELD

20 Mar	1848	50994	Alma Plate
20 Mar	1848	50994	Moultan Plate
20 Mar	1848	50994	Cable Plate
20 Mar	1848	50994	Blackberry Plate
20 Mar	1848	50994	Unnamed Plate

WILLIAM BROWNFIELD

10 Feb	1851	76664	Bouquet Plate
10 Oct	1851	80910	Plain ewer (Clarendon)
		80911	Bowl
16 Oct	1851	80989	Fuschia jug
4 Mar	1852	84133-4	Water jug & Water Bowl
25 Oct	1852	87228	Mazeppa jug
1 Apr	1854	95510	Kent jug
8 May	1854	95751	Vine Jardinière
2 Oct	1854	96980	Plate
26 Apr	1855	99972-4	Plain jug, Plate, Linenfold jug
28 Nov	1855	102785	Wicker jug
30 Apr	1856	104602-3	Ivy jug, Plain jug
27 Nov	1856	107714	Sauce Tureen
5 Jun	1857	110096-7	Jug, Jardinière
9 Dec	1857	112354	Arrowhead jug
2 Jun	1858	113905-6	Tureen, Plate
24 Aug	1858	114763	Jug
5 Oct	1858	115902	Jewel jug
20 May	1859	119968	Shamrock jug
5 Nov	1859	123816	Fern jug
6 Jun	1860	129681	Eglantine jug
6 Jun	1860	129680-2	Plate & Dinner service
29 Oct	1860	134968	Floral jug
6 Jul	1861	141732	Donatello jug
6 Sep	1861	143313	Plate
4 Dec	1861	147309-10	Union jug, Passion Flower
11 Jan	1862	148517	Plate
25 Jan	1862	148870	International jug
14 Mar	1862	149957-8	Dinner Service, Plate
		*	(Mother and Child jug)
5 Dec	1862	158091	Denmark Plate
8 Jun	1863	163189	Gothic jardinière
20 Jul	1863	164353	Veg dish table service
14 Oct	1863	167289	Albion jug
26 Nov	1863	169553	Plate
23 Dec	1863	170418	Plain jug
5 Jan	1864	170759	Dinner service
29 Apr	1864	174168	Argos jug
30 Jun	1864	175927	Geneva plate
12 Oct	1864	179656	Tyrol jug
1 Apr	1865	185520	Florence jug
30 Oct	1865	191407-8	Veg Dish, Tiverton jug
20 Apr	1866	196672-3	Alloa jug, Veg Dish

15 Mar	1867	206762-6	Glenny Jardinière, Vase, Veg Dish, Plate/Comport, Candle Holder
21 Jun	1867	209057	Napoleon jug
11 Jan	1868	215725	Butter dish
12 Jun	1868	219316-7	Cone Teapot, Hampton jug
21 Oct	1868	223308	Westminster jug
12 Dec	1868	225425	Butter dish
2 Apr	1869	228377	Barlaston jardinière
19 Jun	1869	230183-4	Teapot, Severn Teapot
10 Nov	1869	235974	Dinner Service
3 Dec	1869	236829	(Item missing from records)
10 Jun	1870	242392-4	Nile jug, Plain jug, Nile Teapot
9 Aug	1870	243807	Dessert service
19 Sep	1870	244976	Toilet Ewer
27 Sep	1870	245229	Jardinière
22 Oct	1870	246149	Cup and Saucer
10 Nov	1870	247079-80	Dinner Service, Marne jug
1 Dec	1870	248242	Cheese Stand
27 Mar	1871	251246	Teapot

WILLIAM BROWNFIELD AND SON

2 May	1871	252177-80	Worcester jug, Ewer & Basin, Marmalade pot & Cake stand
6 May	1871	252258	Jug
6 Jun	1872	263162	Dinner Service
22 Jun	1872	263565	Fruit Shell service
16 Aug	1872	65167-8	Veg dish, Dessert Comport
14 Nov	1872	267893-5	Candelabra, Teapot, Fern Case
14 Dec	1872	268806	Cupid jug
		268807	Paroquet Dinner Service
3 May	1873	272642-6	Foot pan, Slop pail, Dessert Centre, Ice Stand
29 Sep	1873	276566	Severn Teapot & Infuser
5 Dec	1873	278867	Flower Holder
22 Apr	1874	281902	Sauceboat
6 Jun	1874	282799 -802	Salt cellar, Menu & Flower Holders, Aston Tea Pot and Lamp Holder
8 Aug	1874	284254-5	Vase, Plant Bucket
10 Sep	1874	285013	Bangor jug, Lincoln Ewer, Mandarin, Hong Kong, Audley jugs.
30 Sep	1874	285776	Flower holders
6 Nov	1874	286759	Dessert Ware
20 Jan	1875	288553-6	Breakfast, Tea & Coffee Services, Menu & Flower Holder, Fruit Shell, Cruet Set.
5 Mar	1875	289769	Flower stand & Scent Ornament.
31 Mar	1875	290209-10	Flower holder, Fruit fan
9 Apr	1875	290393-4	Candelabrum, Menu Holder

5 Jun	1875	291870-1	Children Ornaments
10 Jun	1875	292005	15 Sylvan plates (& jug)
5 Jul	1875	292542	Fruit & Flower Basket
1 Dec	1875	296475	Flower vase

WILLIAM BROWNFIELD AND SONS

29 Jan	1876	298027-9	Yeddo jugs, Sisyphus jardinière
1 Feb	1876	298049	Flower holder
6 Sep	1876	303309	Water jug
7 Oct	1876	304129-31	Flower Basket & Holders
31 Oct	1876	304910-4	Three Teapots, Fruit Tray, Spittoon
8 Nov	1876	305090	Elephant Flower Holder
24 Jan	1877	307213	Puck Dessert Set (12)
7 Feb	1877	307570-2	Medieval jug, Plate, Cheese Stand
19 Feb	1877	307877	Table Service
16 May	1877	310175	Flower Holder
22 May	1877	310359-61	Flower Holders
10 Oct	1877	315104-5.	Toilet Ware, Olympus Jug
6 Nov	1877	315954-6	Leek jug, Vase, Flower Holder
22 Dec	1877	317427-8	Hudson jug, Honey Pot
25 Jan	1878	318107-8	Spoon Warmer, Flower Holder
24 Apr	1878	320669	Strawberry Tray
9 Sep	1878	325992-4	Flower Stand, Candelabrum, Cache-pot
26 Oct	1878	328320	Tea Ware
4 Dec	1878	329939	Jardinière
9 Jan	1879	330997-8	Swirling Fish Jug, Yesso Jug
19 May	1879	335308-9	Flower Holder, Spitoon
17 Sep	1879	339685-6	Dinner Services
28 Nov	1879	343530	Menu Holder
26 Jan	1880	345719	Basket Teapot
12 Feb	1880	346363	Teacup and Saucer
3 May	1880	349438-43	Cake Plate, 4 Cake Stands
25 May	1880	350098	Missouri Jug
11 Sep	1880	355091-100	Ten Vase designs
15 Dec	1880	359668-71	Sceau, Vase, Menu Holder, Flower Holder
8 Feb	1881	361538-41	Pastimes Kettle, Water Jug, Two Teapots
4 May	1881	364625-7	Mistletoe jug, Dessert Plate, Mistletoe Teacup
4 Oct	1881	370885	Water Jug
29 Oct	1881	372485	New York Cathedral Cup
4 Apr	1882	379212-3	Jug & Flower Holder
9 May	1882	380558	Tureen
6 Jul	1882	383020-1	2 Decorative Designs — Pottery
5 Aug	1882	384353-4	Box for Potted Meats, Design for Pottery Decoration
29 Aug	1882	385623	Trinket or Flower Tray
24 Jan	1883	393108-9	Two Vegetable Dishes
29 Jan	1883	393310	Bear Umbrella Stand
18 Jun	1883	399555-9	Gentleman Jug, Jug (556-7), Cruet set, Potted Meat Dish
25 Jun	1883	399897-8	Candlestick, Flower Holder
4 Jul	1883	400348	Tray
30 Jul	1883	401553	Lamp
25 Aug	1883	402839	Montana Jug
5 Sep	1883	403298-9	Two Toast Racks
13 Oct	1883	405363-4	Treetrunk Jug, Teapot
20 Oct	1883	405725-9	Four Oyster Trays, Candelabrum
10 Nov	1883	406781-2	Lamp Design, Soup Plate

REGISTRATIONS 1884-1894

WILLIAM BROWNFIELD AND SONS
1884-1892

Date		Reg No.	Item
Jan	1884	617	Salad Bowl
Feb	1884	1629	Ewer
Feb	1884	2026	Cribbage Board
May	1884	7043-4	Two Dinner Sets
Jun	1884	7626-7	Ice Tray, Jug
Jul	1884	9461-2	Plate, Ewer
Aug	1884	10361	Dessert Service
Sep	1884	12805-6	Tea Set
Oct	1884	14058	Tea Set
Oct	1884	15551	Plate Design
Jan	1885	20555	Jug
May	1885	27539	Biscuit Box
Jul	1885	29193	Plain Water Jug
Sep	1885	32609	Centre Dish
Sep	1885	33829	Design for Pattern
Sep	1885	34018	Design for Pattern
Dec	1885	39334	Toilet Set
Feb	1886	43302	Teacup
Mar	1886	45261-3	Teaset, Two Teapots
Mar	1886	46084	Pattern Design
May	1886	49737	Dessert Plate
Jul	1886	51594	Bed Pan
Sep	1886	57551	Menu Holder
Dec	1886	63054	Plate
Jan	1887	65227	Plate
Mar	1887	71415	Jug
Jul	1887	77821	Plain Jug Shape
Sep	1887	79562	Bowl
Oct	1887	83253	Teapot
Nov	1877	88370	Biscuit Box
Dec	1887	91243	Dish shape
Jan	1888	93597	Plate
May	1888	100839	Jug
Jun	1888	102493	Dish
Jun	1888	101303	Cake Dish
Oct	1888	111693	Soup Plate
Nov	1888	114320	Plate
Dec	1888	117214	Cup
Jan	1889	118288	Plate
Jul	1889	128561	Jug
Sep	1889	133052	Vase
Mar	1890	146658	Jug
Mar	1890	147186	Vase
Jun	1890	150703-6	Jug, Coffee Pot, Teapot, Teaset
Jul	1890	151655-6	Ewer
Aug	1890	154429	Plate
Jul	1890	—	Plate
Aug	1890	155409-10	Pie Ventilators
Sep	1890	155580	Bowl
Sep	1890	156777	Bowl
Oct	1890	159188	Cup and Saucer
Dec	1890	163772	Bowl
Mar	1891	167431	Bowl
Mar	1891	168509-10	Cups
Apr	1891	169523	Cup
Jun	1891	173111-4	Cups and Saucers
Jun	1891	173210	Cup and Saucer
Aug	1891	174555	Not found
Oct	1891	180593	Design NOT issued
Nov	1891	183744	Dish
Dec	1891	185255	Dish

	Date	Pat No.	Item
Apr	1892	190591	Jug
Apr	1892	190816	Plate Pattern

BROWNFIELD GUILD POTTERY SOCIETY LTD: 1892-1899

Oct	1892	200390.	Jug
Dec	1892	204656	Tray
Feb	1893	208185-6	Plate
Mar	1893	210702	Cheese Stand
Mar	1893	210792	Plate
Sep	1893	218156	Plate Patterns
Nov	1893	223134	Jug
Jan	1894	226227	Plate
Jan	1894	226669	Design NOT issued
Mar	1894	229505	Coffee Set and Bowl
Jun	1894	233711	Plate
Sep	1894	240962	Design NOT issued
Jun	1897	299919	
Jul	1897	300873	

BROWNFIELD POTTERY LTD

Jan	1899	332663
Feb	1899	332864
Apr	1899	333569
Nov	1899	336798

WOOD AND BROWNFIELD (AGENTS)

Apr	1900	355747	
May	1900		Cromer, Stuart and Mimosa.
Apr	1900	358427	

APPENDIX 2

PORCELAIN PATTERN AND SHAPE NUMBERS 1871-1900

Title	Pat No.	Date	
CUP & SAUCER	247	8/78	
FLORAL PLATE	650	9/77	
ORIENTAL LADIES PLATE	662	/74	RD 6/11/74
ORIENTAL LADIES COMPORT	664	11/74	RD 6/11/74
FLORAL PLATE	—		RD 6 /11/74
PAIR OF VASES	—		RD 30/10/75
GOAT & PRAM	—		RD 7/10/76
(SULTAN MIRZA PLATE	769	2/79	

Made for the second son of the Shah of Persia.)

Title	Pat No.	Date	
SYLVAN-HAUNT OF SNIPE PLATE	927	/78?	
SYLVAN-WILD LIFE IN THE ALPS	927	1/78	
SWALLOWS & PIGEON PLATE	1145	9/78	
CUP & SAUCER	1187		RD 20/1/75
SWALLOWS & SAILING SHIP PLATE	1192	–/80	
SWALLOWS & MOUNTAIN LAKE	1192	–/80	
SWALLOWS & WATERFALL	1192	–/80	
SWALLOWS & WINDMILL	1192	–/80	
DRAGONFLY & HAWTHORN CUP/SAUCER	1346	7/82	
STORK TEAPLATE	1428		
PASTIMES COMPORT	1448		

There are at least six different designs in this set.

Title	Pat No.	Date	
TULIP PLATE	1450	/79?	
ROSE PLATE	1450 ?	/79	
STORK TEAPLATE	1528	8/79	
CHRISTENING PLATE	1529	1/83	
LABURNUM PLATE	—	10/81	
FLORAL TEA SERVICE	1584	11/81	RD /81
FLORAL TEA SERVICE	1780	11/82	RD 5/81
FLORAL TEA SERVICE	—		RD 4/5/81
SWALLOW CUP & SAUCER	2072	8/79	
FLORAL ROSE PLATE	2074	/88	
BIRD & BUTTERFLY TEACUP	2195	12/79	RD 26/10/78
PASTIMES PLATE	2213	10/80	
FLORAL DINNER SERVICE	2234	1890s	RD 8/84

(Made for Tiffany's of New York.)

Title	Pat No.	Date	
DRAGONFLY & HAWTHORN CUP/SAUCER	2336	7/82	
ACORN LEAF TREMBLER	2437	11/80	
BLUE,GOLD & WHITE FLORAL PLATE	2530	10/81	
FLORAL PLATE	2533	c1884	
REG NO 10361			RD — 8/84

There are at least ten different designs in this set.

Title	Pat No.	Date	
FLORAL PLATE	2613	6/83	
BLUE/RUST/GREEN	2622	7/82	
FLOWERHEADS CUP & SAUCER	—		
LABURNUM PLATE	2631	10/81	
PINK FLOWERHEADS CUP		12/82	
SILVER & GOLD TREE CUP		1/83	
DRAGONFLY & HAWTHORN CUP	—	7/85	

Title	Pat No.	Date		
ORANGE/BROWN/SILVER FLOWERHEADS CUP/SAUCER		6/86		
JENNETT JONES CUPS & SAUCERS		11/83	4/84	11/84
	3239	2/86		
PINK & BROWN FLORAL CUP	—	5/91		
BLUE FOLIAGE/ BROWN EDGE CUP	—	8/93		

PORCELAIN PIECE SHAPE NUMBERS

The bracketed number indicates its shape number in the 1880 Brownfield Catalogue.

Item	Shape No	Height	Regd date
PAIR OF VASES			All regd 1/12/75
VASE	(1)		
VASE	(2)		
VASE	(3)		
VASE	(6)		
VASE	(7)		
VASES	(8-9)		
VASES	(10-12)		
VASE	(14)		
CHERUB WITH FLOWER POT ON HEAD	(15)		
WINGED CHERUBS CAKE DISH	(21)	12"	RD — 14/11/74
TRIPLE CANDLESTICKS	(24)	22¼"	RD — 14/11/72
WINGED CHERUB CAKE DISH	(31)	9"	
RECLINING CHERUB CAKE DISH	(32)	5½"	
SEATED CHERUB CAKE DISH	(33)		
CERES AND SHEAVES	(34)	11½"	
CERES AND GRAPES	(34)	11½"	
RECLINING CHERUB FRUIT SHELL	(40)		RD — 22/6/72
RECLINING DRYAD (?) FRUIT SHELL	(40)		RD — 22/6/72
RECLINING PAN FRUIT SHELL	(40)		RD — 22/6/72
STARTLED CHERUB AND LOBSTER	(41)	14½"	
CHERUB SUPPORTING OIL LAMP	(43)	29½"	
POODLE CARRYING BASKET	(44)		
BEAR SUPPORTING ICE STAND	(48)	13"	RD — 3/5/73
CHERUB AND TRIPLE SHELLS STRAWBERRY DISH	(52)	6½"	RD — 3/5/73
STYLISED CASTLE	(57)		
OPEN WINGED PARROT ON STAND	(59)		
CAKESTANDS	(67-8)		
CHERUB FLOWER HOLDER	(69)	7¾"	RD — 5/12/73
TWIN OIL LAMPS	(71)	24"	
LADY SUPPORTING			

Item	Shape No	Height	Regd date
OIL LAMP	(73)	34½"	
CANDLESTICK	(78)		
CANDLESTICK	(79)		
POODLE BEGGING			
MENU HOLDER	(83)		RD — 6/6/74
CHERUB			
FLOWER HOLDERS	(86)		RD — 30/9/74
COCKEREL	(91)	22½"	
COCKEREL	(92)	19¼"	
CHAINED BEAR			
CANDLESTICK	(96)	9½"	RD — 9/4/75
KITTEN & BALL FLOWER			
STAND/SCENT HOLDER	(99)	9"	RD — 5/3/75
CHERUB AND SHELL	(105)		
MONKEY AND SHELL	(106)		
SHELL	(107)		
FRUIT FAN	(108)		RD — 31/3/75
KITTENS PLAYING			
FLOWER STAND	(109)	10"	RD — 31/3/75
KITTENS TRIPLE			
FLOWER STAND	(110)		RD — 31/3/75
MAMA AND PAPA			
FIGURES	(112-3)	10½"	
TWIN CHERUBS			
CARRYING FISHING NET	(120)	9"	RD — 5/7/75
FLOWER POT	(121)		
VASES	(122-3)		
VASE	(127)		
VASES	(128-9)		
CHILDREN AND PANNIER BASKET			
FLOWER HOLDERS	(130)		RD — 1/2/76
TWIN LADIES			
CAKE STAND	(131)	15½"	
VASES	(132-3)		
KITTEN			
CLUTCHING BASKET	(135)		
VASE	(137)	8"	
CONFIDENCE STATUETTE	(142)	18"	
"LOVE" STATUETTE	(143)	18"	
"SPRING" STATUETTE	(144)	14"	
BOY WITH BASKET			
ON HEAD	(148)		
GIRL WITH BUNDLE			
ON HEAD	(149)		
GOAT AND PRAM	(150)		RD — 7/10/76
GOAT AND PANNIERS	(151)		RD — 7/10/76
PARROT AND SHELL	(153)		RD — 7/10/76
VASES	(155-6)		
FOX, CHICKENS &			
PANNIERS	(154)		

Item	Shape No	Height	Regd date
ELEPHANT			
FLOWER HOLDER	(157-8)		RD — 8/11/76
CAT, FLOWER POTS	(160-1)		
CHICKEN &			
PANNIER BASKET	(171)		
KITTEN &			
PANNIER BASKET	(171)		
WOMAN WITH BIRD			
IN HANDS	(173)		
CHILD STATUETTE			
FLOWER HOLDER	(176)		
CROSSED LEG MONKEY			
ON A TURTLE	(178)		RD — 22/5/77
VASES	(179-82)		
FLOWER BASKET	(183)		RD — 16/5/77
FLOWER HOLDER	(185)		
TRIPLE CHERUB			
ORNATE VASE	(186)	46"	
TYROLEAN (?) GIRL			
AND WATER FOWL	(193)		
CAT FLOWER POT	(194)		
TWO JAPANESE LADIES			
IN KIMONOS	(198-9)		
TWIN CHERUBS SUPPORTING			
LARGE VASE	(200)	36"	
CHERUBS AND			
DECORATED VASE	(200)	36"	
BEAR BISCUIT BARREL	(201)		
CHERUB AND			
NAUTILUS SHELL	(208)		
CHERUB AND			
NAUTILUS SHELL	(209)		
CHERUB AND			
NAUTILUS SHELL	(210)		
WINGED CHERUB			
AND FLOWER POT	(211-2)		
KNEELING CHERUBS			
AND SHEAVES	(213-4)		
TRIPLE CANDELABRA	(216)	15"	RD — 9/9/78
VASES	(1116)		
VASES	(1117)		
VASES	(1173)		
OPEN WINGED EAGLE	(2050)	24"	
CHERUBS			
SUPPORTING PAN	(2068)		

N.B. The recent discovery of a porcelain vase with a shape number 440 indicates that this list only covers a small proportion of Brownfield porcelain pieces. All those in the range 220-440+ are not reviewed in the 1880 catalogue.

APPENDIX 3

? indicates questionable attribution.

INDEX OF PLATE DESIGNS

ROBINSON, WOOD & BROWNFIELD
1837-37

Date		Pat No.	Marks	Pattern name
cJun	1837	22	RW&B	Floral
cJun	1837	24	RW&B	Floral
cSep	1837	31	RW&B	Floral
c1837		—	RW&B	Canton
c1837			RW&B	Mansion Tea Set
c1837		—	RW&B	Zoological
c1837		—	RW&B	Versailles

WOOD AND BROWNFIELD: 1837-1850

Date				
cFeb	1838	54	W&B	Amoy
	c1840-50		W&B	Albion Service.
	c1840-50		W&B	Eastern Plants
	c1840-50		W&B	Grecian Statue
	c1840-50		W&B	Juvenile
	c1845-50		W&B	Navarro
	c1845-50		W&B 3	Palmyra
	c1840-50		W&B	Venetian Scenery.
	c1840-50	?		Three Orientals??
cApr	1842	279		Ironstone??
cMay	1842	303	W&B	Ironstone Amoy
cJun	1842	328	W&B	Ironstone
cJun	1842	338	W&B	Amoy Bowl
cNov	1842	397	W&B	Rose
cJun	1843	642	3	Precursor No 35
cJul	1843	718.	W&B	Floral Rose
cSep	1843	788		Sandon??
cDec	1843	917	W&B	Hindostan
cMay	1845	2/1636	Alba	
cJun	1845	1676	W&B	Pomona
cJun	1845	1690	W&B	Oriental
cJan	1846	2030	W&B	Windsor Wreath
	c1846		W&B	Chiswick
cJul	1846	2/2314		Alba??
cDec	1846	2602	3	Precursor No 35
cApr	1847	2768	o	Chinoiserie
cSep	1847	3005	W	Formosa
cOct	1847	6/3117		Plate
(Thomas & Higginbotham, Wellington Quay, Dublin.)				
cDec	1847	3159	W&B	Floral Scroll
cDec	1847	3218 B		Plate??
20 Mar	1848	?	*	Alma
20 Mar	1848	3738	W&B	Moultan
20 Mar	1848?		W&B B	Cable
20 Mar	1848		W&B B	Blackberry
cSep	1848	3631		Plate??
cOct	1848	2/3688	*	Comport??
cMar	1849	3905/2		Plate
cMay	1849	4142/7		Convolvulus
cNov	1849	4338	W	Fruit Bowl??
cNov	1849	D/4369		Plate & Comport??
cDec	1849	4410/2	*	Musicians??
cJun	1850	4682		Plate RD 20/3/48

WILLIAM BROWNFIELD: 1850-1871

Date		Pat No.	Marks	Pattern name
cDec	1850	5146		Alba
cDec	1850	5160/4		Bouquet
cDec	1850	2/5169	W	Smyrna??
	c1850-60?		WB	Bude/Inkerman
	c1850-60?		WB	Ascot
	c1850-60?		WB	Pekin
	c1850-60?		*WB	Magenta
cFeb	1851	5217/O	WB	Eureka
10 Feb	1851	5267	p	Bouquet
10 Feb	1851	5346	*	Bouquet
10 Feb	1851	5346	*	Bouquet
cApr	1851	5438		Plate
cMay	1851	5590		Bouquet
cDec	1851	5914		Plate & Comport
cFeb	1852	6035/2		Comport
cFeb	1852	6038	!	Bouquet
cFeb	1852	6075	o	Plate
cMar	1852	6181	10	No 7
cMar	1852	6187		No 8
cMar	1852	6189		No 8
cAug	1852	6370	*	Plate & Comport
cAug	1852	6410?	*o	No 7
cAug	1852	6411	WB	No 7
cSep	1852	6487	*	No 12
cOct	1852	6510		No 9
cOct	1852	6514	*o	No 9
cOct	1852?	6566/2	(ú?)	Floral.??
cFeb	1853	6707	*	No 13 Dish
cFeb	1853		3	No 13
cMay	1853	6817		No 8 Soup Bowl
cJun	1853	6875	*o	Savona Service
cAug	1853	6923		No 13 Platter
cNov	1853	7081	W	Ellesmere??
cNov	1853	7146		No 15 Tureen Base
cApr	1854	7449	*	Bouquet Comport
cApr	1854	7459	*o	Bouquet
cJun	1854	7589	*o	Dog Rose
cJul	1854	7646		Alba (2/5169)
cJul	1854	7691	x	Comport RD 2/10/54
cAug	1854?	7726	COA	Smyrna??
cAug	1854	7727	*o	Comport RD 10/2/51
cAug	1854	727/11	*	Bouquet
cAug	1854	7732		Bouquet
cAug	1854	7738	*o	Bouquet
cAug	1854	7749	*o	Alma
cAug	1854	7750		Alma
cAug	1854	7764/1		Moltke Comport
2 Oct	1854	(7870-7900?)		First of 15 designs
cOct	1854	7875/0		A La Paix Specimen plate?
cDec	1854	8057	*o	Azoff Dish
cDec	1854	8079	*o	Bouquet
	c1855	(WB)	*o	Eupatoria platter
	c1855	(WB)	*o	Gordon platter
6 Apr	1855	(8390?)		
cAug	1855	8413	*	Sweaborg Service
cAug	1855	8443	*o	No 27
cAug	1855	8500	:.	Dog Roses.??
cAug	1855	8512		Plate
cAug	1855	8627	*o	Dog Rose
cAug	1855	8649	*	Six Roses
cSep	1855	8714		No 15
cOct	1855	8740	*v	Kinburn
cOct	1855	8755/0	*	No 26

Date		Pat No.	Marks	Pattern name
cNov	1855	8829	*v	Eupatoria
cDec	1855	8907	v	Pre-Cursor No 35
cDec	1855	8940	*	No 27
cDec	1855	8947	*o	No 27
c Mar	1856	9046/2	W	Floral
cApr	1856	9146/6	*W	Kars
cJun	1856	9202	*	No 34
cJun	1856	9234	*B	No 28 Bouquet
cJul	1855	9285		Comport
cSep	1856	9417	S	No 8 Bowl.
cNov	1856	9556		Comport
cNov	1856	9568	*om	Thrace
27 Nov	1856	—	(Alba)	No 46 Service
cDec	1856	9630	Alba	Comport
cDec	1856	9632	::	No 35
cDec	1856	9694-5	*	Fruit Comports
cJan	1857	9706	*	Fruit Bowl
cMar	1857	9930	S	Alba
cMay	1857	10,108	*W	No 40
cSep	1857	10,414		No 46
cSep	1857	10,414		No 46 Tureen 27/11/56
cNov	1857	10,585	*o	Floral Wreath
cNov	1857	10,592	*W	Floral Wreath
cNov	1857	10,597	*o	Floral Wreath
cJan	1858	10,714	WB	Plate
c Mar	1858	10,870	WB	Calpee
c Mar	1858	10,910	W	No 48
c Mar	1858	10,949	*	No 47
c Mar	1858	10,951	*	No 47
cApr	1858	10,979/1	W	Crimson
cMay	1858	11,047/1	*o	No 60
2 Jun	1858			Dinner Service
cJan	1859	11,703	p oB	Floral
cJan	1859	11,707	*o	Plate
cJan	1859	11,728	*B	No 61 Bouquet
cApr	1859	12,034/7	*	Montebello Tureen Base.
cJun	1859	12,456	RD	Dinner Service
cAug	1859	12,551	B!	No 54
cAug	1859	12,573	*W	No 54
cAug	1859	12,56?	*o	No 54 Comport
cSep	1859	12,630		Turkish Design
	1859?			No 58
	1859?			Albert Ribbon/ Victoria
c Feb	1860	13,167	M	No 55
c Feb	1860	13,173		No 56
c Feb	1860	13,189	*o	Fruit Bowl
6 Jun	1860		WB	Dinner Service
Jun	1860	13,457	WB	Dinner Service
6 Sep	1861			
cMay	1861	14,399	*	Bouquet -
11 Jan	1862			
11 Mar	1862	14,847	*E	Compiegne
14 Mar	1862			Mother & Child
14 Mar	1862			Mother & Child
14 Mar	1862			Berlin Platter
5 Dec	1862	—	* G	Denmark

(Family Crest indicates a special order for George Willoughby Hemans.)

Date		Pat No.	Marks	Pattern name
5 Dec	1862	16,423		Dinner plates
26Nov	1863 T			No 79 Platter

NEW PATTERN NUMBERING SYSTEM — 1864

Date		Pat No.	Marks	Pattern name
5 Jan	1864	166	EL	No 73
5 Jan	1864			Dinner Service
	1864	—		No 74 Bowl
	1864?	—		No 76
30 Jun	1864			Geneva comport
c	1867	270	WB	Green Border
c	1867?	370 T		Floral
10 Nov	1869	SK	WB	Plate
10 Nov	1869	SK	WB	Meat Platter
10 Jun	1870	SK	WB	Rome
9 Aug	1870.	2269/2	WB.	Comport
10 Nov	1870	T5970/2	WB	No 131
?		7050	WB	Texas
10 Nov	1870	7497	TM	Smyrna
	1870-1880?	T1790		Shakespeare
	1870-1880?	T2801		Cressy

WILLIAM BROWNFIELD & SON: 1871-1876

Date		Pat No.	Marks	Pattern name
	1872-1880	—		Harlequin plates
6 Jun	1872			Dinner Service
14 Dec	1872			Dinner Service
10 Sep	1874			Audley
10 Sep	1874			Hong Kong
10 Sep	1874			Mandarin
10 Sep	1874			Dorking
10 Jun	1875	292005		Sylvan (1258-7)
10 Jun	1875	No 1		Wild Life in the Alps
10 Jun	1875	No 2		The Woodland Fountain
10 Jun	1875	No 3		The Haunt of the Snipe
10 Jun	1875	No 4		The Australian Bush
10 Jun	1875	No 5		Monarch of the Glen
10 Jun	1875	No 6		Retrieving
10 Jun	1875			The Partridge Family
10 Jun	1875	AVAILABLE		The Timid Hare
10 Jun	1875	AS		Wild Ducks at Home
10 Jun	1875	DINNER PLATES		With The Pheasants

WILLIAM BROWNFIELD & SONS:1876-1892

Date		Pat No.	Marks	Pattern name
Jan	1876	T4319		No 114 Bowl
Jan	1876			No 115
	1876?		WB	No 131
	1876?		WB	No 132
	1876?	T4787/11		Marsala (SK)
	1876?	T5199/6		Plate (SK)
7 Feb	1877			Medieval Scenes Collection
7 Feb	1877			(A) Pastimes in the Garden (6)
7 Feb	1877			(B) Washing in the Garden (2)
7 Feb	1877			(C) Activities in the Kitchen (2)
7 Feb	1877			(D) Children's Activities (4)
7 Feb	1877			(E) Activities — Countryside (4)
7 Feb	1877			(F) Leisure Time (4)
	c1877			Merton

Date		Pat No.	Marks	Pattern name
	c1877			Spring
	c1877			Porcelain Rose
	c1877			Porcelain Tulip
cFeb	1878?			Bird (No 1) 2/78
cFeb	1878?			Bird (No 2) 2/78
cFeb	1878?			Bird (No 3) 2/78
cFeb	1878?			Bird (No 4) —
Mar	1878	8578		Tycoon 3/78
Mar	1878	8645		Tycoon 3/78
cMay	1878			No 92 5/78
cSep	1878	1145		Porcelain Swifts 9/78
Feb	1879			Sultan Mirza Service
Oct	1879			Merton 10/79
cApr	1880.?	9191/12		Denver 4/80
Apr	1880	9050/15		Texas 4/80
Feb	1881	2894/1		Merton cake stand 2/81
8 Feb	1881			Pastimes 1 2/85
		922/1		Pastimes 2 10/83
		922/1		Pastimes 3 10/83
4 May	1881			
Oct	1881	2630		Laburnam 10/81
29 Oct	1881			
	1882			W Bourne Wall Plaque /81
Jan	1883	1529		Storks Christening
Dec	1883			Malo 12/83

NEW REGISTRATION SYSTEM — 1884

Date		Reg No.	Pat Name
Jan	1884		Ning Po 1/84
May	1884	7044	Merton 9/85
May	1884	7044	No 57 11/87
May	1884	7044	Alaska 1/87
Jun	1884	3948	Orange Border 6/84
Jul	1884	9461	
Oct	1884	14058	Woodland 9/85
Oct	1884	15551	
Sep	1885	33829	

Date		Pat No.	Marks	Pattern name
Sep	1885	34018		
Mar	1886	46084		
May	1886	49737		
Dec	1886	63054		
Jan	1887	65227		
Jan	1888	93597		
Jun	1888	5285		Orange Floral
Nov	1888	114320		
Jan	1889	118288		
Aug	1890	154429		
Apr	1892	190816		

BROWNFIELD GUILD POTTERY SOCIETY LTD

Date		Reg No.	Pat No.	Manufacturer
Feb	1893	208185-6		The Guild
Mar	1893	210792		The Guild
Sep	1893	218156		The Guild
Jan	1894	226227		The Guild
Jun	1894	233711		The Guild

BROWNFIELD POTTERY LIMITED

Dec	1898		Tongue 12/98

OTHER KNOWN PATTERNS

Madras (Art Journal Advert 1884)
Laburnham (Art Journal Advert 1884)
Niel (Art Journal Advert 1884)
Rienzi (Art Journal Advert 1884)
Cyprus (Art Journal Advert 1884)

PLATE DESIGNS IN THE 1880 CATALOGUE SPODE MANUSCRIPTS — UNIVERSITY OF KEELE

Taunton, Sylvan, Bangor, St Germain, Dartmouth, Bangor, Marble, Rose Leaf, Richelieu, Cambridge, Suez.

APPENDIX 4

LIST OF BROWNFIELD JUGS: 1837-1900

Bracketed Numbers are Estimated Pattern Numbers
(p indicates a photo in the book; e is an engraving)

ROBINSON, WOOD & BROWNFIELD:
1837-1837

Date		Photo	Design name	Pat No
cSep	1837	p	Transfer Printed Jug	30
	c1837	p	Transfer Printed Jug	70
	c1837		Versailles Water Ewer	
	c1837	p	Canton Water Jug	
	c1837		Zoological Ewer	
1 Sep	1839	p	Vertical Columns jug	

WOOD & BROWNFIELD: 1837-1850

Date		Photo	Design name	Pat No
cJul	1839	p	Chinoiserie jug	103
1 Jan	1841	p	Willie	
30 Sep	1841	p	Solomon	
	c1842		Chinoiserie jug??	275
	c1842	p	Painted Floral jug	—
	c1842	p	Oriental jug	
1 Mar	1842	p	Jas Dixon jug??	
cJun	1842	p	Amoy jug	333
cNov	1842		Chinoiserie jug	388
22 Sep	1842	p	James Dixon jug	
cApr	1842		Chinoiserie jug??	580
cAug	1843	p	Nankin	773
cDec	1843		Japanese	885
cFeb	1844	p	Viola	1009
cMar	1846		Oriental jug	2109
c	1846	p	Portland Jug	(2150)
cAug	1847	p	Water Ewer??	2985
cSep	1847	p	Chinoiserie jug	3008
cNov	1847	p	'Portland' I	3134
cApr	1848	p	Portland II	3368
cApr	1848	p	'Portland' III	3371
Oct	1848	p	Snipe jug	3665
cJun	1849	p	Turin jug	4088
cSep	1849		Bouquet Water jug	4210
	1840-50	p	Precursor Lotus Jug	—

OCTOBER 1850 : 5000 PATTERNS APPROX.
WILLIAM BROWNFIELD 1850 - 1871

Date		Photo	Design name	Pat No
cNov	1850	p	'Portland' IV	5049
cFeb	1851	p	Eureka Water Jug	5272
cFeb	1851	p	Portland V	5348
cFeb	1851	p	Chinoiserie Jug	5348
10 Oct	1851	p	Plain Ewer (1st Reg Diamond)	
16 Oct	1851	p	Fuschia	5675?
cApr	1851	e	Water Ewer	5469
cJan	1852	p	Patent No 1 Jug (as No 38)	
cMar	1852	p	Bouquet Jug	6099
cMar	1852	p	No 7 Jug	6150/6
cMar	1852		Eupatoria Jug	
cJun	1852	p	'Rope' jug	6287/H
25 Oct	1852	e	Mazeppa	(6575?)
cMay	1853	p	Moldavia Water Ewer	6827
cOct	1853	p	Cuba Floral Jug	6932
cOct	1853	p	No 17 Chinoiserie Jug	6950
1 Apr	1854	p	Kent	841
cAug	1854	p	Clarendon Ewer	7787/4

Date		Photo	Design name	Pat No
	c1854	p	Kew Ewer	
8 May	1854	e	Jardinière	
cSep	1854	p	No 17 Jug	
cSep	1854	p	No 18 Floral Jug	7867
cSep	1854	p	No 18 Floral Jug	7871
cSep	1854	p	No 18 Floral Jug	7872
cMar	1855	p	No 21 Floral jug	8377
cApr	1855	p	Barley Ear Jug	8428#
26 Apr	1855	p	'Linenfold'	(8450?)
26 Apr	1855	p	Plain jug	
	1855	p	Wicker	(8900?)
	c1855	p	Cape Ivy Ewer	
30 Apr	1856	p	Ivy	9070
Apr	1856	p	Plain jug	
	c1856		'Farmer's Arms Jug' — made on this exact shape and moulding — no attributive marks.	
cSep	1856	p	No 28 Water Ewer	9474
cDec	1856	p	No 38 Jug	9638
cDec	1856		No 46 Alba Jug	9660
5 Jun	1857	p	'Tradescantia'	10,227
cSep	1857	p	No 45 Floral Jug	10,408
9 Dec	1857	p	'Arrowhead'	10,681
24 Aug	1858	p	Water Jug	
5 Oct	1858	p	Jewel	11,341
20 May	1859	p	Shamrock 1st	11,940
c Jul	1859	p	Greek	12.379
c Jul	1859		Antique	12,397
c Nov	1859	p	Fern 1 —	
5 Nov	1859	p	Fern 2	12,856
6 Jun	1860	p	Eglantine	(13,250?)
29 Oct	1860	p	'Floral'	13,902
6 Jul	1861	p	Donatello SK	13,495
4 Dec	1861	p	Union	14,918
4 Dec	1861	e	Passion Flower (jardinière)	
25 Jan	1862	p	International	15,376
14 Mar	1862	p	Mother & Child jug (Printed Mark)	
cJan	1863	p	Swiss I	(16,050)
cMar	1863	p	Universe	16,164/3
cMar	1863	p	Burton	16,176
cApr	1863	p	Swiss II	16,205
8 Jun	1863	e	Gothic (jardinière)	
14 Oct	1863	p	Albion	(16,620?)
23 Dec	1863		Plain jug shape	

INTRODUCTION OF NEW PATTERN
NUMBERING SYSTEM — 1864

Date		Photo	Design name	Pat No
29 Apr	1864	p	Argos	23
cMay	1864	p	No 35 variant	70
	c1864	p	Tyrol	103
	c1864	p	Tyrol	113
1 Apr	1865	p	Florence	244
30 Oct	1865	p	Tiverton	1898
7 Apr	1866	p	Alloa	209
15 Mar	1867	e	Glenny (jardinière)	
15 Mar	1867	p	Cashmere	285
21 Jun	1867	e	Napoleon	
12 Jun	1868	p	Cone Teapot	1054
12 Jun	1868	p	Hampton	
21 Oct	1868	p	Westminster	445
2 Apr	1869	e	Barlaston (jardinière)	
19 Jun	1869	p	Severn	639

Date		Photo	Design name	Pat No
	c1870	e	Lotus	
	c1870	e	Strawberry	
	c1870	e	Alexandra	
	c1870	e	Coblentz	
	c1870	e	Bayonne	
10 Jun	1870	p	Nile	784
10 Jun	1870		Plain jug	
10 Nov	1870	p	Marne	

WILLIAM BROWNFIELD & SON: 1871-1876

Date		Photo	Design name	Pat No
2 May	1871	p	Worcester	1008
6 May	1871	p	Greek Key jug (WP & GP)	
pre Oct	1871	p	Cockatoo	
14 Dec	1872	p	Cupid 1	1348
14 Dec	1872	p	Cupid 2	
16 Jun	1874	p	Aston Teapot	
10 Sep	1874	p	Bangor 1 (Twin Globes & RD)	
10 Sep	1874	e	Bangor 2	
10 Sep	1874	p	Mandarin 1	
10 Sep	1874	p	Mandarin 2	
10 Sep	1874	e	Hong Kong 1	
10 Sep	1874	—	Hong Kong 2	
10 Sep	1874	—	Hong Kong 3	
10 Sep	1874	e	Audley	
10 Sep	1874	—	Bangor Marble Ware	
10 Sep	1874	p	Lincoln Water Ewer	
10 Sep	1874	e	Kent Water Ewer	
preNov	1874	p	Bass	
10 Jun	1875		Sylvan jug (Bangor shape)	

WILLIAM BROWNFIELD & SONS: 1876-1892

Date		Photo	Design name	Pat No
29 Jan	1876	p	Yeddo 1 (1st Cartouche), (RD Twin Globes)	
29 Jan	1876	p	Yeddo 2	
29 Jan	1876	p	Yeddo 3	1695
29 Jan	1876	p	Audley	T1757
29 Jan	1876	p	Sisyphus	10/76
6 Sep	1876		Water jug	
7 Feb	1877	p	Medieval	
7 Feb	1877		Carnival	
10 Oct	1877	p	Olympus 9/79	5414
10 Oct	1877	p	Suez	
6 Nov	1877	e	Leek	
22 Dec	1877	p	Hudson No 1	
22 Dec	1877	p	Hudson 2	
22 Dec	1877	p	Hudson 3	
22 Dec	1877	p	Hudson 4	
22 Dec	1877	p	Hudson 5	
pre Dec	1877	p	Alsopp	
pre Mar	1878		Tycoon	
4 Dec	1878		Jardinière	
9 Jan	1879	p	Swirling Fish.i.e Dolphin jug?	
9 Jan	1879	p	Yesso Jug 11/80	
9Jan	1879	p	Sado 7/79	
9 Jan	1879	p	Ranga 12/79	
9Jan	1879		Denver	
9 Jan	1879	p	Daisy	5277
9 Jan	1879		Green Leaves Jug	
9 Jan	1879		Tudor	
9 Jan	1879	p	Unnamed	
pre Nov	1879	p	Merton I & II	
pre Feb	1880	p	Goose and Monkey jug	
26 Jan	1880	p	Basket	
25 May	1880	p	Missouri	

Jugs identified from the Brownfield Photographic Catalogue 1880

Date		Photo	Design name	Pat No
pre Jan	1881	p	Adonis	
pre Jan	1881	p	Clyde	
pre Jan	1881	p	Corinth B/81	
pre Jan	1881	p	Dunedin	
pre Jan	1881	p	Exe	
pre Jan	1881	p	Stanley	
pre Jan	1881	p	Stratford	
pre jan	1881	p	Tasso	
pre Jan	1881	p	Truro (two impressed 1885 B&E)	
pre Jan	1881	p	Solon	
pre Jan	1881	p	Oxford	
pre Jan	1881	e	Dorking	
pre Jan	1881	p	Taunton	
pre Jan	1881	p	Dartmouth	
pre Jan	1881	p	St Germain	
pre 1881		p	Prunus	
	1881	p	Neil (Niel?)	
8 Feb	1881	e	Pastimes	
8 Feb	1881	e	Wisconsin	
4 May	1881	p	Mistletoe	
4 Oct	1881		Water jug	
4 Ap	1882	e	'Pumpkin' (?) Jug Reg No 379212	
pre Nov	1882	p	Ayr	
24 Jan	1883	e	Jug	393106
18 Jun	1883	e	Jug	399556
18 Jun	1883	e	Gentleman Jug	399557
25 Aug	1883	p	Montana	
13 Oct 1883		e	Tree Trunk jug	405363
pre Feb	1884	p	Gypsy I	

Jugs identified from the new Registration System Archives, Kew

Date		Photo	Design name	Pat No
Feb	1884	e	Ewer	1629
Jun	1884	e	Jug	7627
Jan	1885	e	Jug	20555
Mar	1887	e	Jug	71415
Jul	1887		Plain Jug Shape	77821
May	1888	e	Jug	100389
Jul	1889	e	Jug	128561
Mar	1890	e	Jug	14665
8 Jun	1890	e	Jug	15070
pre	1892		Perforated Celtic jug	
Mar	1892	e	Jug	190591
pre Oct	1892	p	Devon water ewer	

BROWNFIELD GUILD POTTERY SOCIETY COMPANY LTD 1892-1898

Date		Photo	Design name	Pat No
Oct	1892	e	Jug	200390
Nov	1893	e	Jug	223134

BROWNFIELD POTTERY LTD: 1898-1900

1900?	Cromer	Advertised	
1900?	Stuart	in the	
1900?	Mimosa	Pottery Gazette	

PRECISE DATE OF INITIAL PRODUCTION UNKNOWN

	Photo	Design name
?	p	Gypsy
?	p	Tiber Mosaic jug?
?	p	Wye Mosaic jug

APPENDIX 5

Factory Marks on Brownfield products

Robinson, Wood & Brownfield (1837-1837)

1. Printed RW&B — 'Opaque Stone China' plate Pat No 24.
2. Printed RW&B — Transfer Printed jug — Pat No 30.
3. 'Published by RW&B' — 'Vertical Columns' jug.
4. Printed Coronet, Printed 'RW&B' — 'Canton' Ewer.

Wood & Brownfield (1837-1850)

1. Printed W&B. 'Pearl Ware', 'Amoy' and Painted Pattern Number — plate Pat No 54.
2. 'Published by Wood & Brownfield' — 'Willie' and 'Solomon' jugs.
3. Printed Garter Mark with Crown and 'WB' — 'Alma' plate.
4. Impressed 'W&B' — (J P Cushion — Ceramic Marks).
5. Printed Cartouche with Plate Pattern Name (with or without 'W&B').
6. Printed Coat of Arms 'W&B' — 'Real Ironstone' plate.
7. Printed Garter Mark and Jug Pattern Name and 'W&B' — 'Turin' jug.
8. Printed Coronet, Printed 'Canton' and Printed 'W&B'.
9. Painted Pattern Number and Factory Sunburst Mark '*' — Comport Pattern Number '4140 / 4'.
10. Impressed Cartouche, 'W&B', 'Cobridge' and 'Opaque Stone China'.
11. Printed Factory Marks alone — '*', 'o'.
12. Printed Cartouche with Arrow, Pattern Name and 'W&B' — 'Snipe' jug.

William Brownfield (1850-1871)

1. Printed Garter Mark with Crown and 'WB' — 'Alma' plate.
2. Circular Impressed 'Brownfield', Printed Pattern Name and 'WB' — 'Bude' plate.
3. Printed Cartouche and 'WB' — 'Bouquet' plate.
4. Registration Diamond only — 'Fuchsia', 'Mazeppa', 'Kent', 'Wicker', 'Linenfold', 'Tradescantia', 'Arrowhead' and 'Jewel' (1851-59).
5. Moulded Registration Diamond and Printed 'No ...' — 'No ...'.
6. Potter's Marks and Painted Pattern Number — 'Barley Ear' jug.
7. Staffordshire Knot alone — 'Barley Ear' jug.
8. Staffordshire Knot and Registration Diamond — 'Fern', 'Shamrock' and 'Eglantine' jugs.
9. Cartouche, Reg Diamond and Staffs Knot — 'Donatello', 'Union' jugs.
10. Cartouche and Staffs Knot — 'Swiss' and 'Universe' jugs.
11. Printed Registration Diamond alone — 'Mother and Child' jug.
12. Circular Trade Mark and Reg Diamond — 'Argos', 'Albion', 'Tyrol', 'Florence' jugs (1863-72).
13. Cartouche only — 'Hampton' jug (Kathy Hughes).
14. Cartouche, Reg Diamond and 'WB' — 'Westminster' jug.
15. Impressed Pattern Name only — 'Clyde', 'Burton' jugs.
16. Painted Pattern Number, Printed Factory Sunburst Mark '*'. Printed Number '...' — 'No 46' Comport.
17. Painted Pattern Number ('12,397') and Factory Printed Sunburst Mark '*' — 'Antique' jug.
18. Printed 'No ...' and Factory Sunburst Mark '*' — 'No 7' plate.
19. Moulded Registration Diamond and Painted Pattern Number — ('16,038').
20. Erroneous Pattern Name 'Severn' on 'Westminster jugs.

William Brownfield & Son (1871-1876)

1. Twin Globes Trade Mark, Reg Diamond and Cartouche — 'Bangor', 'Yeddo', 'Hudson' jugs.
2. Printed Garter Mark and Crown, Moulded Staffs Knot, 'WB', Printed 'WB&S' — 'Paroquet' Dinner Service.
3. Moulded Staffordshire Knot and 'WB' and Printed No '...' — 'No 132' plate.

William Brownfield & Sons (1876-1892)

1. Impressed Pattern Name only — 'Truro', 'Bass', 'Burton', 'Alsopp' jugs.
2. Twin Globes Trade Mark and Cartouche — 'Sisyphus' jug.
3. Printed Twin Globes Trade Mark and Reg Diamond — 'Mandarin' jug.
4. Moulded Twin Globes, Cartouche and Printed Reg Diamond — 'Audley' jug.
5. Moulded Reg Diamond and Printed Twin Globes Trade Mark — 'Yesso', 'Ranga', 'Sado' jugs.
6. Impressed Jug Pattern Name and 'Brownfield' — 'Medieval', 'Carnival' jugs.
7. Impressed 'Brownfield' only — 'Pastimes' jug.
8. Impressed 'Brownfield', 'Dublin' alone — 'Dublin' jug.
9. Printed Twin Globes Trade Mark, Printed Reg Pattern Number, Impressed Reg Pat No (Erroneous), Impressed Date (85) — 'Woodland' plate.
10. Printed Twin Globes Trade Mark, Printed Reg Pat No, Impressed Date '9/85' — 'Merton' plate.
11. Printed Garter Mark, 'Brownfields', 'England' — 'Grecian Statue' plate.
12. Impressed 'Brownfield' and Impressed Factory Shape Number — Porcelain Figures.
13. Impressed Reg Diamond and Factory Shape Number — Porcelain Figures.
14. Printed 'Brownfields China', Printed 'Tiffany & Co, New York', Painted Pattern Number, Printed Reg Diamond Pattern Number (10361).
15. Erroneous Impressed Registration Diamond — 30/10/75 and Impressed 'Brownfield' — Porcelain Vases. Proper Registration Date — 1/12/75.
16. Printed Registration Diamond and Pat No only — 'Clamshell' Teapot (1883).
18. Shape Number alone — Some Porcelain Figures.

Brownfield Guild Pottery Society Company (1892-1897)

1. Printed Monogram.
2. Impressed 'BGP Co.'.

Brownfield Pottery Limited (1898-1900)

1. Printed 'Brownfields' within Circular Cartouche.
2. Impressed Pattern Name only — 'Solon' jug.

APPENDIX 6

BROWNFIELD PATTERN NUMBERS:
1837-64

An explanation of the painted numbers on the base of jugs, plates etc is now possible owing to some invaluable clues provided first by surviving products from the period 1837-40 and secondly by the foreman William Shaw who retired from the firm at the end of 1863 after 22 years of service. As explained in Chapter 7, the pattern numbers for 1837-40 show that items produced after Noah Robinson's death in September 1837 were no longer marked with RW&B only with W&B. From product Number 54 onwards, internal company policy was to omit any printed reference on their products to Noah Robinson's widow, who remained a partner until the Spring of 1841. The ONLY known exception to this rule is the registered 'Vertical Columns' jug of September 1839. It is, of course, impossible to calculate precisely at what pace new patterns were introduced in these early, formative years. We do, however, know from William Shaw that by the beginning of 1842, when he joined Wood & Brownfield, 200 patterns had already been used.

In his retirement speech in late 1863 William Shaw said that 16,700 patterns had been introduced by the firm. A vital clue in unravelling this numbering system came with the discovery of a "Swiss" jug with the number 16,256 on it. Other evidence showed that the Staffordshire knot (also on its base) indicated a manufacture date of between 1855-63. As Shaw retired at the end of September 1863, 16,256 is just 440 short of the number achieved by the firm by October or November (the end of the potter's year). Other similar case studies fitted into the same pattern — an "International" jug first produced in January1862 was found with the painted number 15,378, what one would expect for that month and year. The "Union" jug of December 1861 has a number 14,918, a number that accords with the approximate production level for the end of this year.

The estimates for the years 1841-56 do depend on some carefully reasoned assumptions — one of which is that Wood and Brownfield introduced far less patterns per year during the poor business years of the 1840s, an opinion supported by the annual review of the pottery trade given each Martinmas in the Staffordshire Advertiser. Another, is that William Brownfield accelerated the introduction of new patterns in the 1850s and early 1860s, seemingly before the 1855 Paris Exhibition and especially so prior to the 1862 International Exhibition in London, for which alone he offered 150 new designs some in different colour ranges and each different colour would have its own pattern number. A working hypothesis for the years 1842-51 shows a gradual build up from 400 patterns in November 1842, to 2550 in November 1846, to 5100 in November 1850, the time at which William Brownfield had just taken over sole control of the firm.

In February 1991 the author evolved a hypothetical numbering system for those enamelled jugs that had not yet been discovered and the calculation for the 'Tradescantia' jug of 5th June 1857 was 10,300. (These are the bracketed numbers found in Appendix 6.) Five months later an enamelled version of this jug was discovered with the number 10,227 — only 73 wide of the hypothetical figure. Appendix 6A provides an attempt to gauge just how many patterns Brownfields had introduced by the end of each potter's year — in November. Evidence taken from the jugs and plates themselves ensures that the calculations for the years 1856-63 are reliable to within 3-4 months.

The enamelled "Eglantine" of 1860 has not yet been found with a painted number, but the two jugs from 1859 have. The "Shamrock" of May 1859 has the number 11,940 while the "Fern" jug of Nov 1869 has the number 12,856 — approximately what one would expect on a jug introduced just over five months later. The "Fern" jug has, however, been discovered with no less than six different painted numbers — 12,856, 12,868, 12,869, 12,877, and under the new pattern numbering system 270 and 870. The reason for the many different numbers is straightforward — each enamelled version of "Fern" had a separate pattern number. However, there is still a problem — how to identify the first pattern number — ie that appropriate to its initial production when it was first registered and produced. In the case of "Fern" where many different enamelled jugs have survived, 12,856 is very probably the one introduced in Nov 1859.

The potter's year November 1861-62 was an especially busy time for new patterns in preparation for the coming London Exhibition. This 'extra busy' period raises a further problem in estimating the annual production level at the end of each year throughout the period 1837-64. The estimates contained in Appendix 6A are substantially based on a relatively steady progression in output and the dating of patterns is based on that progression. Occasional spurts in production (or a corresponding slowing down) will inevitably upset the calculations by up to 2 -4 months. This is unavoidable without any factory pattern book, but a carefully assessed approximation of pattern introduction dates is much better than none at all. The dinner service "Sweaborg" is a good example of this problem of pinpointing the date of introduction precisely. On a steady output progression, a date of approximately May 1855 would be indicated whereas other evidence strongly suggests that it was, in fact, probably introduced in late August 1855 — some three months later.

It should therefore be remembered that in using all the data in Appendices 6A-6C, an allowance of two to four months should be made in dating the introduction of a pattern numbered product.

PATTERN NUMBERS ON EARTHENWARE
AND STONEWARE: 1864-1894

It is much more difficult to explain the new pattern numbering system introduced in late 1864. The first reason for this is the paucity of jugs and plates etc which have a painted pattern number. Even those that have one do not always facilitate a clear dating of the year of the pattern's introduction, as opposed to its year of manufacture. A plate with a pattern number initially dating from 1864 could in a re-issued form have an impressed date for 1888. It is clear that a separate numbering was adopted for porcelain wares after 1871, but there is some doubt as to whether a whole range of pattern numbers preceded by the letter T constitute a separate entity or are an integral part of the post 1864 earthenware and stoneware numbering system.

The pace at which new pattern numbers were introduced clearly varies from one period to another, perhaps influenced by the introduction of porcelain in 1871 and also by the need to exhibit new patterns at the various International Exhibitions which William Brownfield (& Sons) attended in the years 1867-1888. Most problematical of all is the dearth of evidence for products manufactured in the late 1880s and 1890s. The highest numbered Brownfield pattern identified post 1864 is "9193" and this probably emanated from about 1892, just before the Co-Operative was launched. Nothing is known about the number of new patterns introduced per year after 1880 and some assumptions have had to be made about a steady rate of new patterns per year. Further research will be needed to clarify pattern introduction after 1880. Surviving marked examples mean that the figures for the years 1864-1876 are accurate to within a few months. Thereafter question marks must remain for the present. Even within the earlier period there are still some anomalies to be explained and these too will need further investigation and analysis.The figures given below relate to pattern production achieved by the end of November each year.

APPENDIX 6A

BROWNFIELD PATTERN NUMBERS: 1837-1864					
NOV 1837	40	NOV 1848	3750	MAY 1855	8470
NOV 1838	80	FEB 1849	3900	AUG 1855	8650
NOV 1839	120	MAY 1849	4050	NOV 1855	8830
NOV 1840	160	AUG 1849	4200	FEB 1856	9010
NOV 1841	200	NOV 1849	4350	MAY 1856	9200
NOV 1842	400	FEB 1850	4530	AUG 1856	9410
MAY 1843	640	MAY 1850	4680	NOV 1856	9590
NOV 1843	880	AUG 1850	4860	FEB 1857	9800
FEB 1844	1010	NOV 1850	5100	MAY 1857	10,150
MAY 1844	1140	FEB 1851	5375	AUG 1857	10,360
NOV 1844	1400	MAY 1851	5600	NOV 1857	10,580
FEB 1845	1530	AUG 1851	5780	FEB 1858	10,830
MAY 1845	1670	NOV 1851	5900	MAY 1858	11,050
AUG 1845	1810	FEB 1852	6075	AUG 1858	11,380
NOV 1845	1950	MAY 1852	6250	NOV 1858	11,550
FEB 1846	2100	AUG 1852	6425	FEB 1859	11,890
MAY 1846	2250	NOV 1852	6600	MAY 1859	12,235
AUG 1846	2400	FEB 1853	6735	AUG 1859	12,580
NOV 1846	2550	MAY 1853	6870	NOV 1859	12,940
FEB 1847	2700	AUG 1853	6980	FEB 1860	13,175
MAY 1847	2850	NOV 1853	7130	MAY 1860	13,450
AUG 1847	3000	FEB 1854	7350	AUG 1860	13,725
NOV 1847	3150	MAY 1854	7580	NOV 1860	14,000
FEB 1848	3300	AUG 1854	7800	NOV 1861	14,900
MAY 1848	3450	NOV 1854	8020	NOV 1862	15,950
AUG 1848	3600	FEB 1855	8240	NOV 1863	16,700

THE DATING OF PATTERN NUMBERS: 1864-1892 (EXCLUDING PORCELAIN)

Nov 1864	120	Nov 1879	(Sydney)	3280
1865	180	1880	(Melbourne)	3810
1866.	240	1881	(Adelaide)	4380
1867	400 (Paris)	1882		4910
1868	550	1883		5280
1869	750 (Amsterdam)	1884	(Crystal Palace) (Calcutta)	5790
1870	900	1885		6230
1871	1150 (London)	1886		6670
1872	1320 (Lyons)	1887		7110
1873	1430 (Vienna)	1888	(Paris)	7550
1874	1540	1889		7990
1875	1650 (Paris)	1890		8430
1876	1850 (Philadelphia)	1891		8870
1877	2280	1892		9300
1878	2750 (Paris) (Cancelled)			

APPENDIX 6B

PAINTED PATTERN MARKS ON BASE OF BROWNFIELD PRODUCTS.

(Found only on enamelled products)
(BRACKETED FIGURES = CONJECTURE)
(?? = Questionable attribution)

ROBINSON, WOOD & BROWNFIELD: 1837-37

Title	Pat No	Marks	Date
MANSION SUGAR BOWL			c1837
ZOOLOGICAL PLATE		7	c1837
CANTON PLATE			c1837
CANTON JUG			c1837
VERSAILLES WATER			c1837
JUG AND BASIN			c1837
NANKIN PLATE			c1837
VENETIAN SCENERY			c1837
OPAQUE STONE	22		cJul 1837
CHINA PLATES	24		cJul 1837
TR PRINTED JUG	30		cSep 1837
STONE CHINA PLATE	31		cSep 1837

WOOD & BROWNFIELD: 1837-1850

Title	Pat No	Marks	Date
GRECIAN STATUE PLATE		W&B	1837-50
ALBION PLATTER		W&B	1837-50
VENETIAN SCENERY		W&B	1837-50
EASTERN PLANTS		W&B	1837-50
MACAO PLATE		W&B	1837-50
AMOY PLATE	54	W&B	cFeb 1838
TR PRINTED JUG	70		Aug 1838
AMOY JUG	104	v	cJul 1839
WILLIE JUG		W&B	cJan 1841
JUDGEMENT— SOLOMON		W&B	cSep 1841
AMOY PLATE	303	COA	cMay 1842
IRONSTONE PLATE	309	COA	cMay 1842
IRONSTONE PLATE	328	COA	cJun 1842
AMOY JUG	333		cJun 1842
AMOY SERVICE	335	COA	cJun 1842
AMOY PLATE	338	COA	c Jun 1842
CHINOISERIE JUG	388		cNov 1842
ROSE PLATE	397	W&B	cNov 1842
CHINOISERIE DESSERT SET	428	W&B	cDec 1842
CHINOISERIE JUG ??	580	U	c Apr 1843
PRECURSOR No 35	642	3	cJun 1843
FLORAL PLATE	718	W&B	cJul 1843
NANKING JUG	773	v	cAug 1843

Title	Pat No	Marks	Date
SANDON PLATE ??	788	—	cAug 1843
JAPANESE JUG	885	W&B	cDec 1843
JAPANESE PLATE	885	W&B	cDec 1843
HINDOSTAN PLATE	917	W&B	cJan 1844
VIOLA JUG	1009		cFeb 1844
POMONA PLATE	1676	W&B	cJun 1845
ORIENTAL PLATE	1690	W&B	cJun 1845
TRANSFER PRINT JUG ??	1883	::	cAug 1845
WINDSOR WREATH	2030	W&B	cJan 1846
ORIENTAL JUG	2109	W&B	cMar 1846
CAKE DISH ??	2169		cFeb 1846
ALBA PLATE ??	2/2314		cJul 1846
PRECURSOR No 35	2602	3	cDec 1846
CHISWICK PLATE	2613	W&B	cDec 1846
WATER EWER ??	2614		cDec 1846
CHINOISERIE PLATE ??	2768	o	cApr 1847
WATER EWER ??	2985		Aug 1847
FORMOSA PLATE. ??	3005	W	cSep 1847
CHINOISERIE JUG	3008	U3	cSep 1847
CHINOISERIE JUG	3008	AA*	cSep 1847
PORTLAND SHAPE I.	3134		cNov 1847
FLORAL SCROLL	3159	W&B	cNov 1847
PLATE ??	3218	B	cJan 1848
ALMA PLATE	(3360)?	RD	20 Mar 1848
CABLE PLATE	(3361)?	RD	20 Mar 1848
PORTLAND SHAPE II	3368		cApr1848
PORTLAND SHAPE III	3371/1	—	cApr 1848
PLATE ??	3631	—	cSep 1848
SNIPE I JUG	3665	W&B *	cOct 1848
SNIPE II JUG	3665	W&B *	cOct 1848

(These two jugs are produced in quite different shapes.)

Title	Pat No	Marks	Date
MOULTAN PLATE	3738	RD	cNov 1848
BLACKBERRY PLATE		RD	c1848
MINI WATER JUG? ??	3890	H	cFeb 1849
PLATES & COMPORTS ??	3905/2		cMar 1849
FRUIT BOWL ??	3921	*	cMar 1849
TURIN JUG	4088	W&B *::	cJun 1849
CHINOISERIE JUG	4132/1	*	cJul 1849
FLORAL COMPORTS	4140	*	cJul 1849
FLORAL PLATE	4142/4		cJul 1849
FLORAL DESSERT SET	4150	*	cJul 1849
WATER JUG & BASIN	4210		cSep 1849
CHINOISERIE PLATE ??	4255	W::	cSep 1849
STRAWBERRY BLOSSOM	4314	* +	cNov 1849
FLORAL PLATE	4384		cNov 1849
COMPORT	4592	*M	cMar 1850
DOG ROSE PLATE	4595	*	cMar 1850
DOG ROSE PLATE	4598/4		cMar 1850
PLATE RD 20/3/48	4682		cJun 1850

WILLIAM BROWNFIELD: 1850-1871

Title	Pat No	Marks	Date
PORTLAND SHAPE V	5049	::	cNov 1850
ALBA PLATE	5146	::	cDec 1850
BOUQUET EDGED PLATE	5160/4		cDec 1850
ALBA COMPORT	5166	M	cDec 1850
ASCOT PLATE	—	P	c1850-55
EUREKA PLATE	5217/O	WB	cFeb 1851
BOUQUET EDGED PLATE	5267	p	cFeb 1851
EUREKA JUG	5272	H*	cFeb 1851
BOUQUET EDGED PLATE	5346/x	* JT	cFeb 1851
PORTLAND SHAPE V	5348x		cFeb 1851
PLATE	5438		cFeb 1851
BOUQUET EDGED PLATE	5590		cMay 1851
BOUQUET EDGED PLATE	5733		cAug 1851

Title	Pat No	Marks	Date
CLARENDON EWER	(5850)?		10 Oct 1851
FUCHSIA JUG	(5875)?		16 Oct 1851
FLORAL PLATE	5915/4		cDec 1851
EALING TOILET SET	5920	WT	cDec 1851
MONTANA SHAPED JUG ??	5946	B	cDec 1851
COMPORT ??	2/6035		cFeb 1852
BOUQUET EDGED PLATE	6038	!	cFeb 1852
PLATE	6055	*o	cFeb 1852
PLATE	6075	o	cFeb 1852
BOUQUET JUG	6099	H	cMar 1852
No 7 JUG (SET)	6150/6	*+	cMar 1852
No 7 PLATE.	6174	10	cMar 1852
No 7 PLATE	6176/2		cMar 1852
No 7 PLATE	6181	10	cMar 1852
No 8 PLATE	6189	R	cMar 1852
PLATTER	6189	m	cMar 1852
'ROPE' JUG	6280/2	H	cJun 1852
'ROPE' JUG	6287/4	GP	cJun 1852
PLATE	6370	*	cAug 1852
No 7 PLATE	6411		cAug 1852
No 7 PLATE	6412		cAug 1852
No 12 PLATE	6487	*	cSep 1852
No 9 PLATE	6510		cOct 1852
No 9 PLATE	6514	*o	cOct 1852
No 9 JUG & BOWL	RD		cOct 1852
FLORAL PLATE ??	6566/2	:: ú	cOct 1852
MAZEPPA JUG	(6575 ?)		25 Oct 1852
No 13 BOWL	6707	::	cFeb 1853
No 8 SOUP BOWL	6817		cMay 1853
MOLDAVIA EWER	6827	*	cMay1853
SAVONA SERVICE	6875	WB	cJun 1853
No 13 SWEET DISH			cJul 1853
No 13 PLATE		3	cJul 1853
No 13 SIDE PLATE	6918		cJul 1853
No 13 PLATTER	6923		cJul 1853
CUBA JUG	6932	::o	cAug 1853
CHINOISERIE JUG	6950		cAug 1853
No 15 TUREEN BASE	7146		cDec 1853
No 15 SOUP PLATE	7148		cDec 1853
POMPEII PLATE	7324/1		cFeb 1854
WATER EWER ??	7347/1		cFeb 1854
RASSOV POT	7373	*	cMar 1854
COMPORT	7447	*	cMar 1854
BLUE EDGED PLATE	7459	*o	cMar 1854
KENT JUG	RD 1/4/54		1 Apr 1854
FLORAL PLATE	7589/1	*o	cJun 1854
FLORAL PLATE	7598	*o	cJun 1854
ALBA PLATE ??	7646		cJul 1854
COMPORT RD 2/10/54	7691.		cJul 1854
BOUQUET EDGED PLATE	7727/11	*v	cAug 1854
BOUQUET EDGED PLATE	7732		cAug 1854
BOUQUET EDGED PLATE	7738	*o	cAug 1854
ALMA PLATE	7749	*=	cAug 1854
ALMA PLATE	7750	*o	cAug 1854
ALMA PLATE	7752	*	cAug 1854
MOLTKE COMPORT	7764	10/75	cAug 1854
CLARENDON BOWL	7787/4	*	cAug 1854
No 18 PLATE	(7865)?		cSep 1854
No 17 JUG	—		cSep 1854
No 18 FLORAL JUG	7867	*o	cSep 1854
No 18 FLORAL JUG/PLATE)	(7875/0)		(cSep 1854)
AZOFF PLATE	8057		cDec 1854
WATFORD PLATE	8073		cDec 1854
BOUQUET EDGED PLATE	8079	#	cDec 1854
BOUQUET EDGED PLATE	8152	*	c Jan 1855
ANAPA TOILET SET	8221	10*o	cFeb 1855

Title	Pat No	Marks	Date	Title	Pat No	Marks	Date
No 21 FLORAL JUG	8377	*o	cMar 1855	PLATE	10,714	WB	c Jan 1858
No 21 FLORAL JUG/ PLATE	(8400)?		cMar 1855	CALPEE PLATE	10,870	WB	cMar 1858
SWEABORG DINNER SET	8413	*	cMay 1855	No 48 PLATE	10,910	W	cMar 1858
KENT JUG RD 1/4/54	8416		cMay 1855	No 47 PLATE	10,949	* !	cMar 1858
KENT JUG RD 1/4/54	8418/7	3	cMay 1855	No 47 PLATE	10,951	W	cMar 1858
BARLEY EAR JUG	8428	#	cMay 1855	PLATE RD 2/6/58	10,979/1	W	cMar 1858
'LINENFOLD' JUG	(8430)?		cMay 1855	No 58 PLATE	(10,990)?		cMar 1858
No 27 PLATE	8443	*o	cMay 1855	No 60 PLATE	11,047/1	*o	cMay 1858
ALBA ROSE PLATE ??	8500	:	cJun 1855	DETROIT PLATE	11,250	WB	cJul 1858
CHARIOT JUG ??	8614/2	F	cAug 1855	JEWEL JUG	11,341	/D	cOct 1858
DOG ROSE PLATE	8627	*o	cAug 1855	JEWEL JUG	11,342		cOct 1858
FLORAL PLATE	8649	*	cAug 1855	JEWEL JUG	11,348		cOct 1858
No 15 PLATE	8714		cSep 1855	JEWEL JUG	11,352		cOct 1858
KINBURN PLATE	8740	*	cOct 1855	JEWEL JUG	11,354		cOct 1858
No 26 PLATE	8755/0	* P	cOct 1855	JEWEL JUG	11,358		cOct 1858
No 26 PLATE SK		WB	cOct 1855	FLORAL PLATE	11,703	/p B	cJan 1859
EUPATORIA PLATTER		WB	c1855	FLORAL PLATE	11,707	*o	c Jan 1859
WICKER JUG	(8820)?		cNov 1855	No 61 PLATE	11,728	* B	c Jan 1859
EUPATORIA PLATE	8829	*v	cNov 1855	SHAMROCK JUG	11,926		cFeb 1859
PRECURSOR NO 35	8907	v	cFeb 1856	SHAMROCK JUG	11,936		cFeb 1859
No 27 PLATE	8940/1	*	cFeb 1856	SHAMROCK JUG	11,940		cFeb 1859
No 27 PLATE	8947	/:: *o	cFeb 1856	SHAMROCK JUG	11,949		cFeb 1859
No 27 PLATE	—	*o W	cFeb 1856	MONTEBELLO TUREEN	12,030/7	*	cApr 1859
No 18 FLORAL PLATE	9046/2	W	cMar 1856 I	No 53 PLATE	12,068		cApr 1859
VY JUG RD 30/4/56	9070		cApr 1856	GREEK JUG	12,379	* o	cJul 1859
T-PRINTED FLORAL JUG	(9100)?		cApr 1856	ANTIQUE JUG	12,397	*	cJul 1859
KARS PLATE	9146/6	*W	cApr 1856	DINNER SERVICE	12,456		cApr 1859
IVY JUG RD 30/4/56	9149		cApr 1856	No 54 PLATE	12,545		cApr 1859
T-PRINTED FLORAL JUG	9161	* o	cApr 1856	No 54 PLATE	12,551	B !	cAug 1859
No 34 PLATE	9202	* o	cJun 1856	No 54 PLATE	12,563/8	S *o	cAug 1859
No 28 PLATE RD 10/2/51	9233	* o	cJun 1854	No 54 PLATE	12,573	*o	cAug 1859
No 28 PLATE	9234	*	cJun 1856	TURKISH PLATE	12,630	B	cSep 1859
COMPORT	9285	W	cJul 1856	FERN JUG	12,856		cNov 1859
IVY JUG	9401/2	M	cSep 1856	FERN JUG	12,865		cNov 1859
No 8 SOUP BOWL 10/80	9417	S	cSep 1856	FERN JUG	12,868		cNov 1859
IVY JUG RD 30/4/56	9418		cSep 1856	FERN JUG	12,869/3		cNov 1859
IVY JUG	9419		cSep 1856	FERN JUG	12,872		cNov 1859
T-PRINTED FLORAL JUG	9429		cSep 1856	FERN JUG	12,877		cNov 1859
No 28 EWER	9474		cSep 1856	GREEK JUG	12,883	*v	cNov 1859
COMPORT	9556		cNov 1856	No 21 FLORAL JUG	12,883	*	cNov 1859
THRACE PLATE	9568	*o	cNov 1856	No 55 PLATE	13,167	M	cFeb 1860
ALBA COMPORT	9630 .	/	cNov 1856	No 56 PLATE	13,173	B	cFeb 1860
No 35 PLATE	9632	::	cDec 1856	FRUIT BOWL	13,189	*o	cFeb 1860
No 38 EASTERN JUG	9638		cDec 1856	EGLANTINE	(13,250 ?)		cJun 1860
No 35 PLATE	9632	::	cDec 1856	DINNER SERVICE	13,457	WB	cJun 1860
No 38 EASTERN JUG	9638		cDec 1856	DONATELLO	13,495		cJun 1860
SUGAR BOWL	9649	*5	cDec 1856	DONATELLO	13,501		cJul 1860
COMPORT	9656		cDec 1856	DONATELLO	13,504		cJul 1860
No 46 ALBA JUG	9660	46	cDec 1856	EGLANTINE	13,50—		cJul 1860
FRUIT PLATE	9694	*o	cDec 1856	DONATELLO	13,533		cJul 1860
FRUIT COMPORT	9695	*o	cDec 1856	FLORAL PLATE	13,899	RD	cJul 1860
FRUIT COMPORT	9696	*o	cDec 1856	FLORAL JUG	13,902		cJul 1860
FRUIT PLATE	9706	*	cDec 1856	FLORAL JUG	13,909		cOct 1860
ALVA (?) PLATE	9930	s	cMar 1857	FLORAL JUG	13,921		cOct 1860
No 40 PLATTER	—	* o	cMay 1857	FLORAL JUG	13,923		cOct 1860
No 40 COMPORT	10,102		cMay 1857	PLATE	14,397		cMay 1861
No 40 COMPORT	10,108	*	cMay 1857	PLATE	14,399		cMay 1861
'TRADESCANTIA' JUG	10,227		cJun 1857	DESSERT SERVICE	14,406	*	cMay 1861
No 45 FLORAL JUG	10,408		cSep 1857	F 63 PLATE	14,670	*o	cAug 1861
No 46 PLATE	10,414		cSep 1857	COMPIEGNE PLATE	14,847	* E	cNov 1861
No 46 TUREEN	10,414		cSep 1857	UNION JUG	14,910		cDec 1861
No 46 PLATTER	10,417	*	cSep 1857	UNION JUG	14,918		cDec 1861
PLATE	10,585		cNov 1857	INTERNATIONAL	15,378		cJan 1862
PLATE	10,592	*	cNov 1857	INTERNATIONAL	15,406		cJan 1862
PLATE RD 2/10/54	10,597	:: *o	cNov 1857	INTERNATIONAL	15,478		cFeb 1862
'ARROWHEAD' JUG	10,681		cDec 1857	BERLIN PLATTER RD 14/3/62	—		c1862

Title	Pat No	Marks	Date
PLATE	16,038	RD	cDec 1862
DENMARK PLATE	(16,050)? * G		cDec 1862
UNIVERSE	16,164/3 K		cFeb 1863
BURTON	16,176		cFeb 1863
SWISS	16,205		cMar 1863
SWISS	16.238		cMar 1863
SWISS	16,254		cApr 1863
SWISS	16,256		cApr 1863
DINNER PLATES	16,423		cJun 1863
ALBION	(16,620?)		cOct 1863

(Oct 1863 — Retiring Foreman pinpoints 16,700 patterns)

INTRODUCTION OF NEW PATTERN NUMBERING SYSTEM —1864

Title	Date	Pat No	Marks
JEWEL JUG	1864	19	RD 5/10/58
ARGOS	1864	23	RD 29/4/64
ARGOS	1864	39	RD 29/4/64
ARGOS	1864	55	RD 29/4/64
GENEVA PLATE	1864	—	RD 30/6/64
No 38 JUG	1864	70	
No 68 PLATE	1864	—	
ALLOA JUG	1864	103	RD 20/4/64
ALLOA JUG	1864	113	RD 20/4/64
WESTMINSTER	1864	140	RD 21/10/68
WESTMINSTER	1864	151/1	RD 21/10/68
No 73 DINNER SET	1864	166	RD 5/1/64
No 74 BOWL	1864	—	
No 76 CAKE PLATE	1864?		
No 79 PLATE	1864	—	RD 26/11/63
TIVERTON	1865	189	RD 30/10/65
FLORENCE	1865	244	RD 1/4/65
FERN JUG	1865	270	RD 5/11/59
TIVERTON	1865	—	RD 30/10/65
ALLOA	1866	204	RD 20/4/66
ALLOA	1866	209	RD 20/4/66
ALLOA	1866	218	RD 20/4/66
PLATE	1867	278	(SK)
CASHMERE	1867	279	RD 15/3/67
CASHMERE	1867	285/3	RD 15/3/67
CASHMERE	1867	295/4	RD 15/3/67
WESTMINSTER	1868	350,	RD 21/10/68
ALLOA	1868	402	RD 20/4/66
WESTMINSTER	1868	445/3	RD 21/10/68
HAMPTON	1868	446.	RD 12/6/68
WESTMINSTER	1868	550	RD 21/10/68
SEVERN	1869	639	RD 19/6/69
SEVERN	1869	658	RD 19/6/69
SEVERN	1869	659	RD 19/6/69
CLYDE	1869	662	
SEVERN	1869	679	RD 19/6/69
NILE	1870	763	RD 10/6/70
NILE	1870	784	RD 10/6/70
ALLOA	1870	812	RD 20/4/66
FERN JUG	1870	870	RD 5/11/59
MARNE	1870	—	RD 10/11/70
SMYRNA PLATE	1870	—	RD 10/11/70
CRESSY PLATE	1870?	T2801	
No 114 BOWL	1870?	T4319	
MARSALA PLATE	1870?	T4787	
No 131 PLATE	1870?	T5970/2	RD 10/11/70
WORCESTER	1871	1008	RD 2/5/71
WORCESTER	1871	1018	RD 2/5/71
WORCESTER	1871	1019	RD 2/5/71
CONE TEAPOT	1871	1054.	RD 12/6/68

WILLIAM BROWNFIELD & SON: 1871-1876

Title	Date	Pat No	Marks
No 7 BOWL	1872 ?	1218	2/86
CUPID	1872	1348	RD 14/12/72
CUPID	1872	1376	RD 14/12/72
PAROQUET DINNER SET	1872		RD 14/12/72
BANGOR	1874	—	RD 10/9/74
LINCOLN	1874	—	RD 10/9/74
SYLVAN (PLATE)	1875?	1258/7	
SYLVAN PLATE	1875	1275	RD 10/6/75

WILLIAM BROWNFIELD & SONS: 1876-92

Title	Date	Pat No	Marks
YEDDO JUG	1877	1695	RD 29/1/76
No 57 PLATE	1877	1753	11/87
AUDLEY JUG	1877	1757-T	RD 29/1/76
SHAKESPEARE PLATE	1877	1790-T	
HUDSON	1877	1880	RD 22/12/77
HUDSON	1877	1886/T	RD 22/12/77
TIVERTON	1877	1898	RD 30/10/65
HUDSON	1877	1899.	RD 22/12/77
MEDIEVAL PLATE	1877	8403/III	RD 7/2/77
MEDIEVAL PLATE	1877	T/8403	RD 7/2/77
No 92 PLATE	1878	2690	WB 5/78
TYCOON PLATE	1878	8645	3/78
LABURNUM PLATE	1878	—	4/78
MERTON JUG	1879	2001	
CRIMSON EDGED COMPORT	1879?	D2269/2	
MERTON JUG	1879	2146	
MERTON JUG	1879	2739	10/79
DAISY JUG	1879	5277	RD 9/1/79
OLYMPUS JUG	1879	5414 *	7/79
PLATE	1880	2740	1/80
TEXAS PLATE	1880	4050	4/80
YEDDO JUG	1880	6201	6/83
TEXAS PLATE	1880	7050	4/80
SMYRNA PLATE	1880?	7497	RD 10/11/70
DENVER PLATE	1880	9191/12	1/80
DAYTON PLATE	1880	9572	11/80
MISTLETOE JUG	1881	2382	11/81
MERTON CAKE STAND	1881	2894/1	2/81
MERTON PLATE	1881	3020	
SADO JUG	1881		RD 9/1/79
MERTON PLATE	1885	— 9/85	RD 5/84
WOODLAND PLATE	1885	— 3/85	RD 10/84
CYPRUS PLATE	1885?	8899/3	
CYPRUS PLATE	1885?	8895/T	–/89
CYPRUS BOWL	1885?	8899/10	4/8
ALASKA PLATE	1887		RD 7044 1/87
ORANGE FLORAL PLATE	1888	5285p	6/88

APPENDIX 6C

AUTHENTICATION OF NUMBERED ITEMS 1-150?

No	Pat No	Authentication
No 1 Jug	—	Same jug shape and transfer print as No 38.

[PRINTED ON THE BOTTOM 'PATENT No 1'.]

No	Pat No	Authentication
No 7 Jug	6150	RD 10/10/51
No 7 Jug	6150	RD 10/10/51
No 7 Plate	6181	Same pattern
No 7 Plate	6411	Impressed Brownfield
No 7 Plate	?	Factory marks *o
No 7 Bowl	1218	Same No 7 pattern
No 8 Plate	6189	Same pattern as No 7
No 8 Bowl	6817	Same pattern as No 7
No 8 Bowl	9417	Same pattern as No 7
No 9 Plate	6510	Printed mark
No 9 Plate	6514	Printed marks * / o
No 9 Jug	—	Illegible RD
No 12 Plate	6487	Printed marks * / o
No 13 Dish	—	Printed marks * / —
No 13 Bowl	6707	Painted marks ::.
No 13 Platter	6923	Otherwise unmarked
No 15 Platter	7146	Factory mark *
No 15 Plate	8714	Same Printing No 15
No 16 Jug	6932	Printed WB
No 17 Jug	—	Same scene as Portland Shape IV. Impressed 17
No 18 Jug	7867	Same shape regd 14/3/62
No 18 Jug	7871	Same shape regd 14/3/62
No 18 Jug	7872	Same shape regd 14/3/62
No 19 Jug	5272	Impressed 19 (Eureka Jug) Garter Mark — "WB"
No 21 Jug	8377	Same shape regd 14/3/62.
No 21 Jug	—	Same shape regd 14/3/62.
No 24 Plate	—	"24" Printed WB
No 26 Plate	8755/0	Staffs Knot, WB
No 27 Plate	8443	Factory marks * / o
No 27 Plate	8940	Factory marks * / o
No 27 Plate	8947	Appropriate Pat No
No 28 Plate	9233	Reg D 10/2/51
No 28 Plate	9234	Reg D 10/2/51
No 28 Ewer	9474	Reg D 10/2/51
No 34 Plate	9202	Factory mark *
No 35 Plate	9632	Painted marks ::
No 38 Jug	9638	Factory mark *
No 40 Comport	10,108	RD 2/10/54
No 40 Plate	—	RD 2/10/54
No 45 Jug	10,408	Factory mark *
No 46 Jug	9660	Pat No, Painted 46
No 46 Tureen	10,414	Reg D 27/11/56
No 46 Plate	10,414	Same pattern as Tureen
No 46 Comport	10,414	Same pattern as Tureen
No 47 Plate	10,949	Factory marks */o
No 47 Plate	10,951	Factory marks */W
No 48 Jug	8,221	RD 26/11/55
No 48 Plate	10,910	Border as No 47 Plate
No 53 Plate	12,068	Pat No — proximity to No 54
No 53 Comport	12,068	Pat No — proximity to No 54
No 54 Tureen	12,56?	WB

No	Pat No	Authentication
No 54 Plate	12,551	Pattern as Tureen Base
No 54 Comport	12,56?	SK — W.B
No 54 Plate	12,573	Factory Marks *o
No 55 Plate	13,167	Pat No & impressed M
No 56 Plate	13,173	Pat No & impressed B
No 57 Plate	1,753	RD 7044
No 58 Plate	—	Unmarked specimen —
No 60 Plate	11,047	RD 2/10/54
No 60 Plate		RD 2//10/54
No 61 Plate	11,728	RD 2/10/54
No 68 Plate	—	Number & Coronet
No 73 Service	166	RD 5/1/64
No 74 Bowl	—	Same pattern as No 73
No 76 Cake plate	—	Unmarked Example
No 79 Platter	—	RD 26/11/63
No 87 Comport	—	Unmarked Example —
No 89 Plate	—	Unmarked Example —
No 92 Plate	2690	Impressed Brownfield
No 93 Comport	1365	Unmarked Example
No 104 Service	—	Unmarked Example
No 110 Jug	—	Unmarked Example
No 112 Plate	—	Unmarked Example
No 114 Bowl	T4319	Unmarked
No 115 Plate	—	Impressed Brownfield
No 115 Platter	—	Twin Globes WB & Son.
No 125 Jug	—	Unmarked Example
No 131 Plate	T5970/2	RD 10/11/70
No 132 Plate		Staffs knot & WB

TOTAL NUMBER OF DIFFERENT 'NUMBERED ITEMS FOUND TO DATE **(49)**

TOTAL NUMBER OF SPECIFIC BROWNFIELD FACTORY MARKS FOUND TO DATE **(39)**

A. REGISTRATION DIAMOND **(11)**
(7, 28, 40, 46, 48, 57, 60, 61, 73, 79, 131)

B. MOULDED STAFFS KNOT **(3)** (26, 54, 132)

C. IMPRESSED BROWNFIELD **(2)** (92, 115)

D. FACTORY MARKS "*" "o", or "§" **(12)**
(9, 12, 13, 15, 17, 18, 27, 34, 35, 38, 45, 47)

E. PRINTED BROWNFIELD **(3)** (16, 19, 24)

F. SHAPE REGISTERED LATER **(1)** (21)

G. IDENTICAL T/P PATTERN **(4)** (1, 8, 48, 74)

H. KNOWN PATTERN SERIES **(3)** (53, 55, 56, 114)

CERTAIN AUTHENTICATION **(39)**

UNMARKED EXAMPLES EXCEPT NUMBER **(10)**
(58, 68, 76, 87, 89, 93, 104, 110, 112, 125.)

TOTAL **49**

TEAPOT DESIGNS
(INCLUDING BROWNFIELDS)

Date		Reg No	Maker	Title
14 Jun	1843	7505	S Alcock	—
14 Dec	1843	12331	G F Bowers	—
1 Mar	1844	16687	Hamilton & Moore	—
7 Mar	1844	16871	T & J Lockett	—
11 Apr	1844	17714	Hilditch & Hopwood	—
26 Nov	1844	1844 22883	Ray & Wynn	—
7 Nov	1844	23210	Thos Edwards	—
5 Jul	1845	28671	George Phillips	—
26 Sep	1846	37421	J Ridgway	—
3 Nov	1846	37935	W Ridgway	—
25 Sep	1847	45992	John Wedge Wood	—
20 Jan	1849	57506	Davenport	—
27 Mar	1849	59245	Cope & Edwards	—
17 Mar	1851	77488	J Ridgway	—
21 Jul	1851	79753	T & R Boote	—
24 Jul	1851	79782	T Till	—
22 Nov	1852	87883	Pankhurst & Dimmock	—
14 Jan	1853	88987	Davenport	Niagara
7 May	1853	11123	J Alcock	—
18 Jul	1853	91737	J Edwards	—
5 Oct	1853	92768	Venables&Mann	Baltic
12 Oct	1853	92869	Livesey, Powell & Bishop	—
24 Dec	1853	93708	J Alcock	Bluebell
6 Oct	1854	97141	Davenport	Cambridge
5 Mar	1855	99579	Elsmore & Forster	—
27 Nov	1856	107708	Davenport	Union
8 Dec	1858	117336	T & R Boote	New Grenade
29 Mar	1859	119137	T & R Boote	Atlantic
20 Nay	1859	119968	W B	SHAMROCK

(This was based on the jug design and not registered separately.)

Date		Reg No	Maker	Title
12 Apr	1861	139714	Davenport	Eric
30 Aug	1862	154221	T & R Boote	Floral
6 Mar	1863	160319	G L Ashworth	Halifax
17 Oct	1863	167374	T & R Boote	Mocho
31 Oct	1863	167762	E T Wood	Corn-on-the-Cob
18 May	1864	174795	G Ray	—
28 Jul	1864	176916	Holland & Green	—
10 Nov	1864	181214	Elsmore & Forster	Olympic
29 Nov	1864	181843	Hope & Carter	—
4 Apr	1866	207201	Elsmore & F	Laurel Wreath
25 Sep	1867	211874	Powell & Bishop	—
6 Nov	1867	213430	W J A Bailey	Key
28 Feb	1868	217112	W J A Bailey	Victoria
12 Jun	1868	219317	WB	CONE
19 Jun	1868	230184	WB	SEVERN
21 Oct	1868	223308	WP & G P	WEST-MINSTER

(This was a Brownfield design registered by a London retailer.)

Date		Reg No	Maker	Title
6 Apr	1869	228430	Baker & Chetwynd	USA
10 Jun	1870	242394	WB	NILE
22 Sep	1870	233527	W J A Bailey	O'Connell
7 Feb	1870	238628	W J A Bailey	G Peabody
27 Jun	1870	242715	G Jones	Pineapple
27 Mar	1871	251246	WB	—
18 Jan	1872	259801	Worcester	Japanese
18 Jun	1872	263497	G Ashworth	Alton
19 Aug	1872	265255	W JA Bailey	Rustic
11 Nov	1872	267806	W E Cartlidge	Wheat Ears

Date		Reg No	Maker	Title
14 Nov	1872	267894	WB	—
10 Feb	1873	270298	W JA Bailey	Oak
21 Jan	1874	279964	Copeland	—
11 May	1874	282249	Moore Bros	Camel
6 Jun	1874	282802	WB	ASTON
20 Jan	1875	288553	WB	TEA SERVICE
29 Jan	1874	288861	Worthington & Son	Scallop Shell
26 Jun	1874	292367	G Jones	Monkey
24 Jan	1875	297817	Minton	Cockerel
22 May	1876	300683	Wedgwood	Boston
3 Jul	1876	301596	Ford & Challinor	—
31 Oct	1876	304911	WB	MAN & GOURD
31 Oct	1876	304912	WB	FACE & PIGTAIL
31 Oct	1876	304913	WB	FISH
14 Nov	1876	305195	Clementson	Canada
20 Mar	1877	306564	Campbellfield	Wicker
25 Jan	1877	307237	G Jones	—
9 Jun	1877	310775	Baker & Co	—
2 Apr	1878	320030	Belfield & Co	—
17 Apr	1878	320482	Minton	Tortoise
2 Oct	1878	327035	Minton	Porcupine
23 Oct	1878	328144	Pinder, Bourne & Hope	—
26 Oct	1878	328320	WB	TEA SERVICE
12 Mar	1879	333210	Edge Malkin	Cockatoo ?
Oct	1880	345719	WB	BASKET
1 Oct	1880	356014	Wade & Colclough	Gladstone
22 Oct	1880	357039	E F Bodley	Storks ?
8 Feb	1881	361540	WB	MISTLETOE
8 Feb	1881	361541	WB	MISTLETOE

(The first of these was a plain shape designed to take an enamelled picture without any relief moulding The second followed the relief moulded pattern of the Mistletoe jug.)

Date		Reg No	Maker	Title
6 Oct	1881	370998	T & R Boote	Tunis
21 Dec	1881	374955	F Grosvenor	Clover ?
23 Mar	1882	378823	T A Simpson	—
27 May	1882	381568	S Lear	Sunflower ?
28 Jul	1882	384078	Hawley & Co	—
10 Aug	1882	384464	Wright & Rigby	Booth
9 Oct	1882	387772	Dean, Capper & Dean	—
8 Mar	1883	395317	E F Bodley	—
24 Mar	1883	396056	Sampson, Bridgwood	—
20 Jun	1883	399640	T & R Boote	—
13 Oct	1883	405363	W B	CLAMSHELL
15 Dec	1883	408356	T & R Boote	—

The following are taken from the new Design Register introduced in 1884.

Date		Reg No	Maker	Title
Sep	1884	12805	WB	—
Mar	1884	45262	WB	—
Mar	1886	45263	WB	—
Oct	1887	83253	WB	—
Jun	1889	150705	WB	—

In addition to those items identified from the Design Register, there are further Brownfield teapots or tea services found in the 1880 Brownfield catalogue located at the Keele University Library The question remains — if the factory introduced a teacup and saucer, was it intended to be a component part of a tea service that included a teapot?

W BROWNFIELD

Date	Pat name	
pre 1880	BUTTERFLY	Teapot form
pre 1880	RICHELIEU	Teapot form
pre 1880	ARGYLL	Teapot form
pre 1880	ROSE LEAF	Teapot form
pre 1880	CAMBRIDGE	Teapot form
pre 1880	LUBECK	Cup & Saucer
pre 1880	PRINCES RIBBON	Cup & Saucer
pre 1880	BISMARK	Cup & Saucer
pre 1880	SHAMROCK	Cup & Saucer

(This is a painted pattern unlike the relief-moulded Shamrock teapot of 20th May 1859.)

Date	Pat name	
pre 1880	MOLTKE	Cup &Saucer

(A Moltke pattern has also been found in comport form.)

pre 1880	DENMARK	Cup & Saucer

(A Denmark pattern has also been found in plate from.)

pre 1880	MARSALA	Cup and Saucer
pre 1880	BETHOOR	Cup & Saucer
pre 1880	SICILY	Cup & Saucer
pre 1880	DURHAM	Cup & Saucer
pre 1880	STRAWBERRY	Cup & Saucer
pre 1880	THREE LINES UNDER GLAZE	
		Cup & Saucer
pre 1880	BAND AND LINE UNDER GLAZE	
		Cup & Saucer

APPENDIX 8

INTERNATIONAL EXHIBITIONS WITH BROWNFIELD CERAMIC DISPLAYS

WOOD & BROWNFIELD 1837-1850

1845-46	MANCHESTER	NONE KNOWN
1849	PARIS	NONE KNOWN

WILLIAM BROWNFIELD 1850-1871

1851	CRYSTAL PALACE	NONE KNOWN
1853	DUBLIN	NONE KNOWN
1855	PARIS	Brownfield ??
1862	LONDON	Brownfield
1867	PARIS	Brownfield
1869	AMSTERDAM	NONE KNOWN
1871	LONDON	Brownfield

WILLIAM BROWNFIELD & SON(S): 1873-92

1872	LYONS	NONE KNOWN
1873	VIENNA	NONE KNOWN

By 1876 Brownfields had an agent in Vienna (Herr G Bossenroth) which suggests that the firm may well have exhibited there in 1873.

1876.	PHILADELPHIA	Brownfield
1878	PARIS	STAND CANCELLED
1879	SYDNEY	Brownfield
1880	MELBOURNE	Brownfield
1881	ADELAIDE	NONE KNOWN
1884	CRYSTAL PALACE	Brownfield
1884	CALCUTTA	Brownfield
1889	PARIS	Brownfield

Further research will be necessary to establish if W&B and WB used an overseas agent to exhibit the factory's goods at foreign exhibitions, especially prior to 1867.

APPENDIX 9

FACTORIES' PRODUCT MARKING IN THE YEARS 1835-1859

The mark "=" means NO clear identifying marks of manufacturing factory.

The mark "#" indicates an apparent 'co-operative joint venture.

The mark "§" indicates the first use of the NEW registration system of 1842.

(PB) means Published by . . . under the old Act of 1811.

All the unnamed jugs marked * are illustrated in Vol 2 of Kathy Hughes' "A Collector's Guide to Nineteenth Century Jugs".

Date		Factory	Product
1834	20th Jun	Machin &Potts	Rob Burns jug (PB)
1835	1st Sep	Eli Jones	Coral jug (PB)
	1st Oct	W Ridgway	Bundle of Faggots (PB)
	1st Oct	W Ridgway	The Kill jug (PB)
	1st Oct	W Ridgway	Floral Ring jug (PB)
	1st Oct	W Ridgway	Morning Glories (PB)
	1st Oct	W Ridgway	Linenfold jug (PB)
	1st Oct	W Ridgway	Tam O'Shanter jug (PB)
1836	30th Aug	J Ridgway	'Giraffe' Dinner Service (PB)
1837	Jun	RW&B	Opaque Stone China plate
	Sep	RW&B	Stone China plate
1838	Feb	W&B	Amoy plate
	1st Sep	Eli Jones	Vertical Leaves jug (PB)
1839	Jul =	W&B	Chinoiserie jug
	1st Sep	RW&B	Vertical Columns jug (PB)
	1st Nov	C Meigh	Julius Caesar jug (PB)
1840	1st Jul	Eli Jones	Basket jug (PB)
	1st Jul	Eli Jones	Elizabethan jug (PB)
	1st Sep	W Ridgway	Eglinton (PB)
	1st Oct	C Meigh	Roman (PB)
1841	1st Jan	W&B	Willie jug (PB)
	30th Sep	W&B	Judgement of Solomon (PB)
	1st Nov	Jones &Walley	Good Samaritan (PB) =
1842	Jan-Mar =	W&B?	Hand painted Floral jug
	1st Mar	Jas Dixon &Son	Chinoiserie jug (PB)
	17th Mar	C Meigh	Apostles jug (PB)
	May	W&B	Ironstone plate
	Jun =	W&B	Amoy jug
	1st Jul#	Jones &Walley	Gipsey jug (PB)
	1st Jul#	S Alcock	Gipsey jug (PB)
	22nd Sep§	Jas Dixon &Son	Floral jug
	3rd Nov§	Jos Wolstenholme	jug

(Wolstenholmes were Britannia Metal Lid Makers. They did not make the jug.)

	30th Dec	James Edwards	jug
1843	21st Mar§	Jos Wedgwood	jug
	31st Mar	S Alcock.	vase
	13th May§	Jones & Walley	Peacock jug
	Aug	W&B	Nankin jug
	10th Nov§	Minton	Plate
	Dec	W&B	Japanese jug
1844	Feb	W&B	Viola jug
	30th Sep§	C Meigh	Bacchanalian Dance
1845	1st Jan§	T & J Mayer	Rossi jug
		Copeland	Vintage jug
	20th Mar =	Minton =	Dancing Amorini =
	26th Apr #	T & R Boote & Jones & Walley	Dessert Service
	8th May	Minton	Putti jug

Date		Factory	Product
	10th May#	T & R Boote	Ranger jug
	10th May	E Walley	Ranger jug
	Jun	W&B	Pomona plate
	22nd Nov=	Minton =	Climbing Ivy jug
1846	Jan	W&B	Windsor Wreath plate
	2nd Mar	Minton	* jug
	?	S Alcock	Portland jug
	? =	W&B =	Portland jug =
	26th May	Minton	Vintage jug
	16th Jul	Ridgway, Son & Co	Vines jug
	1st Aug	Jos Wedgwood	jug
	3rd Aug	Minton	jug
	29th Sep	T & J Mayer	Gothic Figures jug
	3rd Nov§	Ridgway & Abington	
	12th Nov	C Meigh	Minster jug
	3rd Dec =	Ridgway & Abington =	Oak jug
	30th Dec	T Furnival	Falstaff jug
1847	2nd Feb	T & R Boote	jug
	8th Feb	T & J Mayer	Rossi jug
	3rd Apr	S Alcock	Rustic jug
	27th Apr	S Alcock	Naomi jug
	14th May=	Minton =	Hops jug
	3rd Aug	John Rose	jug
	17th Aug	Copeland	Adam and Eve jug
	Sep	W&B	Chinoiserie jug
1848	7th Mar =	Ridgway & A=	Harvest jug
	7th Mar =	Ridgway & A=	Bulrush jug
	20th Mar	W&B	Pomona plate
	20th Mar	W&B	Moultan plate
	20th Mar	W&B	Cable plate
	20th Mar	W&B	Blackberry plate
	20th Mar	W&B	plate
	18th Sep	C Meigh.	Trellis jug
	17th Oct	T & R Boote	Samuel & Eli jug
	4th Nov	Copeland	Vine jug
	21st Nov=	Minton =	Hops jug
1849	20th Jan§	Davenport	jug
	16th Feb =	Ridgway & A =	Sylvan jug
	26th Feb	John Rose	Shells & Flowers jug
	May	E Walley	Hecate jug (PB)
	Jun	W&B	Turin jug
	11th Aug	Copeland	jug
	15th Aug	Minton.	Squirrel & Bee jug
	9th Nov	Copeland	Lily of Valley jug
	17th Nov	Minton	Bird & Ivy jug
	6th Dec	Copeland	jug
1850	21st Jun	E Walley	Diana jug
	2nd Jul =	T & J Mayer	Birdnesting jug
	9th Sep§	T Till	jug
	9th Oct	Minton	jug
	19th Dec =	T & J Mayer	Convulvulous jug
1851	11th Feb	WB	Bouquet jug
	26th Apr	E Walley	Ceres jug
	30th May=	Copeland =	Nymphea jug
	21st Jul	T & R Boote	jug
	16th Aug=	Ridgway & Abington	Nineveh jug
	16th Oct	WB	Fuchsia jug
	21st Oct	Wm Ridgway	Willie jug
	13th Nov=	C Meigh =	Thistle jug
	2nd Dec =	T & J Mayer	Paul & Virginia jug
1852	1st Apr	T Till	Floral jug

Date		Factory	Product
	5th Jun	Minton	jug
	23rd Jul	Minton	Medieval Revelry jug
	23rd Jul	Minton	jug
	13th Aug	T Till	jug
	25th Aug=	C Meigh =	Four Seasons jug =
	3rd Sep	Minton	Ivy jug
	16th Sep=	Minton =	Mermaid & Cupid jug
	25th Oct	WB	Mazeppa jug
1853	1st Jan	Ridgway & A	Slavery jug (PB)
	14th Jan	Davenport	Niagara jug
	26th Feb	Copeland	Harvest Barrel jug
	7th May	John Alcock	jug
	14th Jun	Livesley, P & Co	Julius Caesar jug
1854	30th Jan	S Alcock	Ivy Leaf jug
	23rd Feb	Copeland	Wellington jug
	27th Mar	Geo Baguley	Garland & Cupid jug
	1st Apr	WB	Kent jug
	15th Apr	Geo.Baguley	jug
	3rd Jun	T Till	David & Goliath jug
	9th Jun	C Meigh	jug
	12th Sep	Copeland	Hop jug
	31st Oct	George Ray	Bird Feeding jug
	27th Dec	S Alcock	
1855	1st Jan	Ridgway & A	The Wedding jug (PB)
	1st Jan	S Alcock	Royal Patriotic jug (PB)
	4th Jan.	Worthington & Green	
			Cup Tosser jug
	17th Feb	Pratt & Co	Cupid & Bow jug
	26th Apr	WB	Linenfold jug
	May	WB	Barley Ear jug
	14th May	Minton	jug
	4th Jul	J Thompson	Three Graces jug
	24th Jul	C Meigh	jug
	1st Aug	Ridgway & A	Three Soldiers jug (PB)
	6th Aug	Dudson	Pineapple jug
	27th Sep	S.Bevington	Sacrifice of Iphigenia
1856	15th Jan	J Pankhurst & Co	Home & Abroad jug
	23rd Jan	Minton	Wheat & Leaf jug
	22nd Feb	Richard W Keene	Here We Are jug

Date		Factory	Product
	18th Apr	Wm Beech	May They Ever Be United jug
	18th Apr	E Walley	George Washington jug
	18th Apr	Ridgway & A	Barleycorn jug
	30th Apr	WB	Ivy jug
	13th Jun	C Meigh	Amphitrite jug
	16th Oct	Minton	jug
	22nd Oct	Copeland	Tulip jug
	29th Nov	E Walley	jug
1857	9th Feb	Minton	Hops & Barley jug
	5th Jun	WB	'Tradescantia' jug
	19th Jun	Copeland	
	14th Oct =	Ridgway & A =	Fuchsia jug
	22nd Oct	Pratt & Co	
	9th Dec	WB	Arrowhead jug
1858	29th Jan	Cockson & Harding	Havelock jug
	29th Jul	S Alcock	Draped Linenfold jug
	24th Aug	WB	Floral jug
	3rd Sep	Sharpe Bros & Co	Corn on the Cob jug
	5th Oct	WB	Jewel jug
	5th Oct	Minton	Pineapple jug
	29th Oct	B Green	jug
	11th Nov	E & W Walley	Gleaner jug
	23rd Dec	J Clementson	
1859	1st Jan	Ridgway & A	Moses jug (PB)
	21st Mar	T & R Boote	Four Panels jug
	7th May	E & W Walley	Vintage jug
	7th May	E & W Walley	* jug
	20th May	WB	Shamrock jug
	27th Aug	S Alcock	Daniel in Lion's Den jug
	5th Nov	WB	Fern jug
	25th Oct	Minton	jug
	14th Dec	E & W Walley	jug
1860	6th Jun	WB	Eglantine jug
	Jun	Sandford Pottery	* jug
	Jun	Sandford Pottery	* jug
	6th Jul	Sandford Pottery	Victoria R jug
	Aug	Sandford Pottery	* jug
	29th Sep	Sandford Pottery	Loyal Volunteers jug

The full title for the Sandford Pottery is Sandford Estate Clay Co Ltd.

APPENDIX 10A PRICE GUIDE TO BROWNFIELD JUGS

The mark * indicates that the jug can be found in parian The two asterisks ** indicate those jugs known to have been produced in majolica. To date (1995) few have been discovered. NK means not known.

ROBINSON, WOOD & BROWNFIELD: 1837

Jug	Date	Size	Plain	Enamelled
Floral Ewer	1837	6"	NK	£45-60
Versailles	1837	12"	NK	£130+
Canton	1837	12"	NK	£130+
Zoological	1837	12"	NK	£170+
Vertical Columns	1839	6"	£100+	NK

WOOD & BROWNFIELD: 1837-1850

Jug	Date	Size	Plain	Enamelled
Chinoiserie	1839	8"	NK	£80-100
Willie	1841	8"	£150+	NK
Judge-Solomon	1841	8"	£125+	NK
Jas Dixon	1842	8"	NK	£80-130
Painted Floral	1842	9"	NK	£140-175
Amoy	1842	8"	NK	£100+
James Dixon	1842	8"	NK	£100+
Nankin	1845	7"	NK	£70-85
Japanese	1845	5"	NK	£25-35
Viola	1845	7"	NK	£45-55
Portland Jug	1845	6"	£40+	£60+
Oriental	1846	7"	NK	£75-90
Chinoiserie	1847	9"	NK	£100+
Portland I	1847	7"	NK	£60-65
Snipe	1848	6"	NK	£75+
Portland II	1848	5"	NK	£60-65
Portland III	1848	6"	NK	£70+
Turin	1849	7"	NK	£60-75
Floral	1849	9"	NK	£80-110
Snipe II	1849	6"	NK	£55
Portland IV	1849	6"	NK	£65+
Lotus shape	1840s	7"	NK	£50

WILLIAM BROWNFIELD: 1850-1871

Jug	Date	Size	Plain	Enamelled
Portland V	1850	7"	NK	£60-75
Bouquet	1851	5"	NK	£50-60
Eureka Ewer	1851	9"	NK	£90-120
Fuchsia	1851	6"	£60+	£90-100
Mazeppa	1851	?	NK	£140-175
Portland VI	1852	7"	NK	£60-80
No 1	1852	5"	NK	£30-45
No 7	1852	12"	NK	£100+
Locking Rope	1852	7"	£40	£60-85
Moldavia Ewer	1853	11"	NK	£70-90
Cuba jug	1853	5"	NK	£40
Kew	1854	10"	NK	£80-110
Kent	1854	7"	£45+	£60-75
Clarendon	1854	10"	NK	£75-100
No 17	1854	8"	NK	£40-60
Barley Ear	pre 1855	7"	£30+	£40-50
Barley Ear	post 1855	7"	£30+	NK
No 18 jugs	1855	7"	NK	£40-65
No 21 Floral	1855	7"	NK	£50-70
Linenfold	1855	6"	£80+	£150+

Jug	Date	Size	Plain	Enamelled
Wicker	1855	6"	£40	£70-80
Ivy*	1856	8"	£50+	£75-100
No 28 jug	1856	12"	NK	£80-100
No 38 jug	1856	7"	NK	£35-50
No 46 jug	1856	7"	NK	£40-60
'Tradescantia'	1857	6"	£40+	£60-85
No 45 Floral	1857	10"	NK	£80-100
Farmer's Arms	1857	8"	NK	£80-100
'Arrowhead'	1857	6"	£60	£80-120
Jewel	1858	7"	£40+	£60-80
Shamrock	1859	7"	£40+	£60-85
Fern*	1859	8"	£40+	£60-100
Greek	1859	7"	NK	£45-65
Antique	1859	7"	NK	£40
'Floral'	1860	7"	£40+	£60-80
Eglantine	1860	7"	£40+	£60-90
Donatello	1861	6"	£40+	£60-85
Union	1861	8"	£40+	£60-100
Mother + Child	1862	8"	NK	£50-70
International*	1862	8"	£40+	£75-100
Swiss**	1863	8"	£40+	£60-85
Universe	1863	6"	£70+	£120-160
Albion	1863	6"	£70+	£100-130
Burton*	1863	6"	£40	£50-60
Argos*	1864	6"	£40+	£60-85
Tyrol	1864	6"	£40+	£60-85
Florence	1865	6"	£40+	£60-90
Tiverton*	1865	7"	£40+	£60-90
Alloa*	1866	6"	£40+	£60-80
Cashmere*	1867	6"	£60+	£75-100
Napoleon	1867	?	£500+	NK
Hampton*	1868	7"	£40+	£60-100
Westminster	1868	6"	£40+	£50-65
Severn*	1869	7"	£40+	£60-85
Lotus	1869?	NK	£25+	£50+
Strawberry	1869?	NK	"	£50+
Alexandra	1869?	NK	"	£50+
Coblentz	1869?	NK	"	£50+
Bayonne	1869?	NK	"	£50+
Nile	1870	7"	£40+	£60-90
Marne*	1870	7"	£40+	£60-80
Worcester*	1871	7"	£40+	£75-85

WILLIAM BROWNFIELD & SON: 1871-1876

Jug	Date	Size	Plain	Enamelled
Cockatoo**	1871	10"	NK	£500+
Cupid	1872	8"	£40+	£60-80
Cupid 2	1872	5"	NK	£150-160
Bangor 1**	1874	7"	NK	£70-85
Bangor 2	1874	7"	NK	£70-85
Mandarin 1	1874	7"	NK	£55-65
Mandarin 2	1874	7"	NK	£55-70
Hong Kong 1	1874	7"	NK	£55-65
Hong Kong 2	1874	7"	NK	£55-65
Hong Kong 3	1874	7"	NK	£55-65
Audley	1874	7"	NK	£55-65
Bangor Marble	1874	7"	NK	£55-65
Bass	1874	6"	NK	£40-50
Sylvan (Bangor)	1875	7"	NK	£55-70
Lincoln	1875	10"	NK	£70+
Yeddo 1	1876	6"	£40+	£65-85
Yeddo 2	1876	7"	NK	£120+

Jug	Date	Size	Plain	Enamelled
Yeddo 3	1876	6"	NK	£120+
Audley	1876	7"	NK	£70+
Sisyphus	1876	7"	£40+	£60-85

WILLIAM BROWNFIELD & SONS: 1876-1892

Jug	Date	Size	Plain	Enamelled
Medieval	1877	7"	NK	£40+
'Leek'	1877	?	£80+	£130+
Hudson	1877	6"	£50+	£80-120
Alsopp	1877	6"	NK	£40+
Olympus	1877	9"	NK	£60-80
Suez	1877	8"	NK	£50-70
Crete	1877	8"	NK	£50-70
'Swirling Fish'	1879	?	NK	£400+
Yesso	1879	7"	NK	£40+
Sado	1879	8"	NK	£40-60
Ranga	1879	8"	NK	£40-60
Denver	1879	7"	NK	£40-60
Daisy	1879	8"	NK	£40-60
Tudor	1879	8"	NK	£40-60
Merton	1879	4"	NK	£40+
Goose&Monkey	1880	9"	£60+	£90+
Missouri	1880	6"	£40+	£70+
Carnival	1880	7"	NK	£35-45

BROWNFIELD MOSAIC JUGS

Jug	Date	Size	Plain	Enamelled
Adonis	pre1880	?	NK	£40+
Clyde	pre1880	6"	NK	£60+

Jug	Date	Size	Plain	Enamelled
Corinth	pre 1880	7"	NK	£50+
Dunedin	pre 1880	?	NK	£40+
Exe	pre 1880	7"	NK	£30+
Stanley	pre 1880	6"	NK	£30+
Stratford	pre 1880	?	NK	£30+
Truro	pre 1880	6"	NK	£30+
Solon	pre 1880	6"	NK	£35+

JUGS FROM THE FACTORY 1880 CATALOGUE

Jug	Date	Size	Plain	Enamelled
Oxford	pre 1880	?	NK	£40+
Dorking	pre 1880	?	NK	£40+
Taunton	pre 1880	?	NK	£40+
Dartmouth	pre 1880	?	NK	£40+
St Germain	pre 1880	?	NK	£40+
Neil	1881	6"	NK	£40+
Pastimes	1881	6"	NK	£30+
Mistletoe	1881	7"	£45+	£70-100
Ayr	pre1882	5"	NK	£25+
Gentleman	1883	10"	NK	£400+
Montana	1883	8"	£40+	£70-90
Tree Trunk	1883	7"	£30+	£55+
Gypsy	pre1884	7"	NK	£30+
Wisconsin	pre1885	5"	NK	£30+
Prunus	pre 1892	5"	£35+	£50+
Devon	1892	10"	NK	£100+
Jipsy	?	5"	NK	£25+

APPENDIX 10B   PRICE GUIDE TO BROWNFIELD PLATES

The plate collector will need to judge each plate on its individual merits, aware that a range of quality almost certainly exists for many individual plates. The price range printed here is set to allow for this variability In general a comport will cost £15-£25 more than a plate of the same design

ROBINSON, WOOD & BROWNFIELD

Product name	Pat No	Date	Price
Opaque Stone China	22	1837	£25-45
Opaque Stone China	24	1837	£25-45
Stone China	31	1837	£25-45
Mansion		1837	£20-30
Canton		1837	£30-40
Versailles		1837	£40-50
Zoological		1837	£40-50
Venetian Scenery		1837	£40-60

WOOD & BROWNFIELD

Product name	Pat No	Date	Price
Amoy	54	1838	£30-50
Real Ironstone	303	1842	£30-50
Real Ironstone	328	1842	£30-40
Floral	397	1842	£30-50
Floral comport	397	1842	£50-70
Precursor No 35	642	1843	£20-30
Floral	718	1843	£20-30
Hindostan	917	1843	£20-30

Product name	Pat No	Date	Price
Grecian Statue		1840-50	£25-35
Albion		1840-50	£30-45
Albion platter		1840-50	£60-95
Venetian Scenery		1840-50	£40-60
Pomona	1676	1845	£25-35
Oriental	1690	1845	£20-£35
Windsor Wreath	2030	1846	£25-35
Chiswick		1846	£20-35
Precursor No 35	2602	1846	£20-30
Alma		1848	£40-50
Moultan	3738	1848	£25-35
Cable		1848	£15-20
Blackberry		1848	£30-40
Unnamed	4682	1848	£30-40

WILLIAM BROWNFIELD

Product name	Pat No	Date	Price
Alba	5146	1850	£30-40
Bouquet edged	5160/4	1850	£30-40
Eureka	5 217	1850	£25-45
Ascot		1850-60	£20-25
Pekin		1850-60	£15-20
Bouquet edged		1850?	£30-40
Bouquet edged	5436	1851	£20-35
Bouquet edged	5590	1851	£30-40
Plate	5914	1851	£30-40
Comport	6035	1852	£40-60
Plate	6055	1852	£25-40
No 7	6411	1852	£30-45

Product name	Pat No	Date	Price
No 8		1852	£20-35
No 9	6510	1852	£30-35
No 9	6514	1852	£20-25
No 12		1853	£20-25
No 13	6707	1853	£30-40
No 13 Comport		1853	£40-55
No 15	7146	1853	£25-40
No 15 Tureen Base	7146	1853	£120-150
Comport	7449	1853	£40-50
Plate	7459	1854	£25-40
Dog Rose	7589/1	1854	£30-40
Alba	7646	1854	£25-45
Comport	7691	1854	£40-50
Bouquet edged	7727	1854	£30-45
Bouquet Comport	7727	1854	£45-55
Alma I	7749	1854	£40-50
Bouquet edged	7738	1854	£30-50
Alma II	7750	1854	£40-50
Moltke	7764	1854	£25-40
Azoff	8057	1854	£25-40
Bouquet edged	8079	1854	£30-45
Palmyra		1850-55	£10-15
Navarro		1850-55	£10-15
Palmyra platter		1850-55	£60-80
Bude		1850-55	£10-15
Inkerman		1850-55	£10-15.
Detroit		1850-55	£15-20
Sweaborg	8413	1855	£40+
Sweaborg Vegetable Dish	8413	1855	£75-100
No 27	8443	1855	£30-40
Alba	8500	1855	£30-40
Dog Rose	8627	1855	£30-40
Six Roses	8649	1855	£25-40
No 26	8755	1855	£30-40
Eupatoria	8829	1855	£30-45
Gordon platter	—	1855	£40-60
Precursor No 35	8907	1856	£20-30
No 27	8940	1856	£30-45
No 27	8947	1856	£30-45
No 18	9046	1856	£30-40
Kars	9146/6	1856	£25-35
No 34	9202	1856	£20-30
Bouquet edged.	9285/2	1856	£25-35
No 28	9234	1856	£25-40
No 8 Bowl	9417	1856	£20-30
Comport	9556	1856	£30-40
Thrace	9568	1856	£25-35
Alba Comport	9630	1856	£40-60
No 35	9632	1856	£20-30
Fruit I	9694	1856	£35-45
Fruit II	9695	1856	£35-45
Fruit Comport	9694	1856	£50-60
Fruit Comport	9695	1856	£50-60
Fruit Comport	9696	1856	£50-60
Fruit III	9706	1856	£35-45
No 40	10,108	1857	£30-40
No 40 Comport	10,108	1857	£45-55
No 46	10,414	1857	£25-40
Fruit Wreath	10,585	1857	£35-45
Fruit Wreath	10,592	1857	£35-45
No 48	10,910	1858	£20-30
No 47	10,949	1858	£15-25
Crimson Border	10,979	1858	£10-20
No 58		1858	£20-35
No 60 Comport		1858	£50-70

Product name	Pat No	Date	Price
No 60 Cherry	11,047/1	1858	£35-50
Flower Border	11,703	1858	£35-45
No 61	11,728	1859	£35-45
Montebello Tureen Base	12,034	1859	£30-40
No 53	12,068	1859	£20-30
No 54	12,551	1859	£30-40
Turkish Design	12,630	1859	£35-45
Albert Ribbon		1859	£30-40
No 55	13,167	1860	£20-30
No 68		1860-64	£20-30
Bouquet edged	14,397	1861	£30-40
Floral Wreath	14,399	1861	£35-45
Dessert Plates	14,406	1861	£30-40
Compiegne	14,847	1862	£20-25
Mother&Child		1862	£20-30
Denmark		1862-65	£20-30
Dinner	16,423	1863	£20-25
Scroll		1864	£20-30

INTRODUCTION OF NEW PATTERN NUMBERING SYSTEM FOR STONEWARE GOODS: 1864

Product name	Pat No	Date	Price
Green Border	270	1864	£10-15
No 73	166	1864	£20-30
No 74 Bowl		c1864	£30-45
No 76		c1864	£20-30
No 79		c1864	£25-35
No 92		c1870	£20-35
No 115	T4319	c1870	£20-30
No 131	T5970/2	1870	£20-30
No 132		1870	£20+
Smyrna	7497	1870	£20
Cressy	T2081	1870-75	£25

WILLIAM BROWNFIELD & SON(S)

* represents a porcelain plate produced after 1871

Product name	Pat No	Date	Price
Sylvan		1874	£10-20
Sylvan Plates (Multi Colour)*	1275	1874	£30-40
Tulip Plate*	—	1874?	£30-40
Rose Plate*	—	1874?	£30-40
Shakespeare	1790/T	c1875	£20-25
Medieval	8403	1877	£20-30
Floral*	650	1877	£30-40
Bird (4)*	—	c1878?	£20-30
Tycoon*	8645	c1878?	£15-20
Cyprus	8899/3	1878	£15-20
Swifts*	1145	1878	£35-45
Christening*	1529	1878	£35-55
Merton (Enamelled)		1879	£20-30
Spring (Enamelled)		1879	£20-30
Sultan Massoud*		1879	£200+
Scenic*	1192	1880	£35-45
Texas	7050	1880	£15-20
Pastimes		1881	£30-40
Pastimes*		1881	£50+
Laburnum*		1881	£35-45
W Bourne Plaque		1882	£80-120
Woodland		1884	£20
Floral	5285	1888	£15-25
Denver	9191/12/	1892?	£20-25

APPENDIX 10C

PORCELAIN AND MAJOLICA FIGURES

Dealers will notice that the best Brownfield porcelain pieces fetch prices comparable to those obtained by Minton. This is confirmed by experience at leading antique fairs throughout 1990-1995.
E is an estimated price.

Item	Height	Shape No	Enamelled?	Price
Cupids Cake Stand	12"	(21)	x	£1000+E
Cherub Vase	8"	(22)	x	£500+E
Cherub Candelabra	22"	(24)	x	£700+E
Ceres & Corn	11"	(34)	x	£600+E
Cherub & Lobster	14"	(41)	x	£800+E
Cherub Oil Lamp	29"	(43)	x	£1000+E
Bear Cake Stand	13"	(48)	x	£750+E
Cherub Shell Dishes	6"	(52)	x	£500+E
Basket Spill	—	(59-60)	✓	£350+
Girl & Boy	—	(66)	✓	£500+
Pr Flower Holders	7"	(69)	✓	£600+
Lady Oil Lamp	34"	(73)	x	£1250+E
Cherub & Rabbit	9"	(86)	✓	£400+E
Chained Bear	9"	(96)	x	£350+E
Cat & Globe	10"	(99)	✓	£800+E
Fan shaped Dish	7"	(108)	✓	£400+
Cats Flower Stand	10"	(110)	✓	£800+
Mama & Papa	10"	(112-113)	✓	£450+
Cherub & Netting	9"	(120)	✓	£600+
Cake Stand	15"	(131)	x	£1000+E
Confidence Figure	18"	(142)	x	£1500+E
Love Figure	18"	(143)	x	£500+E
Spring Figure	14"	(144)	x	£500+E
Goat & Perambulator	—	(150)	x	£200+
Girl & Boy	—	(176)	✓	£400+
Cherubs Vase	46"	(186)	x	£1500+E
Tyrolean Girls	—	(193)	✓	£800+E
Japanese Ladies	9"	(198-9)	✓	£575+
Cherub & Nautilis Shell	—	(209-10)	✓	£750+E
Vase		(200)	✓	£500+
Bird of Prey	24"	(2050)	x	£1200+E
Gentleman Jug	12"	(—)	x	£550+
Cockatoo Jug	12"	)—)	✓	£650+
Swirling Fis Jug	10"	(—)	✓	£500+
Man & Gourd Teapot	—	(—)	✓	£300+
Fish Teapot	—	(—)	✓	£300+
Hotei Teapot	—	(—)	✓	£1500+

BIBLIOGRAPHY

Primary sources

Spode MSS (The 1880 Brownfield Catalogue), Keele University.
PRO. The Design Register — BT 43, Vols 64-74 (1842-1883).
PRO. The Design Register — BT 50, various volumes (1884-1900).
Louis Jahn — Catalogue of Sale of Collection, 1911. Hanley Record Library.
Pottery Gazette — various volumes 1860-1900.
Pottery Gazette (March 1902), List of Sale of Brownfield Patterns.
Art Journal — various volumes.
Pottery and Glass Trades Review (1876).
Staffordshire Advertiser — various volumes.

Secondary sources

Ball, A, Price Guide to Pot Lids (1991).
Battie, D and Turner, M, Price Guide to Nineteenth and Twenty Century Pottery (1990).
Bergesen, V, Price Guide to English Pottery (1992).
Coysh, A W, and Henrywood, D K, Dictionary of Blue and White Printed Pottery, Vols I and II (1993-1994).
Cushion, J P, Pocket book of British Ceramic marks (1959).
Godden, Geoffrey, An Illustrated Encyclopædia of British Pottery and Porcelain (1980).
Godden Geoffrey, Staffordshire Porcelain (1983).
Godden, Geoffrey, Encyclopædia of British Porcelain Manufacturers (1988).
Hampson R and E, Brownfields, Victorian Potters, NCSJ Vol 4 (1980-81).
Harrison, D, William Brownfield — Staffordshire's Forgotten Potters (1971).
Harrison, D, Brownfields of Cobridge — made for the Collector (1972).
Henrywood, R K, Relief Moulded Jugs, 1820-1900 (1984).
Hughes, K, A Collector's Guide to Nineteenth Century Jugs, Vols 1 and 2 (1985) (1991).
Jewitt, Ceramic Art in Great Britain (1878), reprint (1985).
Lewis, G, A Collector's History of English Pottery (1985).
Paton, J, Jugs — A Collector's Guide (1975).
G W and F A Rhead, Staffordshire Pots and Potters (1977).
Rumsey, J, Exhibition Catalogue — Victorian Relief-Moulded Jugs (1987).

INDEX

Many plates have no known pattern name and these will be found by their pattern numbers which are listed here in numerical order under No. They are also listed in Appendix 6C.

Numbers in parentheses refer to illustrations.

A

Abington		7, 16-17,29
'Adonis'	(c1875)	64, **(140)**
Adams		12
'Alaska' plate	(1887)	App 6
'Alba'	(1851)	93, 102, **(221-2)**
'Albion' plate	(1837)	App 6
'Albion'	(1863)	39-40, **(79)**
Alcock		7, 11-13, 16, 20, 29
'Alexandra'	(c1875)	45, **(92)**
'Alloa'	(1866)	41, **(84)**
'Alma'	(1848)	92, **(212-3)**
'Alsopp'	(1877)	52, 59, **(125)**
'Amoy'	(1838)	3-5, 11-12, 88, **(4)**, **(15)**, **(202)**
'Anapa'	(1858)	27, 102
'Antique'	(1859)	33, 35
'Argos'	(1864)	40, **(80)**
'Argyle'	(c1878)	83, **(189)**
Arrol, A		41
'Arrowhead'	(1857)	30, **(59A/B)**
'Ascot'	(c1855)	103, **(256)**
'Aston'	(1874)	50, 82, **(179)**
Ashworth		37, 65, **(145)**
'Audley'	(1874)	50, 53, **(106)**, **(112)**, **(304)**
'Ayr'	(c1882)	67, **(150)**
'Azoff'	(1854)	21, App 6

B

Bagster, J D		29
'Bangor'	(1874)	50, **(101)**, **(104)**
'Barlaston'	(1869)	44, **(90)**
'Barley Ear'	(1855)	27-28, **(50)**
'Basket'	(c1880)	82, **(182)**
'Bass'	(c1874)	52-53, **(108)**
Bates (Walker)		456
'Bayonne'	(c1875)	45, **(92)**
Beech & Hancock		39
Belleuse, C		50, 56, 158
Bell, J & M P		39
'Berlin' plate	(c1862)	App 6b
'Bethoor' cup	(c1875)	160-161, **(470)**
Bevington, S		33-35
Bevington, J		33
Bevington, A		76
'Bismarck' cup		160-161
'Blackberry'	(1848)	92, **(215)**
Bodley, E J		76
Bodley & Harold		39
Bo ness Co-op		76
Boote, T & R		13, 48
Bossenroth, G E		49
'Bouquet'	(1851)	13, 20, 93 et seq., **(35)**, **(224)**, **(242)**
Bourne, W	(1881)	123, **(319)**
Boy & Goat Vase		130, **(331)**
Bradbury, Anderson & Bettany		12
Bridgwood, S		74

Browne, H K		36
Brownfield, E Arthur		56, 68-70 et seq.
Brownfield, W Etches		39, 50 et seq., 80
Brownfield Guild Pottery		76-79
Brownhills		73
Brown, Westhead Moore		37, 41, 56, 119, 161, **(298)**
'Bude'	(c1850)	103, **(255)**
'Burton'	(1863)	38, **(77)**
'Butterfly'	(c1875)	83, **(194)**

C

'Cable'	(1848)	12, 92, **(216)**
Calcutta		50
'Calpee' plate	(1858)	App 6
'Cambridge'	(c1875)	83, **(193)**
'Canton'	(1837)	2, 4, 88, **(3)**, **(201)**
'Cape Ivy'	(1855)	28-29, **(53)**
Careys		11, 89
Cartlidge, A		56
'Carnival'	(c1880)	57
'Cashmere'	(1867)	41-42, **(86)**
'Ceres'	(c1884)	159, **(397-8)**, **(451)**
'Chiswick' plate	(1846)	91
'Clamshell'	(1883)	83, 86, 139, **(354)**
'Clarendon'	(1854)	18, 25
Clews R & J		1
'Clyde'	(c1869)	61, 64, **(137)**
'Coblentz'	(c1875)	45, **(92)**
'Cockatoo'	(1878)	47, 130-131, **(330)**, **(335)**
'Compiegne'	(1861)	118, **(291)**
Cooper, T		39
'Cone'	(1868)	81, **(173)**
'Confidence' Statue		148, **(400)**
'Convolvulous'	(c1849)	90, 92, **(217)**
Copeland		12-13, 20, 37, 91
Cork & Edge		11, 13
'Corinth'	(c1875)	61, **(134)**
'Cressy'	(1870)	119, **(302)**
'Crete'	(1880)	57, **(118)**
'Cromer'	(1899)	App 6b
'Cuba'	(1854)	21, 24, **(40)**
'Cupid'	(1872)	48-49, **(99)**
'Cupid II'	(1872)	49, **(100)**
Cushion, J P		84, 86
'Cyprus'	(1878)	126, **(325)**

D

'Daisy'	(1879)	60, **(129)**
'Dartmouth'	(c1875)	65, **(144)**
Davenport		7, 16
Davison, J		60
'Dayton' plate	(c1880)	68, App 6
'Denmark'	(1862)	118, **(297)**
'Denmark' cup	(c1875)	160-161, **(468)**
'Denver'	(1880)	60, 123, **(317)**
'Detroit' plate	(1880)	App 6
Devon jug	(1892)	77
Dimmock, J		73

Dimmock & Pankhurst		29
Dixon, Jas.	(1842)	5, 7, 10-11, 16, **(12)**, **(14)**
'Dog Rose'	(1850)	92, 99, 103, **(218)**, **(241)**
'Donatello'	(1860)	35, **(69)**
'Dorking' plate	(c1874)	119, 122, **(305)**
'Dorking' jug	(1874)	65, **(143)**
Doulton		11, 41, 56, 73
'Dove' Vase	(c1875)	157, **(447)**
'Dublin'	(c1879)	60-61, 144, **(131-2)**
Dudson, J		15, 33, 73, 83
'Dunedin'	(c1875)	64, **(140)**
'Durham' cup	(c1875)	160-161, **(472)**
E		
'Ealing' plate	(1851)	App 6
'Earth Vase'	(1884)	73, 157-159, **(450)**
'Eastern Plants'	(1837)	App 6b
Edge & Malkin		73
'Eupatoria'	(1855)	102-103, **(249)**
'Eglantine'	(1860)	35 **(67)**
'Eureka'	(1851)	9, 18, 93, **(31)**, **(223)**
'Exe'	(c1877)	64, **(139)**
F		
'Face & Pigtail'	(1877)	82, 139, **(353)**
Factory Catalogue	(1880)	81-82 et seq., 139 et seq.
'Fern'	(1859)	32-33 **(64-5)**
Fielding, S		73
'Fish' Teapot	(1877)	82, 139, **(352)**
'Floral'	(1860)	35, **(68)**
'Floral Scroll'	(1847)	App 6b
'Florence'	(1865)	40, **(82)**
'Formosa' plate	(1847)	App 6b
Forrester, Thos		73
Furnival		30, 73
'Fuchsia'	(1851)	15, 18, **(33)**, **(34)**
G		
Gallimore, W		145, **(375)**
Gardner	(1888)	145
'Geneva' plate	(1864)	118, **(294)**
'Gentleman' jug	(1883)	145, **(375)**
'Gipsy'	(c1880)	64, **(144)**
'Gladstone' Vase	(1880)	72-73, **(161)**
'Glenny'	(1867)	41, **(85)**
Goat & Pram	(1876)	**(389)**
Godden, G		10, 84, 86, 88, 134-135, 138, 143-145
'Goose & Monkey'	(c1875)	130-131, **(334)**
'Gordon'	(1855)	99
'Gothic'	(1863)	39-163, **(78)**
'Grapevine'	(1854)	24, **(43)**
'Grecian Statue'	(c1840)	89, 91, **(207)**
'Greek' jug	(1855)	33, 35, **(66)**
'Greek Key'	(1871)	44, 48, **(98)**
Grimwade		73
H		
Hammersley		65
'Hampton'	(1868)	42, 44, **(88)**
Hampsons		130, 139, 144, 162
Hancock (& Beech)		39
'Hanging Game'	(c1845)	15, **(27)**
Harrison Desmond		84, 90, 103, 123, 130, 135, 139, 149, 159-160
Hartshorn		56
Hassall, G		123

Hemans, G W		118
Henrywood, D K		6, 16, 30, 33, 42
'Hibiscus' plate		94, **(229)**
Higginbotham	(1840)	88-89, 106
'Hindostan'	(1843)	App 6b
Holloway, F		123
'Hong Kong'	(1874)	50, 122, **(105)**
Hope & Carter		65
'Hotei' Teapot	(c1875)	83, 131
'Hudson'	(1877)	57, 59, **(120-4)**
Hughes, K		21, 44, 48-49
I		
'Inkerman'	(c1845)	90, 103
'International'	(1862)	36, **(72)**
'Ivy'	(1856)	15, 29, **(54)**
'Isle of Man' Teapot		83
J		
Jahn Louis		39, 48, 50, 77
'Japanese'	(1843)	12
'Japanese Ladies'	(c1880)	149, **(407-8)**
'Jewel'	(1858)	15, 32, **(62)**
Jewitt		154, 156
Jones & Walley		7, 16
Jones Elijah		3
Jones, George		59
Jones, Jenette		161-162, **(473)**
Judgement — Solomon		5-6, **(10)**
K		
'Kars'	(1856)	106, **(259)**
'Kent'	(1854)	24, **(41-2)**
'Kew'	(c1854)	25, 27, **(46)**
'Kinburn'	(1855)	App 6b
L		
'Laburnum'	(c1880)	144, **(374)**
'Leek'	(1877)	57, **(119)**
Lewis, Griselda		37
'Lincoln'		50, 52, **(107)**
Livesey (& Powell)		15
Lockett, J		37
'Lotus'	(c1875)	15, 45, **(24-5)**, **(92)**
'Love' Statue	(c1880)	148, **(401)**
'Linenfold'	(1855)	25, 27, **(47)**
'Lubeck' cup	(c1875)	160-161, **(461)**
M		
'Macao' plate	(1837)	App 6
Machin & Potts		3
McCintyre, J		33
McMaster		41
'Madras'	(1880)	60, 126, **(326)**
'Magenta' plate	(c1860)	118, **(293)**
Majolica	(c1871)	50, 130 et seq.
'Mama' (& 'Papa')	(c1875)	142, **(356-7)**
Mann, Oetz	(1878)	60
'Man & Gourd'	(1877)	82, 139 **(351)**
'Mandarin'	(1874)	50, 52, **(102-3)**
'Mansion'	(1837)	88, **(198)**
'Marsala' cup	(c1875)	160-161, **(469)**
'Marne'	(1870)	47, **(95)**
'Mazeppa'	(1852)	20, **(37)**
'Massoud Mirza'	(1879)	143, **(366)**
Mayer, T & J		16-17, 20
'Medieval'	(1877)	53, 56-57, 122, **(115)**, **(312)**

Meigh, C		11, 16, 20
'Melbourne'		50, 65, 111, **(269)**
Meissen		33
'Merton'	(1879)	71-72, **(159)**, **(323)**
Micklewright, F		159, **(452)**
'Mimosa'	(1900)	80, **(171)**
Minton		7, 20, 29, 37, 39, 44, 48, 56, 65, 67, 163
'Missouri'	(1880)	61, **(133)**
'Mistletoe'	(1881)	67, 82, **(148)**
'Moldavia'	(1853)	21, **(39)**
Mollart		56
'Moltke'	(1854)	App 6b
'Moltke' cup	(c1875)	160-161, **(467)**
'Monkey & Goose'	(c1875)	130-131, **(334)**
'Montana'	(1883)	70, **(152)**, **(155)**
'Montebello'	(1856)	App 6b
Moore Bros		65
'Mother & Child'	(1862)	18. 114-115, **(73)**, **(284)**
'Moultan'	(1848)	92, **(214)**
N		
'Nankin'	(1843)	2, 8, 11-12, 15, 88, **(4)**, **(16)**
'Napoleon'	(1867)	42, **(87)**
'Navarro'	(c1845)	90, App 6b
'Niel'	(1881)	65, **(146)**
'New York'	(1881)	App 1
'Niel'	(c1880)	126
'Ningpo'	(1880)	126
'Nile jug'	(1870)	45, **(93)**, **(176)**
'Nile' teapot		81
'No 1' jug	(1851)	9, 17, 29, **(30)**
'No 7' jug	(1852)	18, **(32)**
'No 7' plate	(1852)	93-94, **(232)**
'No 8' plate	(1853)	94, **(233)**
'No 9' plate	(1852)	94, **(234)**
'No 12' plate	(1853)	99, **(235)**
'No 13' plate	(1853)	99, **(236)**
'No 15' plate	(1853)	99, **(237-8)**
'No 17' jug	(1854)	25, **(44)**
'No 18' jug	(1854)	18, 25, **(45)**
'No 21' jug	(1855)	18, 27, **(49)**
'No 26' plate	(1855)	102, **(246)**
'No 27' plate	(1856)	99, 103, **(250)**
'No 28' jug	(1855)	25, 28, **(51)**
'No 28' plate	(1855)	106, **(261)**
'No 34' plate	(1856)	106, **(260)**
'No 35' plate	(1856)	90, 106, 111, **(263)**
'No 38' jug	(1855)	17, 29, **(57)**
'No 40' plate	(1857)	111, **(264)**
'No 45' jug	(1857)	30, **(60)**
'No 46' plate	(1857)	93, 111, **(265)**
No 47' plate	(1858)	111, **(271)**
'No 48' plate	(1858)	111, **(272)**
'No 53' plate	(1858)	114, **(277)**
'No 54' plate	(1858)	114, **(278)**
'No 55' plate	(1858)	114, **(280)**
'No 56' plate	(1858)	114, **(281)**
'No 57' plate	(c1858)	114
'No 58' plate	(1858)	114, **(282)**
'No 60' plate	(1858)	111, 114, **(274)**
'No 61' plate	(1859)	114, **(276)**
'No 68' plate	(1860)	115, **(286)**
'No 73' plate	(c1860)	115, **(287)**
'No 74' plate	(c1860)	115, **(288)**
'No 76' plate	(c1861)	115, **(289)**
'No 79' plate	(1863)	118, **(295)**
'No 92' plate	(1864)	118
'No 115' plate	(c1868)	119, **(299)**
'No 131' plate	(1870)	119, **(300)**
O		
'Ophelia'		68
'Olympus'	(1877)	57, **(116)**
'Oriental'	(1842)	9, 12, 15-16, 91, **(26)**, **(210)**
'Oxford'	(c1875)	61, **(136)**
P		
Palmerston Lord		41
'Palmyra'	(c1845)	90, **(205)**
Pankhurst, W		5-6
Paris		28, 30, 37, 41-42, 50, 59, 73-74
'Paroquet'	(1872)	App 6b
'Passion Flower'	(1857)	35-36, **(71)**
'Pastimes'	(1881)	57, 65, 123, 135, 143-144, **(147)**, **(320-1)**, **(368-9-70)**
Pearson		12
'Pekin'	(1864)	103, **(257)**
Pellatt		30
Philadelphia	(1876)	50, 56, 68, 139, **(114)**
Phillips, W P & G	(1868)	44-45, 81, 139
Pinder (Bourne)		65
'Pompeii' plate	(1853)	App 6b
'Pomona'	(1845)	91, **(209)**
'Portland'(shape)	(1846-51)	8-10, 12-15, 17, **(17)**, **(19)**, **(20)**, **(21)**, **(28)**, **(29)**
Pottery Guild	(1894-8)	76 et seq
Powell & Bishop		56
Pratt, F & R		20, 33
Price, J & C		41
'Princes Ribbon'	(c1880)	160, **(464)**
Protat		56
'Prunus'	(c1890)	76, **(167)**
'Pumpkin' jug	(1882)	67, **(149)**
R		
'Ranga'	(1879)	60
'Rassov' pot	(1854)	App 6b
Rhead Frederick		68, 73, 77
Ricardo (MP)		41
'Richelieu'	(c1875)	83, **(192)**
Ridgway, J		17, 20, 41
Ridgway, W		3, 6, 14, 20
'Rienzi'	(c1880)	126, **(326)**
Robinson, N	(1837)	1-3, 87-89
Robinson, Dorothea		6
Robinson & Leadbetter		73
'Rome'		15
'Rope' jug	(1852)	21, **(38)**
'Rose Leaf'	(c1875)	83, **(139)**
Rouse		56
S		
'Sado'	(1879)	60, **(128)**
'St Germain'	(c1875)	65, 126, **(144)**
Salomon		79 et seq.
Sander		56
'Savona'	(1853)	App 6b
'Severn'	(1869)	45, 81, **(91)**, **(174)**
'Shakespeare'	(c1870)	119, **(303)**
'Shamrock'	(1859)	15, 32, 81, 86, **(63)**

'Shamrock'	(1880)	81, 160, (205)
Shaw, Alfred		122
Shaw, W		1, 6
'Sicily' cup	(c1875)	160-161
'Sisyphus'	(1876)	36, 53, 56, (113)
Smart, J R		143
'Smyrna'	(1870)	119, (301)
Sneyd, T		13
'Snipe'	(1849)	8, 14, (22)
'Solomon'	(1841)	5-6, (10)
'Solon'	(c1875)	64, (138)
Southwell (MP)		106
'Spring'	(c1880)	123, 126, 148, (323)
'Spring' Statue	(c1880)	148, (399)
Stallard, J		48
'Stanley'	(c1875)	60, (126)
Stevenson, E		29
'Stratford'	(c1875)	64, (140)
'Strawberry'	(c1875)	45, (92)
'Strawberry Blossom'	(1849)	App 6b
'Stuart'	(1900)	80, (171)
'Suez'	(1879)	57, 126, (117)
'Sweaborg'	(1855)	102, (225)
Swirling Fish jug		130, (332)
'Swiss'	(1863)	37-38, (75-6)
Sydney		50
'Sylvan'	(1874)	50, 52, 122, 135, (308-9), (310-11), (343-44)

T		
'Tasso'	(c1875)	62
'Taunton'	(c1875)	65, 126, (144), (329)
'Texas'	(c1875)	123, (318)
'Thrace'	(1856)	106, (262)
'Tiber'		64, (142)
Tiffany		68, 146
'Tiverton'	(1865)	40-41, (83)
Tourton, J L		67
'Tradescantia'	(1855)	30, (58)
'Tree Trunk' jug		70, (153)
'Truro'	(c1875)	61, (135)
'Tudor'		61

Turners (Longton)		56
'Turin'	(1849)	8, 13-15, (23)
'Tycoon'	(c1878)	60
'Tyrol'	(1864)	40, (81)

U		
'Union'	(1861)	35, (70)
'Universe'	(1855)	30, 37, (74)

V		
Van Leyden		47
'Venetian Scenery'	(1839)	91, (208)
'Versailles'	(1839)	2
'Vertical Columns'	(1839)	3-4, (5)
Vienna		49, 68
'Viola'	(1844)	12, App 6b

W		
Wakefield, H		28
Walley		7, 11
'Watford'	(1854)	99, 102 (224)
Wedgwood		7, 12, 20, 41
'Westminster'	(1868)	44, 81, (89), (175)
'Wicker' jug	(1855)	28, (52)
'Willie', W B	(1841)	3-4, 6, (6)
'Windsor Wreath'	(1846)	91-92, (211)
'Wisconsin'	(1884)	65, (147)
Wolstenholme, J		7
Wood, John	(1837)	1 et seq., 87 et seq.
Wood & Bowers		12
Wood & Sale		33
'Woodland'	(1884)	126, (324)
Worcester Royal Porcelain		65, 73
'Worcester'	(1871)	47-48, (97)
Worthington & Green		33

Y		
'Yeddo'	(1876)	35, 53, (109-11)
'Yesso'	(1879)	60, (127)

Z		
'Zoological'	(1837)	88, (199-200)
'Zurich' plate	(c1880)	App 6b